SKETCHES OF THE HISTORY OF MAN

BOOK II

NATURAL LAW AND
ENLIGHTENMENT CLASSICS

Knud Haakonssen
General Editor

Henry Home, Lord Kames

NATURAL LAW AND
ENLIGHTENMENT CLASSICS

Sketches of the History of Man
Considerably Enlarged by the Last Additions and Corrections of the Author

BOOK II
Progress of Men in Society

Henry Home, Lord Kames

Edited and with an Introduction by
James A. Harris

Major Works of Henry Home, Lord Kames

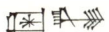

LIBERTY FUND
Indianapolis

This book is published by Liberty Fund, Inc., a foundation established
to encourage study of the ideal of a society of free and responsible individuals.

The cuneiform inscription that serves as our logo and as the design motif for
our endpapers is the earliest-known written appearance of the word
"freedom" (*amagi*), or "liberty." It is taken from a clay document written
about 2300 B.C. in the Sumerian city-state of Lagash.

Frontispiece and cover (detail): Portrait of Henry Home, Lord Kames, by David Martin.
Reproduced with permission of the National Galleries of Scotland.

Introduction, annotations © 2007 by Liberty Fund, Inc.

All rights reserved

Printed in the United States of America

11 10 09 08 07   C   5 4 3 2 1
11 10 09 08 07   P   5 4 3 2 1

Library of Congress Cataloging-in-Publication Data
Kames, Henry Home, Lord, 1696–1782.
Sketches of the history of man/Henry Home, Lord Kames;
edited and with an introduction by James A. Harris.
v. cm.—(Natural law and enlightenment classics)
"Considerably enlarged by the last additions and corrections of the author."
Originally published in 4 v.: Edinburgh: A. Strahan and T. Cadell. 1788.
Includes bibliographical references and index.
Contents: bk. 1. Progress of men independent of society—
bk. 2. Progress of men in society—bk. 3. Progress of sciences.
ISBN 978-0-86597-500-2 (hardcover: set)   ISBN 978-0-86597-505-7 (pbk: set)
1. Civilization—History. 2. Human beings—History.
I. Harris, James A., 1968– II. Title.
CB25.K3 2007
901—dc22   2006028369
ISBN 978-0-86597-502-6 (v. 2: hc)   ISBN 978-0-86597-507-1 (v. 2: sc)

LIBERTY FUND, INC.
8335 Allison Pointe Trail, Suite 300
Indianapolis, Indiana 46250-1684

CONTENTS

SKETCHES OF THE HISTORY OF MAN

BOOK I: Progress of Men Independent of Society	53
BOOK II: Progress of Men in Society	337
SKETCH I: Appetite for Society—Origin of National Societies	339
SKETCH II: General View of Government	371
SKETCH III: Different Forms of Government Compared	375
SKETCH IV: Progress of States from Small to Great, and from Great to Small	389
SKETCH V: Great and Small States Compared	396
SKETCH VI: War and Peace Compared	405
SKETCH VII: Rise and Fall of Patriotism	416
SKETCH VIII: Finances	432
SKETCH IX: Military Branch of Government	491
SKETCH X: Public Police with Respect to the Poor	521
SKETCH XI: A Great City Considered in Physical, Moral, and Political Views	546
SKETCH XII: Origin and Progress of American Nations	555
BOOK III: Progress of Sciences	581

BOOK II

PROGRESS OF MEN IN SOCIETY

CONTENTS[1]

BOOK II.

Progress of Men in Society.

Sk.
1. Appetite for society?—Origin of national societies,   156
2. General view of government,   223
3. Different forms of government compared,   230
4. Progress of states from small to great, and from great to small,   260
5. Great and small states compared,   275
6. War and peace compared,   294
7. Rise and fall of patriotism,   317
8. Finances,   352
    Preface,   352
    Sect.
    1. General considerations on taxes,   354
    2. Power of imposing taxes,   361
    3. Different sorts of taxes, with their advantages and disadvantages,   369
    4. Manner of levying taxes,   381
    5. Rules to be observed in taxing,   384
    6. Taxes examined with respect to their effects,   399
    7. Taxes for advancing industry and commerce, <155>   409

1. The original page numbers from the 1788 edition are retained here.

VOL. III.

Sk.
9. Military branch of government, 1
10. Public police with respect to the poor, 66
11. A great city considered in physical, moral, and political views, 120
12. Origin and progress of American nations, 138

BOOK II
Progress of Men in Society

PREFACE

In the course of explaining this subject, no opportunity is omitted of suggesting an important doctrine, That patriotism is the corner-stone of civil society; that no nation ever became great and powerful without it; and, when extinguished, that the most powerful nation will totter and become a ruin. But I profess only to state facts. From these the reader will not fail to draw the observation: and what he himself observes will sink deeper, than what is inculcated by an author, however pathetically. <156>

∞ SKETCH I ∞

Appetite for Society—Origin of National Societies

That there is in man an appetite for society, never was called in question.* But to what end the appetite serves, whether it embrace the whole species or be in any manner limited, <157> whether men be naturally qualified for being useful members of civil society, and whether they are fitted for being happy in it, are questions that open extensive views into human nature, and yet have been little attended to by writers. I grieve at the ne-<158>glect, because in the present inquiry, these questions, however abstruse, must be discussed.

---

* This appetite is not denied by Vitruvius; but it seems to have been overlooked in the account he gives (book 2. ch. 1.) of the commencement of society, which is as follows. "In ancient times, men, like wild beasts, lived in caves and woods, feeding on wild food. In a certain place it happened, that the trees, put in motion by tempestuous winds, and rubbing their branches one against another took fire. Those in the neighbourhood fled for fear: but as the flame abated, they approached; and finding the heat comfortable, they threw wood into the fire, and preserved it from being extinguished. They then invited others to take benefit of the fire. Men, thus assembled, endeavoured to express their thoughts by articulate sounds; and by daily practice, certain sounds signifying things in frequent use, came to be established. From that casual event, language arose. And thus, fire having attracted many to one place, they soon discovered that they were by nature superior to other animals, differing from them not only in an erect posture, which gave them opportunity to behold the beauties of the heavens as well as of the earth; but also in their hands and fingers, fitted for executing whatever they could invent. They therefore began to cover their habitations with the boughs of trees: some dug caves in the mountains; and, in imitation of a swallow's nest, some sheltered themselves with sprigs and loam. Thus, by observing each other's work, and turning their thoughts to invention, they by degrees improved their habitations, and became daily more and more skilful."

As many animals, beside man, are social, it appeared to me probable, that the social laws by which such animals are governed, might open views into the social nature of man. But here I met with a second disappointment: for after perusing books without end, I found very little satisfaction; though the laws of animal society make the most instructive and most entertaining part of natural history. A few dry facts, collected occasionally, enabled me to form the embryo of a plan, which I here present to the reader: if his curiosity be excited, 'tis well; for I am far from expecting that it will be gratified.

Animals of prey have no appetite for society, if the momentary act of copulation be not excepted. Wolves make not an exception, even where hunger makes them join to attack a village: as fear prevents them singly from an attempt so hazardous, their casual union is prompted by appetite for food, not by appetite for society. So little of the social is there in wolves, that if one happen to be wounded, <159> he is put to death and devoured by those of his own kind. Vultures have the same disposition. Their ordinary food is a dead carcase; and they never venture, but in a body, to attack any living creature that appears formidable. Upon society happiness so much depends, that we do not willingly admit a lion, a tiger, a bear, or a wolf, to have any appetite for society. And in with-holding it from such animals, the goodness of Providence to its favourite man, is conspicuous: their strength, agility, and voracity, make them singly not a little formidable: I should tremble for the human race, were they disposed to make war in company.* <160>

Diodorus Siculus (lib. 1.) says, that men originally led a savage life, without any society; that fear made them join for mutual defence against beasts of prey; that custom by degrees made them social; and that each society formed a language to itself. [["Diodorus Siculus . . . language to itself": added in 2nd edition.]] Has not the celebrated Rousseau been guilty of the same oversight in his essay on the inequality of men? These authors suggest to me the butcher, who made diligent search for his knife, which he held in his teeth.

* The care of Providence in protecting the human race from animals of prey, is equally visible in other particulars. I can discover no facts to make me believe, that a lion or a tiger is afraid of a man; but whatever secret means are employed by Providence to keep such fierce and voracious animals at a distance, certain it is, that they shun the habitations of men. At present there is not a wild lion in Europe. Even in Homer's time there were

Such harmless animals as are unable to defend themselves singly, are provided with an appetite for society, that they may defend themselves in a body. Sheep are remarkable in that respect, when left <161> to nature: a ram seldom attacks; but the rams of a flock exert great vigour in defending their females and their young.* Two of Bakewell's rams, brought to Langholm in the Duke of Buccleugh's estate, kept close together. The one was taken ill, and died, the other gave close attendance, stood beside the dead body, and abstained from food for some days: nor did it recover its spirits

---

none in Peloponnesus, though they were frequent in Thrace, Macedon, and Thessaly, down to the time of Aristotle: whence it is probable, that these countries were not at that time well peopled. And the same probability holds with respect to several mountainous parts in China, which even at present are infested with tigers. When men and cattle are together, a lion always attacks a beast, and never a man. If we can rely on Bosman, a tiger in Guinea will not touch a man if there be a four-footed beast in sight. M. Buffon observes, that the bear, though far from being cowardly, never is at ease but in wild and desart places. The great condor of Peru, a bird of prey of an immense size, bold and rapacious, is never seen but in desarts and high mountains. Every river in the coast of Guinea abounds with crocodiles, which lie basking in the sun during the heat of the day. If they perceive a man approaching, they plunge into the river, though they seldom fly from any other animal. A fox, on the contrary, a pole-cat, a kite, though afraid of man, draw near to inhabited places where they find prey in plenty. Such animals do little mischief; and the little they do, promotes care and vigilance. But if men, like sheep, were the natural prey of a lion or a tiger, their utmost vigour and sagacity would scarce be sufficient for self-defence. Perpetual war would be their fate, without having a single moment for any other occupation; and they must for ever have continued in a brutish state. It is possible that a few cattle might be protected by armed men, continually on the watch; but to defend flocks and herds covering a hundred hills, would be impracticable. Agriculture could never have existed in any shape.

* M. Buffon has bestowed less pains than becomes an author of his character, upon the nature and instincts of animals. He scarce once stumbles upon truth in his natural history of the sheep. He holds it to be stupid, and incapable to defend itself against any beast of prey; maintaining, that the race could not have subsisted but under the care and protection of men. Has that author forgot, that sheep had no enemy more formidable than men in their original hunter-state? Far from being neglected by nature, there are few animals better provided for defence. They have a sort of military instinct, forming a line of battle, like soldiers, when threatened with an attack. The rams, who, in a natural state, make half of the stock, join together; and no lion or tiger is able to resist their united impetuosity. A ram, educated by a soldier, accompanied his master to the battle of Culloden. When a cannon was fired, it rejoiced and run up to it. It actually began the battle, advancing before the troops, and attacking some dogs of the highland army. [["A ram ... highland army": added in 2nd edition.]]

for a long time.[1] The whole society of rooks join in attacking a <162> kite, when it hovers about them. A family of wild swine never separate, till the young be sufficiently strong to defend themselves against the wolf; and when the wolf threatens, they all join in a body. The pecary is a sort of wild hog in the isthmus of Darien: if one of them be attacked, the rest run to assist it. There being a natural antipathy between that animal and the American tiger, it is not uncommon to find a tiger slain with a number of pecaries round him.

The social appetite is to some animals useful, not only for defence, but for procuring the necessaries of life. Society among beavers is a notable instance of both. As water is the only refuge of that innocent species against an enemy, they instinctively make their settlement on the brink of a lake or of a running stream. In the latter case, they keep up the water to a proper height by a dam-dike, constructed with so much art as to withstand the greatest floods: in the former, they save themselves the labour of a dam-dike, because a lake generally keeps at the same height. Having thus provided for defence, their next care is to provide food <163> and habitation. The whole society join in erecting the dam-dike; and they also join in erecting houses. Each house has two apartments: in the upper there is space for lodging from six to ten beavers: the under holds their provisions, which are trees cut down by united labour, and divided into small portable parts (*a*). Bees are a similar instance. Aristotle (*b*) says, "that bees are the only animals which labour in common, have a house in common, eat in common, and have their offspring in common." A single bee would be still less able than a single beaver, to build a house for itself and for its winter food. The Alpine rat or marmot has no occasion to store up food for winter, because it lies benumbed without motion all the cold months. But these animals live in tribes; and each tribe digs a habitation under ground with great art, sufficiently capacious for lodging the whole tribe; covering the bottom with withered grass, which some cut, and others carry. The wild dogs of Congo and <164> Angola hunt in packs, waging perpetual war against other wild

---

(*a*) See the works of the beaver described most accurately by M. Buffon, vol. 8.
(*b*) History of animals, b. 9. c. 40.
1. "Two of . . . long time": added in 2nd edition.

beasts. They bring to the place of rendezvous whatever is caught in hunting; and each receives its share.* The baboons are social animals, and avail themselves of that quality in procuring food; witness their address in robbing an orchard, described by Kolben in his account of the Cape of Good Hope. Some go into the orchard, some place themselves on the wall, the rest form a line on the outside, and the fruit is thrown from hand to hand till it reach the place of rendezvous. Extending the inquiry to all known animals, we find that the appetite for society is with-held from no species to which it is necessary, whether for defence or for food. It appears to be distributed by weight and measure, in order to accommodate the internal frame of animals to their external circumstances.

Society among the more robust animals that live on grass would be useless. So-<165>ciety among beasts of prey would be hurtful; because fifty lions or tigers hunting in company, would have a less chance for prey, than hunting separately. Crows and cranes unite in society while they are hatching their young, in order to defend them from birds of prey.[2]

But on some animals an appetite for society is bestowed, though in appearance not necessary either for defence or for food. With regard to such, the only final cause we can discover is the pleasure of living in society. That kind of society is found among horses. Outhier, one of the French academicians employed to measure a degree of the meridian toward the north pole, reports, that at Torneo all bulky goods are carried in boats during summer; but in winter, when the rivers are frozen and the ground covered with snow, that they use sledges drawn by horses; that when the snow melts and the rivers are open, the horses, set loose, rendezvous at a certain part of the forest, where they separate into troops, and occupy different pasture-fields; that when these fields become bare, they occupy new ground in the same order as at first; that they return home in <166> troops when the bad weather begins; and that every horse knows its own stall. No creature stands less in need of society than a hare, whether for food or for defence. Of food, it has plenty under its feet; and for defence, it is provided both

---

* However fierce with respect to other animals, yet so submissive are these dogs to men, as to suffer their prey to be taken from them without resistance. Europeans salt for their slaves what they thus procure.

2. Paragraph added in 2nd edition.

with cunning and swiftness. Nothing however is more common in a moonlight night, than to see hares sporting together in the most social manner. But society for pleasure only, is an imperfect kind of society; and far from being so intimate, as where it is provided by nature for defence, or for procuring food.* <167>

With respect to the extent of the appetite, no social animal, as far as can be discovered, has an appetite for associating with the whole species. Every species is divided into many small tribes; and these tribes have no appetite for associating with each other: on the contrary, a stray sheep is thrust out of the flock, and a stray bee must instantly retire, or be stung to death. The dogs of a family never fail to attack a stranger dog, bent to destroy him. If the stranger submit, they do him no harm.† Every work of Providence contributes to some good end: a small tribe is sufficient for mutual defence; and a very large tribe would find difficulty in procuring subsistence.

How far brute animals are by nature qualified for being useful members of civil society, or for being happy in it, are questions that have been totally overlook-<168>ed by writers. And yet, as that branch of natural history is also necessary to my plan, I must proceed; though I have nothing to lay before the reader but a few scattered observations, which occurred when I had no view of turning them to account. I begin with the instinctive conduct of animals, in providing against danger. When a flock of sheep in the

---

* Pigeons must be excepted, if their society be not necessary either for food or habitation, of which I am uncertain. Society among that species is extremely intimate; and it is observable, that the place they inhabit contributes to the intimacy. A crazy dove-cot moved the proprietor to transfer the inhabitants to a new house built for them; and to accustom them to it, they were kept a fortnight within doors, with plenty of food. When they obtained liberty, they flew directly to their old house; and seeing it laid flat, walked round and round, lamenting. They then took wing and disappeared, without once casting an eye on their new habitation. Some brute animals are susceptible of affection even to those of a different species. Of the affection a dog has for his master, no person is ignorant. A canary bird, so tame as to be let out of its cage, perched frequently on another cage in the same room inhabited by a linnet; and the birds became good friends. The linnet died: the canary bird was inconsolable, and forbore singing above a year. It recovered its spirits, and now chants as much as ever. [["Some brute animals . . . much as ever": added in 2nd edition.]]

† Columella, treating of goats, observes that it is better to purchase an entire flock, than goats out of different flocks, that they may not divide into different parties, but feed cordially together. [[Note added in 2nd edition.]]

state of nature goes to rest, sentinels are appointed; who, on appearance of an enemy, stamp with the foot, and make a hissing sound; upon which all take the alarm: if no enemy appear, they watch their time, return to the flock, and send out others in their stead. In flocks that have an extensive range in hilly countries, the same discipline obtains even after domestication. Though monkeys sleep upon trees, yet a sentinel is always appointed; who must not sleep under pain of being torn to pieces. They preserve the same discipline when they rob an orchard: a sentinel on a high tree is watchful to announce the very first appearance of an enemy. M. Buffon, talking of a sort of monkey, which he terms *Malbrouck,* says, that they are fond of fruit, and of sugar-canes; and that <169> while they are loading themselves, one is placed sentinel on a tree, who, upon the approach of a man, cries, *Houp! Houp! Houp!* loudly and distinctly. That moment they throw away the sugar-canes that they hold in their left-hand, and run off upon that hand with their two feet. When marmots are at work in the field, one is appointed to watch on a high rock; which advertises them by a loud whistle, when it sees a man, an eagle, or a dog. Among beavers, notice is given of the approach of an enemy, by lashing the water with the tail, which is heard in every habitation. Seals always sleep on the beach; and, to prevent surprise, sentinels are placed round at a considerable distance from the main body. Wild elephants, who always travel in company, are less on their guard in places unfrequented: but, when they invade cultivated fields, they march in order, the eldest in the front, and the next in age closing the rear. The weak are placed in the centre, and the females carry their young on their trunks. They attack in a body; and, upon a repulse, retire in a body. Tame elephants retain so much of their original nature, that if one, upon <170> being wounded, turn its back, the rest instantly follow. Bell of Antimony, in his journey through Siberia to Pekin, mentions wild horses that live in society, and are peculiarly watchful against danger. One is always stationed on an eminence, to give notice of an approaching enemy; and, upon notice given, they all fly.[3] Martin, in his description of the island St. Kilda, reports that the Solan geese have always some of their number keeping centry in the night. If a centry hear a noise, it cries softly, *grog, grog,* at which the

---

3. "Bell of Antimony . . . they all fly": added in 2nd edition.

flock move not. But, if the centry see or hear the fowler approaching, it cries quickly, *bir, bir,* upon which the whole flock take wing.[4] Next in order is the government of a tribe, and the conduct of its members to each other. It is not unlikely, that society among some animals, and their mutual affection, may be so entire as to prevent all discord among them; which seems to be the case of beavers. Such a society, if there be such, requires no government, nor any laws. A flock of sheep occupies the same spot every night, and each hath its own resting-place. The same is observable in horned cattle when folded. And, <171> as we find not that any one ever attempts to dislodge another, it is probable that such restraint makes a branch of their nature. But society among brute-animals is not always so perfect. Perverse inclinations, tending to disturb society, are visible among some brute animals, as well as among rational men. It is not uncommon for a rook to pilfer sticks from another's nest; and the pilferer's nest is demolished by the *lex talionis*. Herons have the same sort of government with rooks in preserving their nests. They are singular in one particular, that there is no society among them but in hatching their young. They live together during that time, and do not separate till their young can provide for themselves.[5] Perverse inclinations require government, and government requires laws. As in the cases now mentioned, the whole society join in inflicting the punishment, government among rooks and herons appears to be republican. Apes, on the contrary, are under monarchical government. Apes in Siam go in troops, each under a leader, who preserves strict discipline. A female, carnally inclined, retired from the troop, and <172> was followed by a male. The male escaped from the leader, who pursued them; but the female was brought back, and, in presence of the whole troop, received fifty blows on the cheek, as a chastisement for its incontinence (*a*). But probably there are not many instances among brutes, of government approaching so near to that of men. Government among horned cattle, appears to have no other end but to preserve order. Their government is monarchical; and the election is founded upon personal valour, the most solid of all qualifications in such a society. The bull who aspires to be lord of the herd must fight his

---

(*a*) Memoirs of Count Forbin.
4. "Martin, in his . . . flock take wing": added in 3rd edition.
5. "Herons have the . . . provide for themselves": added in 2nd edition.

way to preferment; and, after all his rivals are beat off the field, the herd tamely submit. At the same time, he is not secured in the throne for life, but must again enter the lists with any bull that ventures to challenge him. The same spirit is observable among oxen, in a lower degree. The master-ox leads the rest into the stable, or into the fold, and becomes unruly if he be not let first out: nay, he must be first yoked in the plough or wagon. Sheep are not employed in work; <173> but, in every other respect, the same oeconomy obtains among them. Where the rams happen to be few in proportion to the other sheep, they sometimes divide the flock among them, instead of fighting for precedence. Five or six score of sheep, two of them rams, were purchased a few years ago by the author of this work. The two rams divided the flock between them. The two flocks pastured in common; being shut up in one inclosure: but they had different spots for rest during night; nor was it known that a sheep ever deserted its party, or even changed its resting-place. In the two species last mentioned, I find not that there is any notion of punishment; nor does it appear to be necessary: the leader pretends to nothing but precedence, which is never disputed. Every species of animals have a few notes by which the individuals communicate their desires and wants to each other. If a cow or a calf give the voice of distress, every beast of the kind runs to give help. If a stranger utter the voice of defiance, many advance for battle. If he yield, he obtains a certain rank in the herd. If a colony of rooks be suffered to make a settlement in a <174> grove of trees, it is difficult to dislodge them. But, if once dislodged, they never return, at least for many years; and yet numbers must have been procreated after banishment. How is this otherwise to be accounted for, but that rooks have some faculty of conveying instruction to their young?

In some animals, love of liberty is the ruling passion: some are easily trained, and submit readily without opposition. Examples of the latter are common: of the former take the following instance. A brood of stone-chatters taken from the nest were inclosed in a cage. The door was left open to give admission to the mother, and then was shut upon her. After many attempts, finding it impossible to get free, she first put her young to death, and then dashed out her own brains on the side of the cage.[6] I blush to

---

6. "Every species of animals . . . of the cage": added in 2nd edition.

present these imperfect hints, the fruit of casual observation, not of intentional inquiry: but I am fond to blow the trumpet, in order to raise curiosity in others: if the subject be prosecuted by men of taste and inquiry, many final causes, I am persuaded, will be discovered, tending more and more to dis-<175>play the wisdom and goodness of Providence. But what at present I have chiefly in view, is to observe, that government among brute animals, however simple, appears to be perfect in its kind; and adapted with great propriety to their nature. Factions in the state are unknown: no enmity between individuals, no treachery, no deceit, nor any other of those horrid vices that torment the human race. In a word, they appear to be perfectly well qualified for that kind of society to which they are prompted by their nature, and well fitted for being happy in it.

Storing up the foregoing observations till there be occasion for them, we proceed to the social nature of man. That men are endued with an appetite for society, will be vouched by the concurring testimony of all men, each vouching for himself. There is accordingly no instance of people living in a solitary state, where the appetite is not obstructed by some potent obstacle. The inhabitants of that part of New Holland which Dampier saw, live in society, though less advanced above brutes than any other known savages; and so intimate is their society, that they gather <176> their food and eat in common. The inhabitants of the Canary Islands lived in the same manner, when first seen by Europeans, which was in the fourteenth century; and the savages mentioned by Condamine, drawn by a Jesuit from the woods to settle on the banks of the Oroonoko, must originally have been united in some kind of society, as they had a common language. In a word, that man hath an appetite for food, is not more certain, than that he hath an appetite for society. And here I have occasion to apply one of the observations made above. Abstracting altogether from the pleasure we have in society, similar to what we have in eating, evident it is, that to no animal is society more necessary than to man, whether for food or for defence. In society, he is chief of the terrestrial creation; in a solitary state, the most helpless and forlorn. Thus, the first question suggested above, viz. To what end was a social appetite bestowed on man, has received an answer, which I flatter myself will be satisfactory.

The next question is, Whether the appetite embrace the whole species, or be limited, as among other animals, to a soci-<177>ety of moderate extent. That the appetite is limited, will be evident from history. Men, as far back as they can be traced, have been divided into small tribes or societies. Most of these, it is true, have in later times been united into large states: such revolutions, however, have been brought about, not by an appetite for a more extensive society, but by conquest, or by the junction of small tribes for defence against the more powerful. A society may indeed be too small for complete gratification of the appetite; and the appetite thus cramped welcomes every person into the society till it have sufficient scope: the Romans, a diminutive tribe originally, were fond to associate even with their enemies after a victory. But, on the other hand, a society may be too large for perfect gratification. An extensive empire is an object too bulky; national affection is too much diffused; and the mind is not at ease till it find a more contracted society, corresponding to the moderation of its appetite. Hence the numerous orders, associations, fraternities, and divisions, that spring up in every great state. The ever-during Blues and Greens in the Roman empire, <178> and Guelphs and Gibelines in Italy, could not have long subsisted after the cause of their enmity was at an end, but for a tendency in the members of a great state to contract their social connections.* Initiations among the ancients were probably owing to the same cause; as also associations of artisans among the moderns, pretending mystery and secrecy, and excluding all strangers. Of such associations or brotherhoods, the free masons excepted, there is scarce now a vestige remaining.

We find now, after an accurate scrutiny, that the social appetite in man comprehends not the whole species, but a part only; and commonly a small part, precisely as among other animals. Here another final cause starts up, no less remarkable than that explained above. An appetite to associate with the whole species, would form states so unwieldy by numbers, as to be incapable of any government. Our appetite is wisely confined within such limits, as to form states of moderate extent, which of all are the best fitted for good government: <179> and, as we shall see afterward, are also the best

---

* The never ceasing factions in Britain proceed, not from a society too much extended, but from love of power or of wealth, to restrain which there is no sufficient authority in a free government.

fitted for improving the human powers, and for invigorating every manly virtue. Hence an instructive lesson, That a great empire is ill suited to human nature; and that a great conqueror is, in more respects than one, an enemy to mankind.

The limiting our social appetite within moderate bounds, suggests another final cause. An appetite to associate with the whole species, would collect into one society all who are not separated from each other by wide seas and inaccessible mountains: and consequently would distribute mankind into a very few societies, consisting of such multitudes as to reduce national affection to a mere shadow. Nature hath wisely limited the appetite in proportion to our mental capacity. Our relations, our friends, and our other connections, open an extensive field for the exercise of affection: nay, our country in general, if not too extensive, would alone be sufficient to engross our affection. But that beautiful speculation falls more properly under the principles of morality: and there it shall not be overlooked.

What comes next in order, is to exa-<180>mine how we stand affected to those who are not of our tribe or society. I pave the way to this examination, by taking up man naked at his entrance into life. An infant at first has no feeling but bodily pain; and it is familiarised with its nurse, its parents, and perhaps with others, before it is susceptible of any passion. All weak animals are endowed with a principle of fear, which prompts them to shun danger; and fear, the first passion discovered in an infant, is raised by every new face; the infant shrinks and hides itself in the bosom of its nurse (*a*).* Thus every stranger is an object of fear to an infant, and consequently of aversion, which is generated by fear. Fear lessens gradually as our circle of acquaintance enlarges, especially in those who rely on bodily strength. Nothing tends more effectually to dissipate fear, than consciousness of security in the social state: in solitude, no animal is more timid than man; in society, none more bold. But remark, that aversion may subsist after fear is gone: it is propagated from people to their chil-<181>dren through an endless succession; and is infectious like a disease. Thus enmity

---

* In this respect, the human race differs widely from that of dogs: a puppy, the first time it sees a man, runs to him, licks his hand, and plays about his feet.

(*a*) Elements of Criticism, Vol. i. p. 441. edit. 5.

is kept up between tribes, without any particular cause. A neighbouring tribe, constantly in our sight, and able to hurt us, is the object of our strongest aversion: aversion lessens in proportion to distance; and terminates in absolute indifference with respect to very distant tribes.[7]

One would naturally imagine, that, after fear has vanished, aversion to strangers cannot long subsist. But it is supported by a principle that we are not at liberty to deny, because it frequently breaks forth even in childhood, without any provocation; and that is a principle of malevolence, distributed indeed in very unequal portions. Observe the harsh usage that tame birds receive from children, without any apparent cause; the neck twisted about, feathers plucked off, the eye thrust out with a bodkin; a baby thrown out at a window, or torn in pieces. There is nothing more common, than flat stones that cover the parapets of a bridge thrown down, the head of a young tree cut off, or an old tree barked. This odious principle is carefully disguised after the first <182> dawn of reason; and is indulged only against enemies, because there it appears innocent. I am utterly at a loss to account for the following fact, but from the principle now mentioned. The Count de Lauzun was shut up by Louis XIV. in the castle of Pignerol, and was confined there from the year 1672 to the year 1681, deprived of every comfort of life, and even of paper, pen, and ink. At a distance from every friend and relation; without light, except a glimmering through a slit in the roof; without books, occupation, or exercise; a prey to hope deferred, and constant horror; he, to avoid insanity, had recourse to tame a spider. The spider received flies from his hand with seeming gratitude, carried on his web with alacrity, and engaged the whole attention of the prisoner. This most innocent of all amusements was discovered by the jailor, who, in the wantonness of power, destroyed the spider and its work. The Count described his agony to be little inferior to that of a fond mother at the loss of a darling child. Custom may render a person insensible to scenes of misery; but cannot provoke cruelty without a motive. <183> A jailor differs only from other

---

7. The 1st edition adds: "Upon the whole, it appears, that the nature of man with respect to those of his own kind is resolvable into the following particulars. First, Affection for our private connections, and for our country in general. Second, Aversion to neighbours who are strangers to us, and to neighbouring tribes in general. Third, Indifference with respect to others" [1:368].

men, in freedom to indulge malignity against his prisoners without fear of retaliation.⁸

As I neither hope nor wish, that the nature of man, as above delineated, be taken upon my authority, I propose to verify it by clear and substantial facts. But, to avoid the multiplying instances unnecessarily, I shall confine myself to such as concern the aversion that neighbouring tribes have to each other; taking it for granted, that private affection, and love to our country, are what no person doubts of. I begin with examples of rude nations, where nature is left to itself, without culture. The inhabitants of Greenland, good-natured and inoffensive, have not even words for expressing anger or envy: stealing from one another is abhorred; and a young woman, guilty of that crime, has no chance for a husband. At the same time, they are faithless and cruel to those who come among them: they consider the rest of mankind as a different race, with whom they reject all society. The morality of the inhabitants of New Zealand is not more refined. Writers differ about the inhabitants of the Marian or <184> Ladrone islands: Magellan, and other voyagers, say, that they are addicted to thieving; and their testimony occasioned these islands to be called *Ladrones*. Pere le Gobien, on the contrary, says, that, far from being addicted to thieving, they leave every thing open, having no distrust one of another. These accounts differ in appearance, not in reality. Magellan was a stranger; and he talks only of their stealing from him and from his companions. Father Gobien lived long among them, and talks of their fidelity to each other. Plan Carpin, who visited Tartary in the year 1246, observes of the Tartars, that, though full of veracity to their neighbours, they thought themselves not bound to speak truth to strangers. The Greeks anciently were held to be pirates: but not properly; for they committed depredations upon strangers only. Caesar, speaking of the Germans (*a*), says, "Latrocinia nullam habent infamiam quae extra fines cujusque civitatis fiunt."* <185> This was precisely the case of our highlanders, till they were brought under due subjection after the rebellion of 1745. Bougainville observes, that the inhabitants

---

* "They hold it not infamous to rob without the bounds of their canton."
(*a*) Lib. 6. c. 23. de bello Gallico.
8. Paragraph added in 2nd edition.

of Otaheite, named by the English *King George's Island,* made no difficulty of stealing from his people; and yet never steal from one another, having neither locks nor bars in their houses. The people of Benin in Negroland are good-natured, gentle, and civilized; and so generous, that if they receive a present, they are not at ease till they return it double. They have unbounded confidence in their own people; but are jealous of strangers, tho' they politely hide their jealousy. The different tribes of Negroes, speaking each a different language, have a rooted aversion at each other. This aversion is carried along with them to Jamaica; and they will rather suffer death from the English, than join with those of a different tribe in a plot for liberty.[9] Russian peasants think it a greater sin to eat meat in Lent, than to murder one of another country. Among the Koriacs, bordering on Kamskatka, murder within the tribe is severely punished: but to murder a stran-<186>ger is not minded. While Rome continued a small state, neighbour and enemy were expressed by the same word (*a*). In England of old, a foreigner was not admitted to be a witness. Hence it is, that in ancient history, we read of wars without intermission among small states in close neighbourhood. It was so in Greece; it was so in Italy during the infancy of the Roman republic; it was so in Gaul, when Caesar commenced hostilities against that country (*b*); and it was so all the world over. Many islands in the South Sea, and in other remote parts, have been discovered by Europeans; who commonly found the natives with arms in their hands, resolute to prevent the strangers from landing. Orellana, lieutenant to Gonzales Pisarro, was the first European who sailed down the river Amazon to the sea. In his passage, he was continually assaulted by the natives with arrows from the banks of the river: and some even ventured to attack him in their canoes.

Nor does such aversion wear away even <187> among polished people. An ingenious writer (*c*) remarks, that almost every nation hate their neighbours, without knowing why. I once heard a Frenchman swear, says that writer, that he hated the English, *parce qu'ils versent du beurre fondu sur leur*

(*a*) Hostis.
(*b*) Lib. 6. c. 15. de bello Gallico.
(*c*) Baretti.
9. "The different tribes . . . plot for liberty": added in 2nd edition.

veau roti.* The populace of Portugal have to this day an uncommon aversion to strangers: even those of Lisbon, though a trading town frequented by many different nations, must not be excepted. Travellers report, that the people of the duchy of Milan, remarkable for good-nature, are the only Italians who are not hated by their neighbours. The Piedmontese and Genoese have an aversion to each other, and agree only in their antipathy to the Tuscans. The Tuscans dislike the Venetians; and the Romans abound not with good-will to the Tuscans, Venetians, or Neapolitans. Very different is the case with respect to distant nations: instead of being objects of aversion, their manners, <188> customs, and singularities, amuse us greatly.†

Infants differ from each other in aversion to strangers; some being extremely shy, others less so; and the like difference is observable in whole tribes. The people of Milan cannot have any aversion to their neighbours, when they are such favourites of all around them. The inhabitants of some South-sea islands, mentioned above (*a*), appear to have little or no aversion to strangers. But that is a rare instance, and has scarce a parallel in any other part of the globe. It holds also true, that nations the most remarkable for patriotism, are equally remarkable for aversion to strangers. The Jews, the Greeks, <189> the Romans, were equally remarkable for both. Patriotism, a vigorous principle among the English, makes them extremely averse to naturalize foreigners. The inhabitants of New Zealand, both men and women, appear to be of a mild and gentle disposition: they treat one another with affection; but are implacable to their enemies, and never give quarter. It is even customary among them to eat the flesh of their enemies.

To a person of humanity, the scene here exhibited is far from being agreeable. Man, it may be thought, is of all animals the most barbarous; for even

---

* "Because they pour melted butter upon their roast veal."

† Voltaire, (Universal History, ch. 40.) observing, rightly, that jealousy among petty princes is productive of more crimes than among great monarchs, gives a very unsatisfactory reason, "That having little force, they must employ fraud, poison, and other secret crimes"; not adverting, that power may be equally distributed among small princes as well as among great. It is antipathy that instigates such crimes, which is always the most violent among the nearest neighbours.

(*a*) Preliminary Discourse.

animals of prey are innoxious with respect to their own kind.* Aversion to strangers makes <190> a branch of our nature: it exists among individuals in private life: it flames high between neighbouring tribes; and is visible even in infancy. Can such perversity of disposition promote any good end? This question, which pierces deep into human nature, is reserved to close the present sketch.

From the foregoing deduction, universal benevolence, inculcated by several writers as a moral duty, is discovered to have no foundation in the nature of man. Our appetite for society is limited, and our duty must be limited in proportion. But of this more directly when the principles of morality are taken under consideration.

We are taught by the great Newton, that attraction and repulsion in matter, are, by alteration of circumstances, converted one into the other. This holds also in affection and aversion, which may be termed, not improperly, *mental attraction* and *repulsion*. Two nations, originally <191> strangers to each other, may, by commerce or other favourable circumstance, become so well acquainted, as to change from aversion to affection. The opposite manners of a capital and of a country-town, afford a good illustration. In the latter, people, occupied with their domestic concerns, are in a manner strangers to each other: a degree of aversion prevails, which gives birth to envy and detraction. In the former, a court and public amusements, promote general acquaintance: repulsion yields to attraction, and people become fond to associate with their equals. The union of two tribes into one, is another circumstance that converts repulsion into attraction. Such conversion, however, is far from being instantaneous; witness the different small states of Spain, which were not united in affection for many years after they were united under one monarch; and this was also the case

---

* "Denique caetera animantia in suo genere probe degunt: congregari videmus et stare contra dissimilia: leonum feritas inter se non dimicat: serpentum morsus non petit serpentes; ne maris quidem belluae ac pisces, nisi in diversa genera, saeviunt. At, Hercule, homini plurima ex homine sunt mala"; *Pliny, lib.* 7. *Prooemium.* [*In English thus:* "For other animals live at peace with those of their species. They gather themselves in troops, and unite against the common enemy. The ferocious lion fights not against his species: the poisonous serpent is harmless to his kind: the monsters of the sea prey but on those fishes that differ from them in nature: man alone of animals is foe to man!"]

of the two kingdoms of England and Scotland. In some circumstances the conversion is instantaneous; as where a stranger becomes an object of pity or of gratitude. Many low persons in Britain contributed cheerfully for maintaining some <192> French seamen, made prisoners at the commencement of the late war. It is no less instantaneous, when strangers, relying on our humanity, trust themselves in our hands. Among the ancients, it was hospitality to strangers only, that produced mutual affection and gratitude: Glaucus and Diomede were of different countries. Hospitality to strangers is a pregnant symptom of improving manners. Caesar, speaking of the Germans (*a*), says, "Hospites violare, fas non putant: qui, quaqua de causa, ad eos venerunt, ab injuria prohibent, sanctosque habent; iis omnium domus patent, victusque communicatur."* The ancient Spaniards were fond of war, and cruel to their enemies; but in peace, they passed their time in singing and dancing, and were remarkably hospitable to the strangers who came among them. It shews great refinement in the Celtae, that the killing a stranger was capital, when the killing a citizen <193> was banishment only (*b*). The Circassians, described by Bell of Antimony as barbarians, are hospitable. If even an enemy put himself under the protection of any of them, he is secure.[10] The Swedes and Goths were eminently hospitable to strangers; as indeed were all the northern nations of Europe (*c*). The negroes of Fouli are celebrated by travellers for the same quality. The native Brazilians are singularly hospitable: a stranger no sooner arrives among them, than he is surrounded by women, who wash his feet, and set before him to eat the best things they have: if he have occasion to go more than once to the same village, the person whose guest he was, takes it much amiss if he think of changing his lodging.

There are causes that for a time suspend enmity between neighbouring states. The small states of Greece, among whom war never ceased, fre-

---

* "They hold it sacrilege to injure a stranger. They protect from outrage, and venerate those who come among them: their houses are open to them, and they are welcome to their tables."

(*a*) Lib. 6. c. 23. de bello Gallico.
(*b*) Nicolaus Damascenus.
(*c*) Saxo Grammaticus. Crantz.
10. "The Circassians, described . . . he is secure": added in 2nd edition.

quently smothered their enmity to join against the formidable monarch of Persia. There are also causes that suspend for a time all animosity between factions in the same state. The fac-<194>tions in Britain about power and pre-eminence, not a little disagreeable during peace, are laid asleep during a foreign war.

On the other hand, attraction is converted into repulsion by various causes. One is, the splitting a great monarchy into many small states; of which the Assyrian, the Persian, the Roman, and the Saracen empires, are instances. The *amor patriae,* faint in an extensive monarchy, readily yields to aversion, operating between two neighbouring states, less extensive. This is observable between neighbouring colonies, even of the same nation: the English colonies in North America, though they retain some affection for their mother-country, have contracted an aversion to each other. And happy for them is such aversion, if it prevent their uniting in order to acquire independence: wars without end would be the inevitable consequence, as among small states in close neighbourhood.

Hitherto the road has been smooth, without obstruction. But we have not yet finished our journey; and the remaining questions, whether men be qua-<195>lified by their nature for being useful members of civil society, and whether they be fitted for being happy in it, will, I suspect, lead into a road neither smooth nor free from obstruction. The social branch of human nature would be wofully imperfect, if man had an appetite for society without being qualified for that state: the appetite, instead of tending to a good end, would be his bane. And yet, whether he be or be not qualified for society, seems doubtful. On the one hand, there are facts, many and various, from which it is natural to conclude, that man is qualified by nature for being an useful member of a social state, and for being happy in it.[11] I instance, first, several corresponding principles or propensities, that cannot be exerted nor gratified but in society, viz. the propensities of veracity, and

---

11. "On the one ... being happy in it": added in 2nd edition. In 1st edition: "In examining the conduct of men, he is to us a disgustful object in his aversion to those of a different tribe; and I violently suspect, that in his behaviour even to those of his own tribe, he will scarce be found an agreeable object. That he is fitted by nature for being an useful member of society, and for being happy in it, appears from facts many and various" [1:375].

of relying on human testimony; appetite for knowledge, and desire to communicate knowledge; anxiety to be pitied in distress, and sympathy with the distressed; appetite for praise, and inclination to praise the deserving.* Such cor-<196>responding propensities not only qualify men for the social state as far as their influence reaches, but attract them sweetly into society for the sake of gratification, and make them happy in it. But this is not all, nor indeed the greater part. Do not benevolence, compassion, magnanimity, heroism, and the whole train of social affections, demonstrate our fitness for society, and our happiness in it? And justice, above all other virtues, promotes peace and concord in that state. Nor ought the faculty of speech to be overlooked, which in an eminent degree qualifies man for society, and is a plentiful source of enjoyment in it.

I have reserved one other particular to be the concluding scene; being a striking instance of providential care to fit men for society. In reading a play, or in seeing it acted, a young man of taste is at no loss to judge of scenes he never was engaged in, or of passions he never felt. What is <197> it that directs his judgement? Men are apt to judge of others by what they have experienced in themselves: but here, by the supposition, there has been no antecedent experience. The fact is so familiar, that no one thinks of accounting for it. As young persons, without instruction or experience, can judge with tolerable accuracy of the conduct of men, of their various passions, of the difference of character, and of the efficacy of motives; the principle by which they judge must be internal: nature must be their guide, or, in other words, an internal sense. Nor is this sense confined to so low a purpose as criticism: it is a sense indispensable in the conduct of life. Every person is connected with many others, by various ties: if instruction and experience were necessary to regulate their conduct, what would become of them in the interim? Their ignorance would betray them into endless inconveniencies. This sense has man for its object, not this or that man: by it we perceive what is common to all, not what distinguishes one individual from another. We have an intuitive conviction, not only that all men have

---

* Appetite for praise is inherent even in savages: witness those of North America, who upon that account are fond of dress. I mean the men; for the women are such miserable slaves as to have no spirit for ornament.

passions and appetites <198> which direct their actions, but that each passion and appetite produceth uniformly effects proper to itself. This natural knowledge is only our guide, till we learn by experience to enter more minutely into particular characters. Of these we acquire knowledge from looks, gestures, speech, and behaviour, which discover to us what passes internally. Then it is, and no sooner, that we are fully qualified to act a proper part in society. Wonderful is the frame of man, both external and internal![12]

On the other hand, there are facts, not fewer in number, nor less various, from which it is equally natural to conclude, that man is ill qualified for society, and that there is little happiness in it. What can be more averse to concord in society than dissocial passions? and yet these prevail among men; among whom there is no end to envy, malice, revenge, treachery, deceit, avarice, ambition, &c. &c. We meet every where persons bent on the destruction of others, evincing that man has no enemies more formidable than of his own kind, and of his own tribe. Are not discord and feuds the chief articles in the history of every state, factions violent-<199>ly bent against each other, and frequently breaking out into civil wars? Appian's history of the civil wars of Rome exhibits a horrid scene of massacres, proscriptions, and forfeitures; the leaders sacrificing their firmest friends, for liberty to suck the blood of their enemies; as if to shed human blood were the ruling passion of man. But the Romans were far from being singular: the polite Greeks, commonly so characterized, were still more brutal and bloody. The following passage is copied from a celebrated author (*a*). "Not to mention Dionysius the elder, who is computed to have butchered in cold blood above 10,000 of his fellow-citizens; nor Agathocles, Nabis, and others, still more bloody than he; the transactions even in free governments were extremely violent and destructive. At Athens, the thirty tyrants, and the nobles, in a twelvemonth, murdered without trial, about 1200 of the people, and banished above the half of the citizens that remained. In Argos, near the same time, the people killed 1200 <200> of the nobles, and afterward their own demagogues, because they had refused to carry their prosecutions farther. The people also in Corcyra killed 1500 of the nobles, and

---

(*a*) Essay of the populousness of ancient nations, by David Hume, Esq.

12. Paragraph added in 2nd edition.

banished 1000. These numbers will appear the more surprising, if we consider the extreme smallness of those states. But all ancient history is full of such instances." Upon a revolution in the Saracen empire, *anno* 750, where the Ommiyan family was expelled by that of the Abassians, Abdolah, chief of the latter, published an act of oblivion to the former, on condition of their taking an oath of allegiance to him. The Ommiyans, embracing the condition, were in appearance cordially received. But, in preparing to take the oath, they were knocked down, every one of them, by the Emperor's guards. And fully to glut the monster's cruelty, these princes, still alive, were laid close together, and covered with boards and carpets; upon which Abdolah feasted his officers, "in order," said he, "that we may be exhilarated with the dying groans of the Ommiyans." During the vigour of the feudal system, when every gentleman was <201> a soldier, justice was no defence against power, nor humanity against bloody resentment. Stormy passions raged every where with unrelenting fury; every place a chaos of confusion and distress. No man was secure but in his castle; and to venture abroad, unless well armed and well attended, would have been an act of high temerity. So little intercourse was there among the French in the tenth century, that an abbot of Clugni, invited by the Count of Paris to bring some monks to the abbey of St. Maur, near that city, excused himself for declining a journey through a strange and unknown country. In the history of Scotland, during the minority of James II. we find nothing but barbarous and cruel manners, depredations, burning of houses, bloodshed and massacre, without end. Pitscottie says, that oppression, theft, sacrilege, ravishing of women, were but a *dalliance*. How similar to beasts of prey let loose against each other in the Roman circus!

Men are prone to split into parties upon the slightest occasions; and sometimes parties subsist upon words merely. Whig and Tory subsisted long in England, upon <202> no better foundation: the Tories professed passive obedience; but declared, that they would not be slaves: the Whigs professed resistance; but declared it unlawful to resist, unless to prevent the being made slaves. Had these parties been disposed to unite, they soon would have discovered, that they differed in words only. The same observation is applicable to many religious disputes. One sect maintains, that we are saved by faith alone; another, that good works are necessary. The difference lies merely in words: the first acknowledges, that, if a man commit sin, he cannot have faith; and, consequently, under faith are comprehended good works: the other acknowledges, that good works imply good intention, or, in other words, faith; and, consequently, under good works, faith is comprehended (*a*). The following instance, solemnly ludicrous, is of parties formed merely from an inclination to differ, without any cause, real or verbal. No people were less interested in the late war between the Queen of Hungary and the King of Prussia, than the ci-<203>tizens of Ravenna. They, however, split into two parties, which abjured all society with each other. After the battle of Rosbach, a leading partyman withdrew for a month, without once showing his face in public.[13] But our catalogue is not yet complete. Differences concerning civil matters make no figure, compared with what concern religion. It is lamentable to observe, that religious sects resemble neighbouring states; the nearer they are to one another, the greater is their mutual rancour and animosity. But, as all histories are full of the cruelty and desolation occasioned by differences in religious tenets, I cannot bear to dwell longer upon such horrid scenes.

What conclusion are we to draw from the foregoing facts, so inconsistent in appearance with each other? I am utterly at a loss to reconcile them, otherwise than by holding man to be a compound of principles and passions, some social, some dissocial. Opposite principles or passions cannot, at the same instant, be exerted upon the same object (*b*); but they may be exerted at the same instant upon different <204> objects, and at different times upon the same object. This observation serves, indeed, to explain a seeming inconsistency in our nature, as being at one time highly social, and at another time no less dissocial: but it affords not a solution to the question, Whether, upon the whole, men be qualified for society, and be fitted for being happy in it? In order to a solution, we find it necessary to take a second view of the natural history of man.

(*a*) See Knox's Ecclesiastical History of Scotland, p. 13.
(*b*) Elements of Criticism, vol. 1. p. 143. edit. 5.
13. The "late war" in question was the Seven Years' War between Frederick the Great of Prussia and a coalition of other European powers, including Maria Theresa's Austria and Hungary. The Battle of Rossbach took place on November 5, 1757; it was one of Frederick's most decisive victories.

In a nascent society, where men hunt and fish in common, where there is plenty of game, and where the sense of property is faint, mutual affection prevails, because there is no cause of discord; and dissocial passions find sufficient vent against neighbouring tribes. Such is the condition of the North American savages, who continue hunters and fishers to this day; and such is the condition of all brute-animals that live in society, as mentioned above. The island Otaheite is divided into many small cantons, having each a chief of its own. These cantons never make war on each other, though they are frequently at war with the inhabitants of neighbouring islands. The inhabitants of the new Phi-<205>lippine islands, if Father Gobien be credited, are better fitted for society than any other known nation. Sweetness of temper, and love to do good, form their character. They never commit acts of violence: war they have no notion of; and it is a proverb among them, That a man never puts a man to death. Plato places the seat of justice and of happiness among the first men; and among them existed the golden age, if it ever did exist. But, when a nation, becoming populous, begins with rearing flocks and herds, proceeds to appropriate land, and is not satisfied without matters of luxury over and above, selfishness and pride gain ground, and become ruling and unruly passions. Causes of discord multiply, vent is given to avarice and resentment; and, among a people not yet perfectly submissive to government, dissocial passions rage, and threaten a total dissolution of society: nothing, indeed, suspends the impending blow, but the unwearied, though silent, operation, of the social appetite. Such was the condition of the Greeks at a certain period of their progress, as mentioned above; and such was the condition of Europe, and of <206> France in particular, during the anarchy of the feudal system, when all was discord, blood, and rapine. In general, wherever avarice and disorderly passions bear rule, I boldly pronounce that men are ill qualified for society.

Providence extracts order out of confusion. Men, in a society so uncomfortable, are taught, by dire experience, that they must either renounce society, or qualify themselves for it—the choice is easy, but how difficult the performance: After infinite struggles, appetite for society prevailed; and time, that universal conqueror, perfected men in the art of subduing their passions, or of dissembling them. Finding no enjoyment but in society, they are solicitous about the good-will of others; and adhere to justice and good manners: disorderly passions are suppressed, kindly affections encouraged; and men now are better qualified for society than formerly, though far from being perfectly qualified.

But, is our progress toward the perfection of society to stop here? are lust of power and of property to continue for ever leading principles? are envy, revenge, treachery, deceit, never to have an end? <207> "How devoutly to be wished, (it will be said), that all men were upright and honest; and that all of the same nation were united like brethren in concord and mutual affection! Here, indeed, would be perpetual sunshine, a golden age, a state approaching to that of good men made perfect in heavenly mansions." Beware of indulging such pleasing dreams. The system of Providence differs widely from our wishes; and shall ignorant man venture to arraign Providence? Are we qualified to judge of the whole, when but a small part is visible? From what is known of that system, we have reason to believe, that, were the whole visible, it would appear beautiful. We are not, however, reduced to an act of pure faith: a glimmering light, breaking in, makes it at least doubtful, whether, upon the whole, it be not really better for us to be as we are. Let us follow that glimmering light: it may perhaps lead us to some discovery.[14]

Strict adherence to the rules of justice would, indeed, secure our persons and our property: robbery and murder would vanish, and locks and guns be heard of no <208> more. So far excellent, were no new evils to come in their stead: but the void must be filled; and mental distresses would break in of various kinds, such particularly as proceed from refined delicacy, and nice sensibility of honour, little regarded while we are exposed to dangers more alarming. And, whether the change would be much for our advantage, appears doubtful: pain, as well as pleasure, is measured by comparison; and the slightest pain, such, for example, as arises from a transgression of civility or good-breeding, will overwhelm a person who has never felt any pain more severe. At any rate, natural evils would remain; and extreme delicacy, and softness of temper, produced by eternal peace and concord, would ren-

14. In the 1st and 2nd editions the next paragraph begins: "I begin with observing, that tho' in our present condition we suffer much from selfish and dissocial passions, yet custom renders our distress familiar, and hardens us not only to bear but to brave them" [1:381].

der such evils insupportable: the slight inconveniencies of a rough road, bad weather, or homely fair, would become serious evils, and afflict the traveller past enduring.¹⁵

But now, let it not escape our thoughts, that, in order to preserve justice untainted, and to maintain concord and affection, dissocial and selfish passions must necessarily be extirpated, or brought under absolute <209> subjection. Attend to the consequences: they deserve our most sober attention. Agitation is requisite to the mind, as well as to the body: a man engaged in a brisk pursuit, whether of business or of pleasure, is in his element, and in high spirits: but, when no object is in view to be attained or to be avoided, his spirits flag, and he sinks into languor and despondence. To prevent a condition so baneful, he is provided with many passions, that impel him to action without intermission, and invigorate both mind and body. But, upon the present supposition, scarce any motive to action would remain; and man, reduced to a lethargic state, would rival no being above an oister or a sensitive plant.

——————Pater ipse colendi
Haud facilem esse viam voluit, primusque per artem
Movit agros, curis acuens mortalia corda,
Nec torpere gravi passus sua regna veterno.
VIRGIL, Georg. 1.¹⁶

It is true that, in our present condition, we suffer much distress from selfish and dissocial passions. But nature provides a remedy: custom renders

---

15. In the 1st and 2nd editions the paragraph continues: "The French, among whom society has obtained a more refined polish than in any other nation, have become so soft and delicate as to lose all fortitude in distress. They cannot bear even a representation of severe affliction in a tragedy: an English audience would fall asleep at the slight distresses that make a deep impression in the French theatre" [1:382]. In the 1st and 2nd editions the next paragraph begins: "But now supposing, that a scrupulous adherence to the rules of morality would be a real improvement in society; yet to me it appears evident, that men as individuals would suffer more by that improvement, than they would gain as members of society" [1:382].
16. "The great Father himself has willed that the path of husbandry should not run smooth, who first made art awake the fields, sharpening men's wits by care, nor letting his kingdom slumber in heavy lethargy": *Georgics,* bk. I, ll. 121–24. Quotation added in 2nd edition.

misfortunes familiar, and hardens us, not only to bear but to brave them. Bentivoglio having govern-<210>ed Bologna forty years, was expelled by Pope Julius II. which was the first distress he had ever met with. My author Guicciardin reports, that he died of a broken heart, attributed to his constant prosperity. It is well said, that, whom the Lord loveth he chasteneth. The French, among whom society has obtained a more refined polish than in any other nation, have become so soft and delicate, as to lose all fortitude in distress. They cannot bear even a representation of severe affliction in a tragedy: an English audience would fall asleep at the slight distresses that make a deep impression in the French theatre.[17]

Nor ought it to be overlooked, that an uniform life of peace, tranquility, and security, would not be long relished. Constant repetition of the same pleasures would render even a golden age tasteless, like an Italian sky during a long summer. Nature has, for wise purposes, impressed upon us a taste for variety (*a*): without it, life would be altogether insipid. Paraguai, when governed by the Jesuits, affords a striking illustration. It was divided into parishes, in each of which a Jesuit presided as <211> king, priest, and prophet. The natives were not suffered to have any property, but laboured incessantly for their daily bread, which was delivered to them out of a public magazine. The men were employed in agriculture, the women in spinning; and certain precise hours were allotted for labour, for food, for prayer, and for sleep.* They soon sunk into such a listless state of mind, as to have no regret at dying, when attacked by disease or by old age. Such was their indifference about what might befal them, that, though they adored the Jesuits, yet they made no opposition, when the Fathers were, anno 1767, attacked by the Spaniards, and their famous republic demolished. Yet this Jesuit republic is extolled by M. de Voltaire, as the most perfect government

---

* Beside Paraguai tea, for which there is great demand in Peru, cotton, tobacco, and sugar-canes, were cultivated in Paraguai, and the product was stored up in magazines. No Indian durst keep in his house so much as an ounce of any of these commodities, under pain of receiving twelve lashes in *honour* of the twelve apostles, beside fasting three days in the house of correction. The fathers seldom inflicted a capital punishment, because it deprived them of a profitable slave.

(*a*) Elements of Criticism, vol. 1. p. 320. edit. 5.

17. "It is true . . . the French theatre": added in 3rd edition.

in the world, and as the triumph of humanity.¹⁸ The monkish life is contradictory to the <212> nature of man: the languor of that state is what, in all probability, tempts many a monk and nun, to find occupation even at the expence of virtue. The life of the Maltese Knights is far from being agreeable, now that their knight-errantry against the Turks has subsided. While they reside in the island, a strict uniformity in their manner of living is painfully irksome. Absence is their only relief, when they can obtain permission. There will not remain long a knight in the island, except such as, by office, are tied to attendance.

I proceed to another consideration. Familiarity with danger is necessary to eradicate our natural timidity; and so deeply rooted is that principle, that familiarity with danger of one sort does not harden us with respect to any other sort. A soldier, bold as a lion in the field, is faint-hearted at sea, like a child; and a seaman, who braves the winds and waves, trembles when mounted on a horse of spirit. Courage does not superabound at present, even in the midst of dangers and unforeseen accidents: sedentary manufacturers, who seldom are in the way of harm, are remarkably pusillanimous. What would men be <213> in the supposed condition of universal peace, concord, and security? they would rival a hare or a mouse in timidity. Farewell, upon that supposition, to courage, magnanimity, heroism, and to every passion that ennobles human nature! There may perhaps be men, who, hugging themselves in security against harm, would not be altogether averse to such degeneracy. But, if such men there be, I pray them only to reflect, that, in the progress from infancy to maturity, all nations do not ripen equally. One nation may have arrived at the supposed perfection of society, before another has advanced much beyond the savage state. What security hath the former against the latter? Precisely the same that timid sheep have against hungry wolves.

I shall finish with one other effect of the supposed perfection of society, more degrading, if possible, than any mentioned. Exercise, as observed above, is no less essential to the mind than to the body. The reasoning faculty, for example, without constant and varied exercise, will remain weak and undistinguishing to the end of life. By what means doth a man acquire

---

18. "Yet this Jesuit . . . triumph of humanity": added in 3rd edition.

<214> prudence and foresight, but by experience? It is precisely here as in the body: deprive a child of motion, and it will never acquire any strength of limbs. The many difficulties that men encounter, and their various objects of pursuit, rouse the understanding, and set the reasoning faculty at work for means to accomplish desire. The mind, by continual exercise, ripens to its perfection; and, by the same means, is preserved in vigour. It would have no such exercise in the supposed perfection of society; where there would be little to be desired, and less to be dreaded: our mental faculties would for ever lie dormant; and we should for ever remain ignorant that we have such faculties. The people of Paraguai are described as mere children in understanding. What wonder, considering their condition under Jesuit government, without ambition, without property, without fear of want, and without desires? The wants of those who inhabit the torrid zone are easily supplied: they need no clothing, scarce any habitation; and fruits, which ripen there to perfection, give them food without labour. Need we any other cause for their <215> inferiority of understanding, compared with the inhabitants of other climates, where the mind, as well as body, are constantly at work for procuring necessaries?* <216>

---

* The blessings of ease and inaction are most poetically displayed in the following description: "O felix Lapo, qui in ultimo angulo mundi sic bene lates, contentus et innocens. Tu nec times annonae charitatem, nec Martis praelia, quae ad tuas oras pervenire nequeunt, sed florentissimas Europae provincias et urbes, unico momento, saepe dejiciunt et delunt. Tu dormis hic sub tua pelle, ab omnibus curis, contentionibus, rixis, liber, ignorans, quid fit invidia. Tu nulla nosti discrimina, nisi tonantis Jovis fulmina. Tu ducis innocentissimos tuos annos ultra centenarium numerum, cum facili senectute, et summa sanitate. Te latent myriades morborum nobis Europaeis communes. Tu vivis in sylvis, avis instar, nec sementem facis, nec metis; tamen alit te Deus optimus optime." *Linnaeus, Flora Lapponica.*—(*In English thus:* "O happy Laplander, who, on the utmost verge of habitable earth, thus livest obscure, in rest, content, and innocence. Thou fearest not the scanty crop, nor ravages of war; and those calamities which waste whole provinces and towns, can never attain thy peaceful shores. Wrapt in thy covering of fur, thou canst securely sleep; a stranger to each tumultuous care; unenvying and unenvied. Thou fearest no danger, but from the thunder of heaven. Thy harmless days slide on in innocence, beyond the period of a century. Thy health is firm, and thy declining age is tranquil. Millions of diseases, which ravage the rest of the world, have never reached thy happy climate. Thou livest as the birds of the wood; thou carest not to sow nor reap, for bounteous Providence has supplied thee in all thy wants.")—So eloquent a panegyrist upon the Lapland life would make a capital figure upon an oyster. No creature is freer from

This suggests a thought. Considering that instinct is a guide much less fallible than reason, why should it be more sparingly bestowed on man, the chief of the terrestrial creation, than on other animals? Whatever appearance this may have at first sight against the human race, it will be found, on consideration, greatly in their favour. Instinct in man is confined within the narrowest bounds, and given only where reason would be ineffectual. Instinct, it is true, is infallible, and so are the laws of matter and motion: but, how low is blind instinct compared with the faculty of reasoning, deliberating, and choosing? Man governs himself, and chooses invariably what appears the best: Brute animals have no self-government, but are led blindly by natural impulse, without <217> having any end in view. Instinct differs only from the laws of matter, by comprehending a greater variety of circumstances; and is far inferior in dignity to the faculty of reason.[19]

That curious writer Mandevil, who is always entertaining, if he does not always instruct, exults in maintaining a proposition seemingly paradoxical, That private vices are public benefits.[20] He proves indeed, most triumphantly, that theft produced locks and bars, and that war produced swords and guns. But what would have been his triumph, had he discovered, that selfish and dissocial vices promote the most elevated virtues; and that, if such vices were eradicated, man would be a grovelling and contemptible being?

Upon the whole, the present state of things, in which evils both natural and moral make a part, contributes more to the enjoyment of life, as well as to the improvement of our faculties and passions, than an uniform state, without variety, and without hopes and fears.[21]

How rashly do men judge of the conduct of Providence! So flattering to the <218> imagination is a golden age, a life of perpetual sunshine, as to have enchanted poets, ancient and modern. Impressed with the felicity of such a state, can we be satisfied with our condition in this life? Such a jumble

---

want, no creature freer from war, and probably no creature is freer from fear; which, alas! is not the case of the Laplander.

19. Paragraph added in 2nd edition.

20. It was not uncommon for Mandeville's name to be misspelled in this way, especially by his opponents.

21. Paragraph added in 3rd edition.

of good and ill, malice mixed with benevolence, friendship alloyed with fraud, peace with alarms of war, and sometimes bloody wars,—is it not natural to think, that, in this unhappy world, chance prevails more than wisdom? Can freethinkers wish a better theme for declaiming against Providence, while good men sigh inwardly, and must be silent?* <219> But be-

* L'homme qui ne peut que par le nombre, qui n'est fort que par sa réunion, qui n'est heureux que par la paix, a la fureur de s'armer pour son malheur et de combattre pour sa ruine. Excité par l'insatiable avidité, aveuglé par l'ambition encore plus insatiable, il renonce aux sentimens d'humanité, cherche à s'entredétruire, se détruit en effet; et après ces jours de sang et de carnage, lorsque la fumée de la gloire s'est dissipée, il voit d'un oeil triste la terre dévastée, les arts ensevelies, les nations dispersées, les peuples affoiblis, son propre bonheur ruiné, et sa puissance réelle anéantie. "Grand Dieu! dont la seule présence soutient la nature et maintient l'harmonie des loix de l'univers; Vous, qui du trône immobile de l'empirée, voyez rouler sous vos pieds toutes les sphères célestes sans choc et sans confusion; qui du sein du repos, reproduisez à chacque instant leurs mouvemens immenses, et seul régissez dans une paix profonde ce nombre infini de cieux et de mondes; rendez, rendez enfin le calme à la terre agitée! Qu'elle soit dans le silence! Qu' à votre voix la discorde et la guerre cessent de faire retenter leurs clameurs orgueilleuses! Dieu de bonté auteur de tous les êtres, vos regards paternels embrassent tous les objets de la création: mais l'homme est votre être de choix; vous avez éclairé son ame d'une rayon de votre lumière immortelle; comblez vos bienfaits en pénétrant son coeur d'un trait de votre amour: ce sentiment divin se répandant par-tout, réunira les natures ennemies; l'homme ne craindra plus l'aspect de l'homme; le fer homicide n'armera plus sa main; le feu dévorant de la guerre ne sera plus tarir la source des générations; l'espèce humaine maintenant affoiblie, mutilée, moissonnée dans sa fleur, germera de nouveau et se multipliera sans nombre; la nature accablée sous le poids de fléaux, stérile, abandonnée, reprendra bientôt avec une nouvelle vie son ancienne fécondité; et nous, Dieu Bienfaiteur, nous la seconderons, nous la cultiverons, nous l'observerons sans cesse pour vous offrir à chaque instant un nouveau tribut de reconnoissance et d'admiration"; *Buffon Histoire Naturelle*, vol. 9. 8*vo edit.*

(*In English thus:* "Man, who is powerful only by numbers, whose strength consists in the union of forces, and whose happiness is to be found alone in a state of peace, has yet the madness to take arms for his own misery, and fight to the ruin of his species. Urged on by insatiable avarice, and blinded by ambition still more insatiable, he banishes from his breast every sentiment of humanity, and, eager for the destruction of his fellow-creatures, in effect destroys himself. When the days of blood and carnage are past, when the vapour of glory is dissipated, he looks around with a sorrowful eye upon the desolated earth, he sees the arts extinct, the nations dispersed, and population dead: his happiness is ruined, and his power is reduced to nothing. 'Great God! whose sole presence sustains the creative power, and rules the harmony of nature's laws! who from thy permanent celestial throne beholdest the motion of the nether spheres, all-perfect in their course which knows no change; who broughtest from out the womb of rest by endless repro-

hold the blindness of man with respect to the dispensations of Providence! <220> A golden age would to man be more poisonous than Pandora's box; a gift, sweet <221> in the mouth, but bitter, bitter, in the stomach. Let us then forbear repining; for the subject before us must afford conviction, if any thing can, that our best course is to submit humbly to whatever befals, and to rest satisfied, that the world is governed by wisdom, not by chance. What can be expected of barbarians, but utter ignorance of Providence, and of divine government? But, as men ripen in the knowledge of causes and effects, the benevolence as well as wisdom of a superintending Being become more and more apparent. How pleasing is that observation! Beautiful final causes without num-<222>ber have been discovered in the material as well as moral world, with respect to many particulars that once appeared dark and gloomy. Many continue to have that appearance; but, with respect to such, is it too bold to maintain, that an argument from ignorance, a slender argument at any rate, is altogether insufficient in judging of divine government? How salutary is it for man, and how comfortable, to rest on the faith, that whatever is, is the best! <223>

---

duction those never-ceasing movements; who rulest in peace the infinity of worlds: Eternal God! vouchsafe at length to send a portion of that heavenly peace to calm the agitated earth. Let every tumult cease: at thy celestial voice, no more be heard around the proud and clamorous shouts of war and discord. All bounteous Creator! Author of being! each object of thy works partakes of thy paternal care; but chief of all, thy chosen creature man. Thou hast bestowed on him a ray of thine immortal light: O deign to crown that gift, by penetrating his heart with a portion of thy love. Soon will that heavenly sentiment, pervading his nature, reconcile each warring and contradictory principle: man will no longer dread the sight of man: the murdering blade will sleep within its sheath: the fire of war will cease to dry up the springs of generation: the human race, now languishing and withering in the bloom, will bud afresh, and multiply: nature, which now sinks beneath the scourge of misery, sterile and desolated, will soon renew her wasted strength, and regain her first ferility. We, O God of benevolence, we thy creatures will second the blessing. It will be ours to bestow on the earth that culture which best can aid her fruitfulness; and we will pay to thee the most acceptable of sacrifices, in endless gratitude and adoration.'")

How natural is this prayer; how unnatural the state thus anxiously requested? M. Buffon's devotional fits are fervent: pity it is, that they are not better directed.

❧ SKETCH II ❧

General View of Government

The progress of government, accurately delineated, would produce a great volume: in the present work there is room but for a few hints. What are the qualities that fit men for society, is explained above; but writers are far from being unanimous about what fits them for government. All agree, that submission to our governors is a duty: but they appear to be at a loss upon what foundation to rest that duty; as if it were not evident, that, by our nature, we are fitted for government as well as for society (*a*). If justice or veracity be essential to society, submission to government is no less so; and each of these equally is declared by the moral sense to be our duty. But, to qualify man for government, the duty of submission is not alone sufficient: diversity of temper, and of talents, are also <224> necessary; and accordingly it is so ordered by Providence, that there are never wanting, in any society, men who are qualified to lead, as well as men who are disposed to follow. Where a number of people convene for any purpose, some will naturally assume authority without the formality of election, and the rest will as naturally submit. A regular government, founded on laws, was probably not thought of, till people had frequently suffered by vicious governors.*

---

* At first, when a certain regimen was one approved, it may be that all was permitted to the wisdom and discretion of those who were to rule; till, by experience, this was found very inconvenient, so as the thing devised for a remedy did increase the sore which it should have cured. They saw, "that, to live by one man's will became the cause of all men's misery." This constrained them to come into laws, wherein all men might see their duty beforehand, and know the penalties of transgressing them; *Hooker's Eccl. Pol. l.* 1. §10.

(*a*) Principles of Equity, p. 177. edit. 2.

During the infancy of national societies, government is extremely simple; and no less mild than simple. No individual is, by nature, entitled to exercise magisterial authority over his fellows; for no individual is born with any mark of <225> pre-eminence to vouch that he has such a privilege. But nature teaches respect for men of age and experience: who accordingly take the lead in deliberating and advising, leaving execution to the young and vigorous.* War indeed cannot be carried on without a commander; but originally his authority was limited to actual war; and he returned home a private person, even when crowned with victory. The wants of men were originally so few and so easily satisfied, as seldom to occasion a controversy among members of the same tribe. And men, finding vent for their dissocial passions against other tribes, were fond to live peaceably at <226> home. Introduction of money made an amazing change. Wealth, bestowed by fortune or procured by rapine, made an impression on the vulgar: different ranks were recognized: the rich became imperious, and the poor mutinous. Selfishness, prevailing over social affection, stirred up every man against his neighbour; and men, overlooking their natural enemies, gave vent to dissocial passions within their own tribe. It became necessary to strengthen the hands of the sovereign, for repressing passions inflamed by opulence, which tend to dissolution of society. This slight view fairly accounts for the gradual progress of government from the mildest form to the most despotic. The second part of the progress is more pleasing. Men long inured to the authority of government, acquire a habit of repressing their turbulent passions; and becoming by degrees regular and orderly, they are easily restrained from doing wrong.

In every nation originally democracy was the first form of government.

---

* Such as are acquainted with no manners but what are modern, will be puzzled to account for the great veneration paid to old age in early times. Before writing was invented, old men were the repositories of knowledge, which they acquired by experience; and young men had no access to knowledge but from them. At the siege of Troy, Nestor, who had seen three generations, was the chief adviser and director of the Greeks. But, as books are now the most patent road to knowledge, to which the old and young have access, it may justly be said, that by the invention of writing and printing, old men have lost much of their pristine importance.

Before ranks were distinguished, every single man was entitled to vote in matters of common concern. When a tribe becomes too nu-<227>merous for making one body, or for being convened in one place, the management falls naturally to the elders of the people; who, after acquiring authority by custom, are termed the *senate*.¹ At first, little more was thought of, but that to govern great numbers a senate is necessary: time unfolded the constitution of that body and its powers. With respect to the senate of old Rome in particular, even the mode of election was long ambulatory; and it is natural to believe that its powers were no less so; till length of time introduced regularity and order. From this form of government, the transition is easy to a limited monarchy. Absolute monarchy, contradictory to the liberty that all men should enjoy in every government, can never be established but by force. Government among all nations has made the progress above delineated. There are exceptions; but these have arisen from singular events.

To a nation accustomed to liberty and independence, arbitrary government is a sore disease. But awe and submission are also natural; and a life of dependence <228> probably sits easy on those who are accustomed to it. Were it not so, Providence would be unkind, as the far greater part of men are dependent.²

During the infancy of a society, punishments must be mild; because government has no sufficient authority over the minds of men to enforce what are severe. But government in time acquires authority; and when its authority is firmly rooted in the minds of the people, punishments more rigorous can be made effectual; and such punishments are necessary among a people not yet well disciplined. When men at last become regular and orderly under a steady administration, punishments become less and less necessary, and the mildest are sufficient (*a*). The Chinese government is extremely mild, and its punishments are in the same tone. A capital punishment is never inflicted, till the sentence be examined by a sovereign

---

(*a*) Historical Law-tracts, tract 1.
1. The Latin *senex* means "old."
2. This and the previous paragraph added in 2nd edition.

court, and approved by the Emperor. Thus government, after passing through all the intermediate degrees from extreme mildness <229> to extreme severity, returns at last to its original temper of mildness and humanity.* <230>

---

* An ingenious writer observes, that as our American settlements are now so prosperous, banishment to these settlements is scarce a punishment. He therefore proposes, that criminals be transported to Hudson's bay, or to some other uncultivated country. My doubt is, that in proportion as manners improve, the severity of punishment ought to be mitigated. Perhaps, the transportation to any of our American colonies, though less dreadful than formerly, may however be now a sufficient punishment for theft, or other crime of no deeper dye.

෴ SKETCH III ෴

Different Forms of Government compared

Of all governments, democracy is the most turbulent: despotism, which benumbs the mental faculties, and relaxes every spring of action, is in the opposite extreme. Mixed governments, whether monarchical or republican, stand in the middle: they promote activity, but seldom any dangerous excess.

Pure democracy, like that of Athens, Argos, and Carthage, is the very worst form of government, if we make not despotism an exception. The people, in whom resides the sovereign power, are insolent in prosperity, timid in adversity, cruel in anger, blind and prodigal in affection, and incapable of embracing steadily a prudent measure. Thucydides relates (*a*), that Agis with a gallant army of Spartans surrounded the army of Argos; and, tho' secure of victory, suffered them <231> to retreat, upon solemn assurances from Thrasyllus, the Argian general, of terminating all differences in an amicable treaty. Agis, perhaps justly, was bitterly censured for suffering victory to slip out of his hands: but the Argians, dreaming of victory when the danger was over, brought their general to trial, confiscated his effects, and would have stoned him to death, had he not taken refuge in a temple. Two Athenian generals, after one naval victory, being intent on a second, deputed Theramenes to perform the last duty to the dead. A violent storm prevented Theramenes from executing the trust reposed in him; but it did not prevent the people of Athens from putting their two generals to death, as if they had neglected their duty. The fate of Socrates is a sad instance of the changeable, as well as violent, disposition of a dem-

(*a*) Lib. 5.

ocratical state. He was condemned to death, for attempting innovations in the established religion: the sentence was grossly unjust: he attempted no innovation; but only, among his friends, expressed purer notions of the Deity than were common in Greece at that time. But his funeral obsequies <232> were scarce over, when bitter remorse seized the people. His accusers were put to death without trial, every person banished who had contributed to the sentence pronounced against him, and his statue was erected in the most public part of the city. The great Scipio, in his camp near Utica, was surrounded with three Carthaginian armies, which waited only for daylight to fall upon him. He prevented the impending blow, by surprising them in the dead of night; which gave him a complete victory. This misfortune, for it could scarce be called bad conduct, provoked the democracy of Carthage, to pronounce sentence of death against Asdrubal their general. Great trading towns cannot flourish, if they be not faithful to their engagements, and honest in their dealings: whence then the *fides Punica?* A democracy is in its nature rash, violent, and fluctuating; and the Carthaginians merited the reproach, not as individuals, but as a democratical state.

A commonwealth governed by chosen citizens, is very different from a democracy, where the mob rules. The solid foundation of such a commonwealth, is <233> equality among the citizens. Inequality of riches cannot be prevented in a commercial state; but inequality of privileges may be prevented, by excluding no citizen from the opportunity of commanding as well as of obeying. The invidious distinction of Patrician and Plebeian was a gross malady in the Roman republic, a perpetual source of dissension between two bodies of men, equally well born, equally rich, and equally fit for war. This ill-poised government would have put an end to the republic, had not the Plebeians prevailed, who were the more numerous. That reformation produced to Rome plenty of able men, qualified to govern both in peace and in war.

A commonwealth is the best form of government for a small state: there is little room for inequality of rank or of property; and the people can act in a body. Monarchy is preferable for a large state, where the people, widely spread, cannot be easily collected into a body. Attica was a kingdom, while its twelve cantons were remote from each other, and but slenderly connected. Theseus, by collecting the people of figure into the city <234> of Athens, and by a general assembly of all the cantons held there, fitted Attica to be a commonwealth.

When a nation becomes great and populous, it is ill fitted for being a commonwealth: ambition is apt to trample upon justice, selfishness upon patriotism, and the public is sacrificed to private views. To prevent corruption from turning incurable, the only remedy is a strict rotation in office, which ought never to be dispensed with on any pretext.* By such rotation, every citizen in his turn governs and is governed: the highest office is limited as to time, and the greatest men in the state must submit to the sacred law of obeying as well as of commanding. A man long accustomed to power, is not happy in a private station: that corrupting habit is prevented by an alternate succession of public and private life; which is more agreeable by variety, and contributes no less to virtue <235> than to happiness. It was that form of government in ancient Rome, which produced citizens without number, illustrious for virtue and talents. Reflect upon Cincinnatus, eminent among heroes for disinterested love to his country. Had he been a Briton, a seat in parliament would have gratified his ambition, as affording the best opportunity of serving his country. In parliament he joins the party that appears the most zealous for the public. Being deceived in his friends, patriots in name only, he goes over to the court; and after fighting the battles of the ministry for years, he is compelled by a shattered fortune to accept a post or a pension. Fortunate Cincinnatus! born at a time and in a country where virtue was the passport to power and glory. Cincinnatus, after serving with honour and reputation as chief magistrate, cheerfully retired to a private station, in obedience to the laws of his country: nor was that change a hardship on a man who was not corrupted by a long habit of power. But wonderful was the change, when the republic by successful wars comprehended great kingdoms. Luxurious and sensual men, who <236> composed the senate, could not maintain their authority over generals who commanded great armies, and were illustrious by conquest. In the civil wars

---

* A commonwealth with such a rotation may be aptly compared to a group of jets d'eau, rising one above another in beautiful order, and preserving the same order in descending: the form of the group continues invariable, but the forming parts are always changing.

accordingly that were carried on after the death of Julius Caesar, the legions called from Spain and other distant provinces to defend the senate, deserted all to Antony, or to Lepidus, or to Octavius Caesar.[1]

Political writers define a free state to be where the people are governed by laws of their own making. This definition is lame; for laws made by the people are not always just. There were many unjust laws enacted in Athens during the democratical government; and in Britain instances are not wanting of laws, not only unjust, but oppressive. The true definition of a free state, is, where the laws of nature are strictly adhered to, and where every municipal regulation is contrived to improve society, and to promote honesty and industry. If that definition be just, despotism is the worst species of government; being contrived to support arbitrary will in the sovereign, without regarding the laws of nature, or the good of society. The lawless cruelty of a King of <237> Persia, is painted to the life by a single expression of a Persian grandee, "That every time he left the King's apartment, he was inclined to feel with his hand whether his head was on his shoulders." In the Russian empire, men approach the throne with terror: the slightest political intrigue is a sufficient foundation for banishing the greatest nobleman to Siberia, and for confiscating his estate. The laws of that empire smell no less rank of slavery than of oppression. No person dares game with money that bears the impression of the present sovereign: a man going along the street that fronts the Emperor's apartment, must pull off his hat; and it is a heinous trespass, to write a letter with the Emperor's name in small characters. Despotism is every where the same: it was high treason to sell a statue of a Roman Emperor; and it was doubted, whether it was not high treason to hit an Emperor's statue with a stone thrown at random (*a*). When Elisabeth Empress of Russia was on death-bed, no person durst inquire about her; and, even after her death, it was not at first safe to speak of <238> it. The deep silence of the Russians upon matters of government, arises from the encouragement given to accusations of treason. The bystanders must lay hold of the person accused: a father arrests his son, a son his father, and nature suffers in silence. The accused with the accuser are hurried to prison,

(*a*) l. 5. ad legem Juliam Majestatis.
1. "But wonderful was . . . to Octavius Caesar": added in 2nd edition.

there to remain till they be tried in the secret court of chancery. That court, composed of a few ministers named by the Emperor, have the lives and fortunes of all at their mercy. The nobles, slaves to the crown, are prone to retaliate upon their inferiors. They impose taxes at pleasure upon their vassals, and frequently seize all at short hand.* <239>

Servility and depression of mind in the subjects of a despotic government, cannot be better marked than in the funeral rites of a Roman Emperor, described by Herodian (*a*). The body being burnt privately, a waxen image representing the Emperor is laid in a bed of state. On the one side sit the senators several hours daily, clothed in black; and on the other, the most respectable matrons, clothed in white. The ceremony lasts seven days, during which the physicians from time to time approach the bed, and declare the Emperor to be worse and worse. When the day comes of declaring him dead, the most dignified of the nobility carry the bed upon their shoulders, and place it in the old forum, where the Roman magistrates formerly laid down their office. Then begin doleful ditties, sung to his memory by boys and women. These being ended, the bed is carried to the *Campus Martius,* and there burnt upon a high stage with <240> great solemnity. When the flames ascend, an eagle is let loose, which is supposed to carry the soul of the Emperor to heaven. Is that farce less ridiculous than a puppet-shew? Is it not much more ridiculous? Dull must have been the spectator who could behold the solemnity without smiling at least, if not laughing outright; but the Romans were crushed by despotism, and nothing could provoke them to laugh. That ridiculous farce continued to be acted till the time of Constantine: how much later, I know not.

---

* The following incident is a striking example of the violence of passion, indulged in a despotic government, where men in power are under no control. Thomas Pereyra, a Portuguese general, having assisted the King of Pegu in a dangerous war with his neighbour of Siam, was a prime favourite at court, having elephants of state, and a guard of his own countrymen. One day coming from court mounted on an elephant, and hearing music in a house where a marriage was celebrating between a daughter of the family and her lover, he went into the house, and desired to see the bride. The parents took the visit for a great honour, and cheerfully presented her. He was instantly smit with her beauty, ordered his guards to seize her, and to carry her to his palace. The bridegroom, as little able to bear the affront as to revenge it, cut his own throat.

(*a*) Lib. 4.

The finest countries have been depopulated by despotism; witness Greece, Egypt, and the lesser Asia. The river Menam, in the kingdom of Siam, overflows annually like the Nile, depositing a quantity of slime, which proves a rich manure. The river seems to rise gradually as the rice grows; and retires to its channel when the rice, approaching to maturity, needs no longer to be watered. Nature beside has bestowed on that rich country variety of delicious fruits, requiring scarce any culture. In such a paradise, would one imagine that the Siamites are a miserable people? The government is de-<241>spotic, and the subjects are slaves: they must work for their monarch six months every year, without wages, and even without receiving any food from him. What renders them still more miserable is, that they have no protection, either for their persons or their goods: the grandees are exposed to the rapacity of the King and his courtiers; and the lower ranks are exposed to the rapacity of the grandees. When a man has the misfortune to possess a tree remarkable for good fruit, he is required, in the name of the King, or of a courtier, to preserve the fruit for their use. Every proprietor of a garden in the neighbourhood of the capital must pay a yearly sum to the keeper of the elephants; otherwise it will be laid waste by these animals, whom it is high treason to molest. From the sea-port of Mergui to the capital, one travels ten or twelve days, through immense plains of a rich soil, finely watered. That country appears to have been formerly cultivated, but is now quite depopulated, and left to tigers and elephants. Formerly, an immense commerce was carried on in that fertile country: historians attest, that, in the middle of the sixteenth <242> century, above a thousand foreign ships frequented its ports annually. But the King, tempted by so much riches, endeavoured to engross all the commerce of his country; by which means he annihilated successively mines, manufactures, and even agriculture. The kingdom is depopulated, and few remain there but beggars. In the island of Ceylon, the King is sole proprietor of the land; and the people are supinely indolent: their huts are mean, without any thing like furniture: their food is fruit that grows spontaneously; and their covering is a piece of coarse cloth, wrapped round the middle. The settlement of the Dutch East India company at the Cape of Good Hope, is profitable to them in their commerce with the East Indies; and it would be much more profitable, if they gave proper encouragement to the tenants and possessors of their lands. But these poor people are ruled with a rod of iron: the product of their land is extorted from them by the company at so low a price, as scarce to afford them common necessaries. Avarice, like many other irregular passions, obstructs its own gratification: were indu-<243>stry duly encouraged, the product of the ground would be in greater plenty, and goods be afforded voluntarily at a lower price than they are at present obtained by violence. The Peruvians are a sad example of the effects of tyranny; being reduced to a state of stupid insensibility. No motive to action influences them; neither riches, nor luxury, nor ambition: they are even indifferent about life. The single pleasure they feel, is to get drunk, in order to forget their misery. The provinces of Moldavia, Walachia, and Bessarabia, situated between the 43d and 48th degrees of North latitude, are defended on three sides by the Niester, the Black Sea, and the Danube. The climate of that region, and the fertility of its soil, render it not inferior to any other country in Europe. Its pastures, in particular, are excellent, producing admirable horses, with an incredible number of sheep and horned cattle; and corn, wine, oil, honey, and wax, were formerly produced there in great plenty. So populous was Walachia, in particular, a few centuries ago, that its Prince was able to raise an army of seventy thousand men. Yet, notwith-<244>standing all these advantages, the wretched policy of the Turkish government has reduced these provinces to be almost a desert. A despotic government stifles in the birth all the bounties of nature, and renders the finest spots of the globe equally sterile with its barren mountains. When a patriotic king travels about to visit his dominions, he is received with acclamations of joy. A despotic prince dares not hope for such a reception: he is locked up in his seraglio, ignorant of what passes; and indolently suffers his people to be pillaged, without even hearing of their distresses. A despotic prince accordingly, whose wants are all supplied with profusion, and who has nothing left him to wish for or desire, carries on a most languid existence. Rousseau says well, "Tout Prince qui aspire au despotisme, aspire à l'honneur de mourir d'ennui. Dans tous les royaumes du monde cherchez-vous l'homme le plus ennuyé du pays? Allez toujours directement au souverain; surtout s'il est très absolu. C'est bien la peine de faire tant de miserables! ne faudroit-il s'ennuyer à moindres fraix?"² <245>

At the same time, despotism, though calculated to elevate the sovereign above the rules of justice, and to make him the only free person in his dominions, tends, above all other governments, to render him insecure. He becomes odious by oppression; and every hand would be raised against him, but for the restraint of fear. A situation so ticklish, lays him open to every bold spirit, prompted by revenge to seek his ruin, or by ambition to usurp his throne. In that respect, Russia and Turky are precisely similar: conspiracies against the sovereign are equally frequent, and equally successful. The moment an usurper seizes the palace, all prostrate themselves before him, without inquiring about his title. In that manner was the present Empress of Russia established, notwithstanding a very unfavourable circumstance, that of dethroning her own husband Peter III. No free spirit regrets such events in a despotic government: the only thing to be regretted, is, that they concern the monarch only; not the people, who remain abject slaves, as formerly. The present Empress, sensible of her precarious situation, is intent to humanize her people, <246> and to moderate the despotism. In that view, she has published a code of laws fit for a limited monarchy; and expressing great regard to the lives, liberties, and property of her subjects.

But a monarchy, with all the moderation that despotism can admit, is inconsistent with the liberty of the press. Political pamphlets, and even newspapers, are no less useful for instructing the King, than for securing his subjects. In France, the ministry are deprived of that means of acquiring knowledge; and are reduced to the necessity of trusting to insinuating men, who cunningly creep into favour, with a view to their own interest. After the late peace 1763, a plan was concerted for establishing a colony in Guiana;

---

2. "Any Prince who aspires to despotism aspires to the honor of dying of boredom. If in any Realm on earth you are looking for the country's most bored man, always go directly to the sovereign, especially if he is very absolute. What a waste to make so many people wretched! couldn't he become bored at less cost?" (*Julie, ou la nouvelle Héloïse*, pt. VI, letter 8, p. 570). "A despotic prince accordingly . . . à moindres fraix?": added in 2nd edition.

and no fewer than twelve thousand persons were landed there all at one time. But, so grossly ignorant were that ministry of the preparations necessary for planting a colony in the torrid zone, that contagious diseases, occasioned by unwholesome food, and want of accommodation, left not a single person alive. This could not have happened in England: every article of management would have been canvassed, <247> and light would have broken in from every quarter.

Government is essential to a society of any extent; and both are equally the work of nature. With a view to government, nature has fitted a small proportion for being leaders, and a great proportion for being led. The form of government accordingly, that is the most consonant to nature, is that which allots to each their proper station. Democracy is contradictory to nature, because the whole people govern: despotism is not less so, because government rests in a single person. A republic, or a limited monarchy, is the best form; because in these every man has an opportunity to act the part that nature destined him for.[3]

I have insisted upon the deplorable effects of despotism longer perhaps than is necessary; but I was fond of the opportunity to justify, or rather applaud, the spirit of liberty so eminent in the inhabitants of Britain. I now proceed to compare different forms of government, with respect to various particulars; beginning with patriotism. Every form of government must be good that inspires patrio-<248>tism; and the best form to invigorate that noble passion is a commonwealth founded on rotation of power; where it is the study of those in office to do good, and to merit approbation from their fellow citizens. In the Swiss Cantons, the salaries of magistrates and public officers are scarce sufficient to defray their expences; and those worthy persons desire no other recompense but to be esteemed and honoured. Thus, these offices are filled with men of ability and character. The revenues of Geneva scarcely amount to L. 30,000 a year; which, however, by a well-regulated oeconomy, is more than sufficient to defray the current expences. And this republic is enabled to provide for the security of its subjects, from an income, which many individuals, both in France and

---

3. Paragraph added in 2nd edition.

England, squander in vain pomp, and vicious dissipation.*[4] A republic so modelled, in-<249>spires virtues of every sort. The people of Switzerland seldom think of a writing to confirm a bargain: a law-suit is scarce known among them; and many there are who have never heard of an advocate nor of an attorney. Their doors are never shut but in winter. It is patriotism that Montesquieu has in view, when he pronounces virtue to be the leading principle in a republic. He has reason to term it so, because patriotism is connected with every social virtue; and, when it vanishes, every virtue vanishes with it.†[5] Demo-<250>cracy will never be recommended by any enlightened politician, as a good form of government; were it for no other reason but that patriotism cannot long subsist where the mob governs. In monarchy, the King is exalted so high above his subjects, that his ministers are little better than servants. Such condition is not friendly to patriotism: it is as little friendly to ambition; for ministers are still servants, however much raised above other subjects. Wealth being the only remaining pursuit, promotes avarice to be their ruling passion. Now, if patriotism be not found in ministers, who have power, far less in men who have no power; and thus,

---

* No human work can be everlasting: The seventy-two bailiages of the extensive Canton of Bern threaten ruin to the republic. These lucrative offices, which the great council appropriates to its own members, occasion a constant influx of riches into the capital. Patriotism is observed of late years to be on the decline among the citizens of Bern; and no wonder, considering that luxury and selfishness are the never-failing offspring of opulence. When selfishness becomes the ruling passion of that people, those in power will pilfer the public treasure, which is immense, and enrich themselves with the spoils of the republic. Confusion and anarchy must ensue, and the state will settle in a monarchy, or, more probably, in an odious democracy.

† Industry and frugality may in some measure have the same effect with patriotism, where riches are gained by labour, not by inheritance. Manchester is one of the greatest manufacturing villages in England. Industry there flourishes, and with it frugality and honesty. It is remarkable, that its numerous inhabitants, amounting to above 40,000, are governed by a magistrate of no higher rank than a justice of peace constable; and, by his authority, small as it is, peace and good order are preserved. The best citizens are not unwilling to be constables; and some are ambitious of the office. There are in England many other great manufacturing villages that are governed pretty much in the same manner. [[Note added in 2nd edition.]]

4. "Thus, these offices ... and vicious dissipation" (but not the appended note): added in 3rd edition.

5. In 1st edition: "and when it vanishes, men regard themselves only, not their fellow-citizens" [1:403].

in monarchy, riches are preferred before virtue, and every vitious offspring of avarice has free growth. The worst sort of monarchy is that which is elective; because patriotism can have no stable footing in such a state. The degeneracy of the Poles is owing to an elective monarchy. <251> Every neighbouring state being interested in the election, money is the great engine that influences the choice. The electors being tempted by every motive of interest, lose sight of the public, and endeavour each of them to make the best bargain he can for his own advantage. This reasoning is verified by the late war of the Russians in Poland. Baron de Manstein, in his memoirs of Russia, says, that, though the Poles were a match for the Saxons, yet that seldom did three hundred Russians go a step out of their way to avoid three thousand Poles.[6]

Sumptuary laws have a fine effect in the small cantons of Switzerland, where every one is known to every one, but are impracticable in a great monarchy.[7]

Without piercing to the foundation, one can have no just notion of the various forms that government assumes in different states. Monarchy is of many different kinds, and so is a republic. Rome and Carthage, the two great rival republics of ancient times, differed widely in their original constitution. Much has been said of these republics by historians and political writers. There is one point of compa-<252>rison, that will set in a clear light the difference of their constitutions with respect to peace and war. Carthage, advantageously situated for commerce, became a great and flourishing trading town. The Carthaginians having no object but riches, admitted none into a participation of their privileges. War was against their genius: but they made war in order to load their new subjects with taxes. Rome, on the contrary, was ill situated for commerce: its inhabitants were from the beginning employed in war, either defensive or offensive. Their great object accordingly was power; to which end, they were always disposed to adopt as citizens the best of those they conquered. Thus Rome became a city of warriors, Carthage of merchants. The subjects of the latter were always ripe for a revolt, while the subjects of the former were always

---

6. "The worst sort . . . three thousand Poles": added in 2nd edition.
7. Paragraph added in 3rd edition.

faithful. Between two such states, there could be no equality in war; and, had the Carthaginians been as skilful in politics as they were in commerce, they would have avoided, with the strictest circumspection, every occasion of difference with the Romans. Rome employed its own ci-<253>tizens in war: Carthage had none to employ but mercenaries. In an offensive war, the object of the latter was riches; that of the former was power and glory, motives much superior, and more animating. In a defensive war, the difference is infinite between mercenaries, who have no interest but to receive pay, and citizens, who fight for their country, and for their wives and children. What then are we to think of Hannibal, who carried on war against the Romans with an army of mercenaries, was successful in every engagement, and pushed them to the very brink of ruin? He certainly was the greatest General the world ever saw. If any one is to be excepted, it is the present King of Prussia.*

I next compare different forms of government, with respect to the influence of <254> opulence. Riches, which, joined with ambition, produce bold attempts for power, are, however, not dangerous in monarchy, where the sovereign is so far superior, as to humble to the dust the most aspiring of his subjects. But riches, joined with ambition, are dangerous in a republic: ambition will suggest the possibility of sowing dissension among the leaders: riches will make the attempt successful; and then adieu to the republic. Wealth, accumulated by commerce in Carthage and in Athens, extinguished patriotism, and rendered their democracies unjust, violent, and tyrannical. It had another bad effect; which was, to make them ambitious of conquest. The sage Plutarch charges Themistocles with the ruin of Athens. "That great man," says he, "inspired his countrymen with desire of naval power. That power produced extensive commerce, and conse-

* The following character of Hannibal is drawn by Titus Livius. "Has tantas viri virtutes ingentia vitia aequabant, inhumana crudelitas, perfidia plusquam Punica, nihil veri, nihil sancti, nullus Deum metus, nullum jusjurandum, nulla religio." [["These admirable qualities of the man were equalled by his monstrous vices: his cruelty was inhuman, his perfidy worse than Punic; he had no regard for the truth, and none for sanctity, no fear of the gods, no reverence for an oath, no religious scruple."]] This betrays the cloven foot of gross prejudice. A man of such a character could never, for so many years, without a single mutiny, have kept on foot a mercenary army, composed of different nations. [[Note added in 2nd edition.]]

quently riches: riches again, beside luxury, inspired the Athenians with a high opinion of their power, and made them rashly engage in every quarrel among their neighbours." Suppress the names, and one will believe it to be a censure on the conduct of Britain. <255> Successful commerce prompted the Carthaginians, against their natural interest, to make war for gain. Had they been successful against the Romans, both nations must have fallen a sacrifice to the ambition of Hannibal: what Carthaginian durst have opposed that glorious conqueror, returning with a victorious army, devoted to his will? That event was long dreaded by Hanno, and the wiser part of the Carthaginian senate; and hence their scanty supplies to Hannibal. But what is only a supposition with respect to Carthage, proved to be the fate of Rome. Inequality of rank, opulence, and luxury, relaxed every principle of the commonwealth, particularly rotation of power, which ought to have been their palladium. Conquest at a distance led them unwarily, in some instances, to suspend that fundamental law, of which Caesar availed himself in his Gallic war, by debauching from their duty the best disciplined army of the republic: and it was that army, under a leader little inferior to Hannibal, which determined the fate of Rome.

A state with a small territory, such as Hamburgh or Holland, may subsist long <256> as a commonwealth, without much hazard from the opulence of individuals. But an extensive territory in the hands of a few opulent proprietors, is dangerous in a commonwealth; because of their influence over numbers who depend on them for bread. The island of Britain is too large for a commonwealth. This did not escape a profound political writer (*a*), who is an honour to his country; and, to remedy the evil, he proposes an Agrarian law. But fondness for a system of his own invention made him overlook a defect in it, that would not have escaped him, had it been the invention of another; which is, that accumulation of land can never be prevented by an Agrarian law: a trust-deed is a ready screen for covering accumulation beyond law: and dark transactions are carried on without end; similar to what is practised, most dishonestly, by those who elect and are elected members of parliament. When such comes to be the condition of land-property, an Agrarian law will be ripe for dissolution.

(*a*) Harrington.

In early times, greater variety of cha-<257>racter is seen than at present; among sovereigns especially, who are not taught to govern their passions. Perusing the history of Spain, in particular, one is struck with an amazing variety of character in the Moorish Kings. In some of them, outrageous cruelty; in others, mildness and affection for their people: in some, unbounded ambition surmounting every obstacle of justice and humanity; in others, strict attention to commerce, and to every moral virtue; some heaping up treasure; some squandering all upon voluptuousness; some cultivating peace; some fond of war. During the nonage of society, men exert their natural bias without reserve: in the progress of society, they are taught to moderate their turbulent passions: at last, mild and courtly behaviour, produced by education and imitation, give an air to men of figure as if they were all copies from one original; which is peculiarly the case in France. The mildness of external behaviour must have a considerable influence on the internal part; for nothing tends more to soften or to suppress a passion, than never to give it vent: for which reason, absolute mo-<258>narchy in France is far from being so dreadful as it was formerly: it is at present far from being violent or sanguinary; the manners of the people having the same influence there that laws have in a free country. The King, delicate with respect to his conduct, and dreading the censure of the world, is guilty of few excesses; and the people, tame and submissive, are easily kept in order. To be discharged the court for any misdemeanour, or to be relegated to his country-seat, is, to a gentleman of rank, more terrible than a capital punishment.

We finish this short essay with a comparison of different governments as to the execution of laws. Laws relative to property and pecuniary interest, are every where preserved in vigour, because the violation of them hurts many. Laws respecting the public are kept alive in a monarchical government; because the King, to whom execution of law is intrusted, seldom benefits by their transgression. For a steady execution of such laws, a democracy has nothing to rely on but patriotism; and, when that subsides, such <259> laws fall asleep. The reason is, that the powers, both of legislation and execution center in the people; and a multitude, frequently no better than a mob, will never, with constancy, direct execution against themselves. <260>

SKETCH IV

Progress of States from small to great, and from great to small

When tribes, originally small, spread wider and wider, by population, till they become neighbours, the slightest differences inflame mutual aversion, and instigate hostilities that never end. Weak tribes unite for defence against the powerful, and become insensibly one people: other tribes are swallowed up by conquest. And thus states become more and more extensive, till they be confined by natural boundaries of seas or mountains. Spain originally contained many small states, which were all brought under the Roman yoke. In later times, it was again possessed by many states, Christian and Mahometan, continually at war, till by conquest they were united in one great kingdom. Portugal still maintains its independency; a blessing it owes to the weakness of Spain, not to advantage of situa-<261>tion. The small states of Italy were subdued by the Romans; and those of Greece by Philip of Macedon, and his son Alexander. Scotland escaped narrowly the fangs of Edward I. of England; and would at last have been conquered by its more potent neighbour, had not conquest been prevented by a federal union.

But, at that rate, have we not reason to dread the union of all nations under one universal monarch? There are several causes that for ever will prevent a calamity so dreadful. The local situation of some countries, defended by strong natural barriers, is one of these. Britain is defended by the sea; and so is Spain, except where divided from France by the Pyrenean mountains. Europe in general, by many barriers of seas, rivers, and mountains, is fitted for states of moderate extent: not so Asia, which being divided by nature into very large portions, is prepared for extensive monarchies.* Russia is the only ex-<262>ception in Europe; a weak kingdom by situation, though rendered formidable by the extraordinary talents of one man, and of more women than one.

A second cause, is the weakness of a great state. The strength of a state doth not increase with its bulk, more than that of a man. An overgrown empire, far from being formidable to its neighbours, falls to pieces by its weight and unwieldiness. Its frontiers are not easily guarded: witness France, which is much weakened by that circumstance, though its greater part is bounded by the sea. Patriotism vanishes in a great monarchy: the provinces have no mutual connection: and the distant <263> provinces, which must be governed by bashaws, are always ripe for a revolt. To secure Nicomedia, which had frequently suffered by fire, Pliny suggested to the Emperor Trajan, a fire-company of one hundred and fifty men. So infirm at that period was the Roman empire, that Trajan durst not put the project in execution, fearing disturbances even from that small body.

The chief cause is the luxury and effeminacy of a great monarchy, which leave no appetite for war, either in the sovereign or in his subjects. Great inequality of rank in an extensive kingdom, occasioned by a constant flow of riches into the capital, introduces show, expensive living, luxury, and sensuality. Riches, by affording gratification to every sensual appetite, become an idol to which all men bow the knee; and, when riches are worshipped as a passport to power as well as to pleasure, they corrupt the heart, eradicate every virtue, and foster every vice. In such dissolution of manners, contradictions are reconciled: avarice and meanness unite with van-

---

* En Asie on a toujours vu de grands empires; en Europe ils n'ont jamais pu subsister. C'est que l'Asie que nous connoissons a de plus grandes plaines: elle est coupée en plus grands morceaux par les montagnes et les mers; et comme elle est plus au midi, les sources y sont plus aisement taries, les montagnes y sont moins couvertes des nieges, et les fleuves, moins grossis, y forment des moindres barriers; [[Montesquieu,]] *L'Esprit des Loix, liv.* 17. *c.* 6.

(*In English thus:* "In Asia there have always been great empires: such could never subsist in Europe. The reason is, that, in Asia, there are larger plains, and it is cut by mountains and seas into more extensive divisions: as it lies more to the south, its springs are more easily dried up, the mountains are less covered with snow, and the rivers proportionally smaller, form less considerable barriers.")

ity; dissimulation and cunning, with splendor. Where subjects are so cor‹264›rupted, what will the prince be, who is not taught to moderate his passions, who measures justice by appetite, and who is debilitated by corporeal pleasures? Such a prince never thinks of heading his own troops, nor of extending his dominions. Mostazen, the last Califf of Bagdat, is a conspicuous instance of the degeneracy described. His kingdom being invaded by the Tartars in the year 1258, he shut himself up in his seraglio with his debauched companions, as in profound peace; and, stupified with sloth and voluptuousness, was the only person who appeared careless about the fate of his empire. A King of Persia, being informed that the Turks had made themselves masters of his best provinces, answered, that he was indifferent about their success, provided they would not disturb him in his city of Ispachan. Schah Hussein, King of Persia, at the beginning of the present century, was so sunk by sloth and luxury in a seraglio life, that, when a victorious army of rebels was approaching to Ispachan, he said to his ministers, "It is your business to repel the rebels, as you have armies provided. As for my part, if they but leave me my ‹265› palace of Farabath with my women, I am content." Hoatsang, the last Chinese Emperor of the Chinese race, hid himself in his palace, while the Tartars were wresting from him his northern provinces, and Listching, a rebel mandarine, was wresting from him the remainder. The Empress strangled herself in her apartment; and the Emperor, making a last effort, followed her example. The ninth Chinese Emperor of the blood of Genhizcan, addicted to women and priests, was despised by his people. A person without a name, who had been a servant in a convent of Bonzes, putting himself at the head of some robbers, dethroned the monarch, and extinguished the royal family.

The Tonquinese, after a long subjection to the Emperor of China, regained their independence, and were governed by kings of their own nation. These princes having by long peace become indolent, luxurious, and effeminate, abandoned the government to their ministers. The governor of Cochinchina, being at a great distance from the capital, revolted first, and that country became a separate kingdom. The governor of Tonquin, in which province ‹266› the King resided, usurped the sovereignty; but respecting the royal family, he only locked up the King in his palace; leaving to the King's descendents the name of *Bova*, or King, with some shadow of royalty. The usurper and his successors content themselves with the title of *Chova,* or Generalissimo; which satisfies the people, who pierce no deeper than what eyesight discovers. A revolution of the same kind happened in Japan. Similar causes produce similar effects. The luxurious and indolent successors of Charlemagne in the kingdom of France, trusting their power and authority with the mairs of their palace, were never seen in public, and were seldom heard of. The great power of these officers inflamed them with an appetite for more. Pepin and his successors were for a long time kings *de facto,* leaving to the rightful sovereign nothing but the empty name. Charles Martel reigned for some time without even naming a king. And at last Pepin the younger, *anno* 751, throwing off the mask, ordered himself to be proclaimed King of France.

Busbequius, who wrote in the days of Philip II. of Spain, has the following ob-<267>servation. "Comparing the Turkish soldiers with ours, I can prognosticate nothing good to Christendom. On their side, a mighty empire, great armies, experience in war, a long series of victories, a veteran soldiery, concord, order, discipline, frugality, vigilance, and patience of labour. On our side, public want, private luxury, contempt of discipline, impatience of labour, drunkenness, and gluttony. Can any one doubt what the event will be? For preventing ruin, we have nothing to depend on but the Persians." How plausible is this reasoning; and yet how false the prognostic! At that early time, the science of politics was but in its infancy in Europe. Busbequius did not discover, nor did any other man discover, a seed of corruption in the Turkish government that in time ripened to its ruin; and that is wealth and luxury in a despotic monarchy. The monarch is sunk in voluptuousness: licentiousness creeps in among the soldiery, and the government becomes entirely military. This progress is far advanced among the Turks; and their troops at present make no figure but by numbers. <268> Our troops, on the contrary, from perpetual wars among Christian Princes, have acquired the perfection of discipline.[1]

Montesquieu, discoursing of luxury in great empires, and effeminacy in the monarchs, describes the danger of revolutions, from ambitious men bred to war, in the following words: "En effet il étoit naturel que des Em-

---

1. Paragraph added in 2nd edition.

pereurs nourris dans les fatigues de la guerre, qui parvenoient à faire descendre du trône une famille noyée dans les delices, conservassent la vertu qu'ils avoient eprouvée si utile, et craignissent les voluptés qu'ils avoient vue si funestes. Mais après ces trois ou quatre premiers princes, la corruption, le luxe, l' oisivété, les declices, s' emparent des successeurs; ils s' enferment dans le palais, leur esprit s' affoiblit, leur vie s' accourcit, la famille decline; les grands s' élévent, les eunuques s' acreditent, on ne met sur le trone que des enfans; le palais devient ennemi de l' empire, un peuple oisif qui l' habite runie celui qui travaille; l'Empereur est tué ou destruit par un usurpateur, qui fonde une famille, dont le troisieme ou quatrieme successeur va <269> dans le même palais se renfermer encore" (a).*

Little reason then have we to apprehend the coalition of all nations into an universal monarchy. We see indeed in the history of mankind frequent instances of the progress of nations from small to great: but we also see instances no less frequent of extensive monarchies being split into many small states. Such is the course of human affairs: states are seldom stationary; but, like the sun, are either advan-<270>cing to their meridian, or falling down gradually till they sink into obscurity. An empire subjected to effeminate princes, and devoid of patriotism, cannot long subsist entire. The fate of all, with very few exceptions, has been the same. The governors of provinces, losing all regard for a voluptuous and effeminate monarch, take courage, set up for themselves, and assume regal authority, each in his own province. The puissant Assyrian monarchy, one of the earliest we read of in history, after having been long a terror to its neighbours, was dis-

---

* "It was indeed natural, that emperors, trained up to all the fatigues of war, who had effected the dethronement of a family immersed in sensual pleasures, should adhere to that virtue of which they had experienced the utility, and dread that voluptuousness whose fatal effects they had seen. But after a succession of three or four such princes, corruption, luxury, and indolence, appear again in their successors: they shut themselves up in their palace, their soul is enervated, their life is shortened, and their family declines: the grandees acquire power, the eunuchs gain credit, and children are set on the throne; the palace is at variance with the empire, the indolent statesmen ruin the industrious people. The Emperor is assassinated, or deposed by an usurper, who founds a new race of monarchs, of which the third or fourth in succession, sinking again into indolence, pursues the same course of ruin, and lays the foundation of a new change."

(a) L'esprit des Loix, liv. 7. chap. 7.

membered by the governors of Media and of Babylon, who detached these extensive provinces from the monarchy. Mahomet and his immediate successors erected a great empire, of which Bagdat became the capital. The later Califfs of that race, poisoned with sensual pleasure, lost all vigour of mind, and sunk down into sloth and effeminacy. The governors of the distant provinces were the first who ventured to declare themselves independent. Their success invited other governors, who stripped the Califf of his remaining provinces, leaving him nothing but the city of Bagdat; and <271> of that he was deprived by the Tartars, who put an end to that once illustrious monarchy. The same would have been the fate of the Persian empire, had it not been subdued by Alexander of Macedon. But after his death it submitted to the ordinary fate: his generals assumed regal power, each of them in the province he governed. Had not the Roman empire been dismembered by the barbarians, it would have been dismembered by the governors of its provinces. The weakness of Charlemagne's successors, hatched in France and in Germany an endless number of petty sovereigns. About the time that a passage to the East Indies by the Cape of Good Hope was discovered, the great peninsula beyond the Ganges was comprehended under the powerful empire of Bisnagar. Its first monarchs had established themselves by valour and military knowledge. In war, they headed their troops: in peace, they directed their ministers, visited their dominions, and were punctual in rendering justice to high and low. The people carried on an extensive and lucrative commerce, which brought a revenue to the Emperor that enabled him <272> to maintain a standing army of 100,000 foot, 30,000 horse, and 700 elephants. But prosperity and opulence ruined all. The Emperors, poisoned with pride and voluptuousness, were now contented with swelling titles, instead of solid fame. *King of kings,* and *Husband of a thousand wives,* were at the head of a long catalogue of such pompous, but empty epithets. Corrupted by flattery, they affected divine honours, and appeared rarely in public; leaving the care of their dominions to their ministers, and to the governors of their provinces. At the beginning of the sixteenth century, neighbouring princes encroached on all sides. In 1565, Bisnagar the capital was taken and sacked by four Moorish kings. The governors of the provinces declared themselves independent; and out of that great empire, sprung the kingdoms of Golconda, Visapour, and several others. The empire of Hindostan, once widely extended, is now reduced to a very small kingdom, under a prince who no longer is entitled to be designed the Great Mogul; the governors of his provinces having, as usual, declared themselves independent. <273>

Our North American colonies are in a prosperous condition, increasing rapidly in population, and in opulence. The colonists have the spirit of a free people, and are enflamed with patriotism. Their population will equal that of Britain and Ireland in less than a century; and they will then be a match for the mother-country, if they chuse to be independent: every advantage will be on their side, as the attack must be by sea from a very great distance. Being thus delivered from a foreign yoke, their first care will be the choice of a proper government; and it is not difficult to foresee what government will be chosen. A people animated with the new blessings of liberty and independence, will not incline to a kingly government. The Swiss cantons joined in a federal union, for protection against the potent house of Austria; and the Dutch embraced the like union, for protection against the more potent king of Spain. But our colonies will never join in such a union; because they have no potent neighbour, and because they have an aversion to each other. We may pronounce with assurance, that each colony will chuse for <274> itself a republican government. And their present constitution prepares them for it: they have a senate; and they have an assembly representing the people. No change will be necessary, but to drop the governor who represents the King of Britain. And thus a part of a great state will be converted into many small states. <275>

SKETCH V

Great and Small States compared

Neighbours, according to the common saying, must be sweet friends or bitter enemies: patriotism is vigorous in small states; and hatred to neighbouring states, no less so: both vanish in a great monarchy.

Like a *maximum* in mathematics, emulation has the finest play within certain bounds: it languisheth where its objects are too many, or too few. Hence it is, that the most heroic actions are performed in a state of moderate extent: appetite for applause, or fame, may subsist in a great monarchy; but by that appetite, without the support of emulation, heroic actions are seldom atchieved.

Small states, however corrupted, are not liable to despotism: the people being close to the seat of government, and accustomed to see their governors daily, talk familiarly of their errors, and publish <276> them every where. On Spain, which formerly consisted of many small states, a profound writer (*a*) makes the following observation. "The petty monarch was but little elevated above his nobles: having little power, he could not command much respect; nor could his nobles look up to him with that reverence which is felt in approaching great monarchs." Another thing is equally weighty against despotism in a small state: the army cannot easily be separated from the people; and, for that reason, is very little dangerous. The Roman pretorian bands were billeted in the towns near Rome; and three cohorts only were employed in guarding that city. Sejanus, prefect of these bands under Tiberius, lodged the three cohorts in a spacious barrack within the city, in order to gain more authority over them, and to wean them from

(*a*) Dr. Robertson.

familiarity with the people. Tacitus, in the 4th book of his Annals, relates the story in the following words. "Vim praefecturae, modicam antea, intendit, dispersas per urbem cohortes una in castra conducendo; ut simul imperia ac-<277>ciperent, numeroque et robore, et visu, inter se, fiducia ipsis, in caeteros metus, crearetur."*

What is said above, suggests the cause of a curious fact recorded in ancient history, "That of many attempts to usurp the sovereignty of different Greek republics, very few succeeded; and that no usurpation of that kind was lasting." Every circumstance differs in an extensive state: the people, at a distance from the throne, and having profound veneration for the sovereign, consider themselves, not as members of a body-politic, but as subjects merely, bound implicitly to obey: by which impression they are prepared before-hand for despotism. Other reasons concur: the subjects of a great state are dazzled with the splendor of their monarch; and as their union is prevented by <278> distance, the monarch can safely employ a part of his subjects against the rest, or a standing army against all.

A great state possesses one eminent advantage, viz. ability to execute magnificent works. The hanging gardens of Babylon, the pyramids of Egypt, and its lake Meris, are illustrious examples. The city of Heliopolis in Syria, named *Balbek* by the Turks, is a pregnant instance of the power and opulence of the Roman empire. Even in the ruins of that city, there are remains of great magnificence and exquisite taste. If the imperial palace, or the temple of the Sun, to mention no other building, were the work of any European prince existing at present, it would make a capital figure in the annals of his reign. And yet so little was the *éclat* of these works, even at the time of execution, that there is not a hint of them in any historian. The beneficence of some great monarchs is worthy of still greater praise. In the principal roads of Japan, hot baths are erected at proper distances, with other conveniencies, for the use of travellers. The beneficence of the

---

* "He extended the power of the prefecture, by collecting into one camp those pretorian cohorts which were formerly dispersed all over the city; that thus, being united, they might be more influenced by his orders, and while their confidence in their power was increased by the constant view of their own numbers and strength, they might at the same time strike a great terror in others."

Chinese government to those who suffer shipwreck, gives a more <279> advantageous impression of that monarchy, than all that is painfully collected by Du Halde. To verify the observation, I gladly lay hold of the following incident. In the year 1728, the ship Prince George took her departure from Calcutta in Bengal for Canton in China, with a cargo l. 60,000 value. A violent storm drove her ashore at a place named *Timpau,* a great way west from Canton. Not above half the crew could make the shore, worn out with fatigue and hunger, and not doubting of being massacred by the natives. How amazed were they to be treated with remarkable humanity! A Mandarin appeared, who not only provided for them victuals in plenty, but also men skilled in diving to assist them in fishing the wreck. What follows is in the words of my author, Alexander Wedderburn of St. Germains, a gentleman of known worth and veracity, who bore office in the ship.

> In a few days we recovered L. 5000 in bullion, and afterward L. 10,000 more. Before we set forward to Canton, the Mandarin our benefactor took an exact account of our money, with the names of the men, furnished us with an es-<280>cort to conduct us through his district, and consigned us dead or alive to one Suqua at Canton, a Chinese merchant well known to the English there. In every one of our resting-places, victuals were brought to us by the villagers in plenty, and with great cordiality. In this manner we passed from one district to another, without having occasion to lay out a single farthing, till we reached Canton, which we did in nine days, travelling sometimes by land, and sometimes by water. Our case had been represented to the court at Pekin, from whence orders came to distribute amongst us a sum of money: which was done by the Chuntuck, Hoppo, and other officers, civil and military, assembled in great state. After a short speech, expressing regret for our calamity, with an eulogium on the humane and generous disposition of their master; to each of us was presented the Emperor's bounty, in a yellow bag on which was inscribed the nature of the gift. The first supercargo received 450 tales in silver, the second 350, myself 250, the mate 75, and each common seaman 15; the whole <281> amounting to about 2000 tales, or L. 800. This is an example worthy of imitation, even where Christianity is professed; though its tenets are often, on like occasions, scandalously perverted.

So far my author: and I add, that this bounty was undoubtedly established by law; for it has not the appearance of an occasional or singular act of benevolence. If so, China is the only country in the world, where charity to strangers in distress is a branch of public police.

Another advantage of a great state I mention with peculiar pleasure, because all who aspire to be eminent in literature, are interested in it. A small kingdom, like Denmark, like Sweden, like Portugal, cannot naturally be productive of good writers; because where there are few readers, there is no sufficient incitement to exert literary talents: a classical work produced at present in the Celtic tongue, would fall little short of a miracle. France is eminent above all other nations for the encouragement it affords to good writers: it is a populous country: it is the chief seat of taste, arts, and sciences; and its language has <282> become universal in Europe, being the court-language every where: why then should not French writers carry the palm? But let not the British despond; for doth not a glorious prospect lie before them? The demand for English books in America is considerable; and is increasing daily. Population goes on vigorously: the number of British already settled upon the river Ohio approach to 10,000; and the delicious country from that river down to the mouth of the Mississippi will be filled with people whose native tongue is English. So fine a climate and so rich a soil will be productive of readers in plenty. Such a prospect ought to rouse our ambition; and our ambition will be highly laudable, if, rejecting local distinctions, we aspire to rival the French writers in real merit.

But the foregoing advantages of a great state, however illustrious, are sadly overbalanced by manifold disadvantages. The first is, the corruption of its kings, which, in a different view, is mentioned in the sketch immediately preceding. A second is, that great monarchs, being highly elevated above their subjects, are acquainted with none but their ministers. And mi- <283>nisters, who in a despotic government are subject to no controul but that of their master, commonly prefer their own interest, without regard to his honour. Solyman Emperor of the Turks, though accomplished above any of his predecessors, could not escape the artifices of his wife Roxalana, and of his Visir Rustan. They poisoned his ears with repeated calumnies against his eldest son Mustapha, a young prince of great hopes. They were not in hazard of detection, because no person had access to the Emperor but by their means. And the concluding scene, was an order from the Emperor to put his son to death (*a*). If a great monarch lie thus open in his own palace to the artifices of his ministers, his authority, we may be certain, will be very slight over the governors of his distant provinces. Their power is precarious; and they oppress the people without intermission, in order to amass wealth: the complaints of the people are disregarded; for they never reach the throne. The Spanish governors of the Philippine islands, afford a deplorable in-<284>stance of this observation. The heat of the climate promotes luxury; and luxury prompts avarice, which rages without controul, the distance of the capital removing all fear of detection. Arbitrary taxes are imposed on the people, and excessive duties on goods imported; which are rigorously exacted, because they are converted by the governor to his own use. An arbitrary estimate is made of what every field may produce; and the husbandman is severely punished if he fail to deliver the appointed quantity, whether his land has produced it or not. Many thousands have abandoned their native country; and the few miserable wretches who remain, have taken refuge among inaccessible mountains.

Third, The corruption of a court spreads through every member of the state. In an extensive kingdom that has no rival, the subjects, having no occasion to exert themselves in defence of their country, lose their manhood, and turn cowards. At the same time, great inequality of rank and fortune engenders luxury, selfishness, and sensuality.* The <285> fine arts, it is true, gain ground, manufactures are perfected, and courtly manners prevail: but every manly virtue is gone; and not a soul to be found, who

---

* The following passage is from a late Russian writer. "It is a truth founded on experience, that commerce polishes manners: but it is also a truth, that commerce, by exciting luxury, corrupts manners. With the increase of foreign fashions and foreign commerce in Russia, foreign luxury has increased there in proportion, universal dissipation has taken the lead, and profligacy of manners has followed. Great landlords squeeze and grind their people, to supply the incessant demands of luxury: the miserable peasant, disabled by a load of taxes, is frequently compelled to abandon his habitation, and to leave his land uncultivated. And thus agriculture and population diminish daily; than which nothing worse can befal a state."

(*a*) See Dr. Robertson's history of Charles V. where this incident is related with uncommon spirit.

will venture his life to save his country. That disease is spreading in Britain; and the only circumstance that guards France from equal pusillanimity, is an established mode, that every gentleman must serve some campaigns in the army.

Fourth, An extensive monarchy is liable to internal convulsions or revolutions, occasioned commonly either by a standing army, or by the governors of distant provinces. With respect to the former, the <286> government of a great kingdom enervated by luxury, must be military, and consequently despotic. A numerous army will soon learn to contemn a pusillanimous leader, and to break loose from every tie of subjection: the sovereign is often changed at the caprice of the army; but despotism continues to triumph. In Turky, Janissaries dethrone the Sultan, without scruple; but being superstitiously attached to the royal family, they confine themselves to it in electing a new Sultan. The pretorian bands were the Janissaries of the Roman empire, who never scrupled to dethrone the Emperor on the slightest disobligation. But as there was no royal family, they commonly carried the crown to market, and bestowed it on the highest bidder. With respect to the latter, the governors of distant provinces, accustomed to act without controul, become greedy of power, and put no bounds to ambition. Let them but gain the affection of the people they govern, and boldness will do the rest. The monarch is dethroned before he is prepared for defence; and the usurper takes his place without opposition. Success commonly attends such underta-<287>kings; for the sovereign has no soul, and the people have no patriotism. In Hindostan formerly, some discontented favourite or souba took up arms to avenge fancied, or perhaps affected wrongs: venturing not however upon independence, he screened himself with setting up some person of the royal blood, whom he proclaimed sovereign. The voluptuousness and effeminacy of the late kings of Persia, has rendered that kingdom a prey to every bold invader. No great state ever lay so open to adventurers, as Persia has done of late years.

In the fifth place, a nation corrupted with luxury and sensuality is a ready morsel for every invader: to attempt the conquest, and to succeed, are almost the same. The potent Assyrian monarchy, having long subsisted in peace without a single enemy, sunk into sloth and effeminacy, and became an easy prey to the kings of Media and Babylon. These two nations, in like circumstances of sloth and effeminacy, were in their turn swallowed up by Cyrus King of Persia. And the great empire of Persia, running the same course, was subdued by Alexander of Ma-<288>cedon with a small army of thirty-five thousand men.*

And this leads to a sixth disadvantage of a great empire, which is, the difficulty of guarding its frontiers. A kingdom, like an animal, becomes weak in proportion to its excess above a certain size. France and Spain would be less fitted for defence, were they enlarged beyond their present extent: Spain in particular was a very weak kingdom, while it comprehended the Netherlands and the half of Italy. In their present extent, forces are soon collected to guard the most distant frontiers. Months are required to assemble troops in an overgrown kingdom like Persia: if an army be defeated at the frontier, it must disperse, fortified places being seldom within reach. The victor, advancing with celerity, lays siege to the capital, before the provincial troops can be formed into a regular army: <289> the capital is taken, the empire dissolved; and the conqueror at leisure disputes the provinces with their governours. The Philippine islands made formerly a part of the extensive empire of China; but, as they were too distant to be protected or well governed, it showed consummate wisdom in the Chinese government to abandon them, with several other distant provinces.

A small state, on the other hand, is easily guarded. The Greek republics thought themselves sufficiently fortified against the Great King, by their courage, their union, and their patriotism. The Spanish Christians, abandoning the open country to the Saracens, retired to the mountains of Asturia, and elected Don Pelayo to be their King. That warlike Prince walled none of his towns, nor did he fortify a single pass; knowing that, while his people were brave, they would be invincible; and that walls and strongholds serve but to abate courage. The Romans, while circumscribed within Italy, never thought of any defence against an enemy but good troops. When they had acquired a vast <290> empire, even the Rhine appeared a barrier too weak: the numberless forts and legions that covered their fron-

---

* In Europe, neighbouring nations differ little in manners, or in fortitude. In Asia, we step instantly from the fierce Tartars, inhabiting a cold and barren country, to the effeminate people of countries warm and fertile. Hence in Asia perpetual conquests from north to south, to which even the great wall of China makes scarce any obstacle.

tiers could not defend them from a panic upon every motion of the barbarians.* A nation, in which the reciprocal duties of sovereign and subject are conscientiously fulfilled, and in which the people love their country and their governors, may be deemed invincible; provided due care be taken of the military branch. Every particular is reversed in a great empire: individuals grasp at money, *per fas aut nefas,* to lavish it upon pleasure: the governors of distant provinces tyrannize without controul; and, during the short period of their power, neglect no means, however oppressive, to amass wealth. Thus were the Roman provinces governed; and the people, who could not figure a greater tyrant than a Roman proconsul, were ready to embrace every change. The Romans accordingly were sensible, that, to force their barrier, and to <291> dismember their empire, were in effect the same. In our times, the nations whose frontiers lie open, would make the most resolute opposition to an invader; witness the German states, and the Swiss cantons. Italy enjoys the strongest natural barrier of any country that is not an island; and yet, for centuries, has been a prey to every invader.

Three plans, at different times, have been put in execution, for securing the frontiers of an extensive empire, building walls, laying the frontiers waste, and establishing feudatory Princes. The first was the ancient practice, proper only for an idle people, without commerce. The Egyptians built a very extensive wall for protecting themselves against the wandering Arabs. The famous wall of China to protect its effeminate inhabitants against the Tartars, is known all the world over; and the walls built in the north of England against the Scots and Picts, are known to every Briton. To protect the Roman territory from German invaders, the Emperor Probus constructed a stone wall, strengthened with towers. It stretched <292> from Ratisbon on the Danube to Wimpsen on the Necker; and terminated on the bank of the Rhine, after a winding course of two hundred miles. To a low state indeed must the Greek empire have been reduced, in the reign of the Emperor Anastasius, when, to repress the Bulgarians, it was necessary to build a wall, at no greater distance from Constantinople than ten leagues, abandoning all without to the barbarians. Such walls, though erected with

---

* The use of cannon, which place the weak and strong upon a level, is the only resource of the luxurious and opulent against the poor and hardy.

stupendous labour, prove a very weak bulwark; for a wall of any extent is never so carefully guarded, as at all times to prevent surprise. And, accordingly, experience has taught that walls cannot be relied on. This, in modern times, has introduced the two other methods mentioned.[1] Sha Abbas, King of Persia, in order to prevent the inroads of the Turks, laid waste part of Armenia, carrying the inhabitants to Ispahan, and treating them with great humanity. Land is not much valued by the great monarchs of Asia: it is precious in the smaller kingdoms of Europe; and the frontiers are commonly guarded by fortified towns. The other frontiers of Persia are guarded by feuda-<293>tory princes; and the same method is practised in China, in Hindostan, and in the Turkish empire. The Princes of Little Tartary, Moldavia, and Wallachia, have been long a security to the Grand Signior against his powerful neighbours in Europe. <294>

---

1. "Three plans, at . . . other methods mentioned": added in 2nd edition. In 1st edition the paragraph begins: "Two methods have been practised for securing the frontiers of an extensive empire: one is, to lay the frontiers waste; the other is, to establish feudatory princes in the distant provinces" [1:425].

SKETCH VI

War and Peace compared

No complaints are more frequent than against the weather, when it suits not our purpose: "A dismal season! we shall be drowned, or we shall be burnt up." And yet wise men think, that there might be more occasion to complain, were the weather left to our own direction. The weather is not the only instance of distrust in Providence: it is a common topic to declaim against war; "Scourge of nations, Destroyer of the human race, Bane of arts and industry! Will the world never become wise! Will war never have an end!" Manifold indeed are the blessings of peace; but doth war never produce any good? A fair comparison may possibly make it doubtful, whether war, like the weather, ought not to <295> be resigned to the conduct of Providence: seldom are we in the right, when we repine at its dispensations.

The blessings of peace are too well known to need illustration: industry, commerce, the fine arts, power, opulence, &c. &c. depend on peace. What has war in store for balancing blessings so substantial? Let us not abandon the field, without making at least one effort.

Humanity, it must be acknowledged, gains nothing from the wars of small states in close neighbourhood: such wars are brutal and bloody; because they are carried on with bitter enmity against individuals. Thanks to Providence, that war, at present, bears a less savage aspect: we spare individuals, and make war upon the nation only: barbarity and cruelty give place to magnanimity; and soldiers are converted from brutes into heroes. Such wars give exercise to the elevated virtues of courage, generosity, and disinterestedness, which are always attended with consciousness of merit and of dignity.* Friend-<296>ship is in peace cool and languid; but, in a war for glory, exerts the whole fire of its enthusiasm. The long and bloody <297> war sustained by the Netherlanders against the tyrant of Spain,

* In the war carried on by Louis XII. of France against the Venetians, the town of Brescia, being taken storm, and abandoned to the soldiers, suffered for seven days all the distresses of cruelty and avarice. No house escaped but that where Chevalier Bayard was lodged. At his entrance, the mistress, a woman of rank, fell at his feet, and deeply sobbing "Oh! my Lord, save my life, save the honour of my daughters." "Take courage, Madam," said the Chevalier, "your life, and their honour, shall be secure while I have life." The two daughters, brought from their hiding-place, were presented to him; and the family reunited bestowed their whole attention on their deliverer. A dangerous wound he had received gave them opportunity to express their zeal: they employed a notable surgeon; they attended him by turn day and night; and, when he could bear to be amused, they entertained him with concerts of music. Upon the day fixed for his departure, the mother said to him, "To your goodness, my Lord, we owe our lives: and to you all we have belongs by right of war: but we hope, from your signal benevolence, that this slight tribute will content you"; placing upon the table an iron coffer full of money. "What is the sum?" said the Chevalier. "My Lord," answered she trembling, "no more but 2500 ducats, all that we have;—but, if more be necessary, we will try our friends."—"Madam," said he, "your kindness is more precious in my eyes than a hundred thousand ducats. Take back your money, and depend always on me."—"My good Lord, you kill me in refusing this small sum: take it only as a mark of your friendship to my family."—"Well," said he, "since it will oblige you, I take the money; but give me the satisfaction of bidding adieu to your amiable daughters." They came to him with looks of regard and affection. "Ladies," said he, "the impression you have made on my heart, will never wear out. What return to make I know not; for men of my profession are seldom opulent: but here are two thousand five hundred ducats, of which the generosity of your mother has given me the disposal. Accept them as a marriage present; and may your happiness in marriage equal your merit." "Flower of chivalry," cried the mother, "May the God who suffered death for us reward you here and hereafter." Can peace afford so sweet a scene!

The following incident is still more interesting: It is of a late date among our countrymen; and will, for that reason, make the deeper impression. The scene of action was in Admiral Watson's ship, at the siege of Chandernagore, where Captain Speke, and his son, a youth of sixteen, were both of them wounded by the same shot. The history is related by Mr. Ives surgeon of the ship; which follows in his own words, only a little abridged. The Captain, whose leg was hanging by the skin, said to the Admiral, "Indeed, Sir, this was a cruel shot, to knock down both father and son." Mr. Watson's heart was too full for a reply; he only ordered both to be carried down to the surgeon. The Captain, who was first brought down, told me how dangerously his Billy had been wounded. Presently after, the brave youth himself appeared, with his eyes overflowing with tears, not for himself, but for his father. Upon my assurance that his father's wound was not dangerous, he became calm; but refused to be touched till his father's wound should be first dressed. Then pointing to a fellow sufferer, "Pray, Sir, dress also that poor man who

made even Dutchmen heroes: they forced their way <298> to the Indies during the hottest period of the war; and gained, by commerce, what supported them against their ferocious e-<299>nemy. What have they gained since by peace! Their immense commerce has eradicated patriotism, and every appetite <300> but for wealth. Had their violated rights been restored without a struggle, they would have continued a nation of frogs and fishermen. The Swiss, by continual struggles for liberty against the potent house of Austria, became a brave and active people, feared and courted by

---

is groaning so sadly beside me." I told him that the man had already been taken care of; and begged that I now might have liberty to examine his wound. He submitted; and calmly said, "Sir, I fear you must amputate above the joint." I replied, "My dear. I must." He clasped his hands together; and, lifting up his eyes toward heaven, he offered up the following short but earnest petition: "Good God! do thou enable me to behave in my present circumstances worthy of my father." He then told me he was all submission. I performed the operation above the joint of the knee; and, during the whole time, the intrepid youth never spoke a word, nor uttered a groan, that could be heard at the distance of a yard. It is easier to imagine than to express the feelings of the father at this time; but, whatever he felt, tears were the only expression. Both of them were carried to Calcutta. The father was lodged in the house of his brother-in-law; and the son was placed with me in the hospital. For the first week I gave comfort to both, carrying good tidings to them of one another. But, alas! all the good symptoms that had attended the young man began to disappear. The Captain perceived all in my countenance; and, so unwilling was he to add to my distress, as seldom to speak about his son. One time he said, "How long, my friend, do you think my Billy may remain in a state of uncertainty?" I replied, that, if he survived the fifteenth day after the operation, there would be strong hopes of his recovery. On the thirteenth he died; and, on the sixteenth, the Captain, looking me stedfastly in the face, "Well, Ives, how fares it with my boy?" Discovering the truth from my silence, he cried bitterly, squeezed my hand, and begged me to leave him for one half-hour. When I returned, he appeared, as he ever after did, perfectly calm and serene. The excellent youth had been delirious the evening before his death; and, at two o'clock in the morning, he sent me a note written with a pencil, of which the following is a copy. "Mr. Ives will consider the disorder a son must be in when he is dying, and is yet in doubt about his father.—If Mr. Ives is not too busy to honour this note, which nothing but the greatest uneasiness could draw from me—The boy waits an answer." I immediately repaired to him; and he had still sense enough to know me. He then said, "And is he dead?"—"Who, my dear?"—"My father, Sir."—"No, my love; nor is he in any danger; he is almost well."—"I thank God: I am now satisfied, and am ready to die." He had a locked jaw, and was in great pain, but I understood every word he uttered. He begged my pardon for having disturbed me at so early an hour; and, before the day was ended, he surrendered a life that deserved to be immortal.—So far my author; and I only add, Does peace afford any scene that can compare with this in moving our sympathetic feelings?

neighbouring princes. Their federal union has secured to them peace and tranquility; which, notwithstanding their mountainous situation, would have sunk them into effeminacy, but for a commerce they carry on of hiring out their men for soldiers. Monks are commonly pusillanimous: their way of life, which removes them from danger, enervates the mind, and renders them spiritless and cowardly.

Industry, manufactures, and wealth, are the fruits of peace; but advert to what follows. Luxury, a never-failing conco-<301>mitant of wealth, is a slow poison, that debilitates men, and renders them incapable of any great effort: courage, magnanimity, heroism, come to be ranked among the miracles that are supposed never to have existed but in fable; and the fashionable properties of sensuality, avarice, cunning, and dissimulation, engross the mind. In a word, man, by constant prosperity and peace, degenerates into a mean, impotent, and selfish animal. An American savage, who treasures up the scalps of his enemies as trophies of his prowess, is a being far superior. Such are the fruits of perpetual peace with respect to individuals.

Nor is the state itself less debilitated by it than its members. Figure a man wallowing in riches, and immersed in sensual pleasure, but dreading the infection of a plague raging at his gate; or figure him in continual dread of an enemy, watching every opportunity to burn and destroy. This man represents a commercial state, that has long enjoyed peace without disturbance. A state that is a tempting object to an invader, without means of de-<302>fence, is in a woful situation. The republic of Venice was once famous for the wisdom of its constitution, and for being the Christian bulwark against the Turks; but, by long peace, it has become altogether effeminate. Its principles of government are conformable to its character: every cause of quarrel with a neighbour is anxiously avoided; and the disturbances at home prevented by watchful spies. Holland, since the days of King William, has not produced a man fit to command a regiment: and the Dutch hath nothing to rely on for independence but mutual jealousy among their neighbours. Hannibal appeared upon the stage too early: had the Romans, after their conquest of Italy, been suffered to exchange their martial spirit for luxury and voluptuousness, they would have been no match for that great general. It was equally lucky for the Romans that they came late upon Macedon. Had Alexander finished his conquest of Greece, and the Romans theirs of Italy, at the same period, they would probably have been confined, each of them, within their own limits. But Asi-<303>atic luxury and effeminacy, which had got hold of the Greeks and Macedonians before the Roman invasion, rendered them an easy prey to the invaders. It was the constant cry of Cato the Censor, *"Delenda est Carthago."* Scipio Nasica was a more subtile politician: his opinion was, to give peace to Carthage, that the dread of that once powerful republic might preserve in vigour the military spirit of his country. What happened afterwards, sets the wisdom of that advice in a conspicuous light. The battle of Actium, after a long train of cruel civil wars, gave peace to Rome under the Emperor Augustus. Peace had not subsisted much above thirty years, when a Roman army, under Quintilius Varus, was cut to pieces in Germany. The consternation at Rome was unspeakable, as there was not a fortified town to prevent the Germans from pouring down upon Italy. Instant orders were given for levying men; but, so effeminate had the Romans already become, that not a single man would enlist voluntarily. And Augustus was forced to use severe measures, before he could collect a small army. <304> How different the military spirit of the Romans during the second Punic war, when several Roman armies were cut off, greater than that of Varus. The citizens who could bear arms were reduced to 137,000; and yet, in the later years of that war, the Romans kept the field with no fewer than twenty-three legions (*a*). The Vandals, having expelled the Romans from Afric, enjoyed peace for a century, without seeing the face of an enemy. Procopius (*b*) gives the following account of them. Charmed with the fertility of the soil, and benignity of the climate, they abandoned themselves to luxury, sumptuous dress, high living, and frequent baths. They dwelt in the theatre and circus, amusing themselves with dancers, pantomimes, and every gay entertainment: their villas were splendid; and their gardens were adorned with water-works, beautiful trees, odoriferous flowers: no regard to chastity, nor to any manly virtue. In that effeminate state, they made scarce any resistence to Belisarius <305> with an army far inferior in number to their own. The Saracens of Asia, corrupted by prosperity and opulence, were able to make no head against

(*a*) Titus Livius, lib. 26. cap. 1.
(*b*) Historia Vandalica, lib. 2.

the Turks. About that time, the Spaniards, equally corrupted, were overpowered by the Saracens of Afric; who, remote from the dissolute manners of Asia, retained their military spirit. The wealth of the kingdom of Whidah in Guinea, from fertility of soil, great industry, and extensive commerce, produced luxury and effeminacy. The King gave himself up to sensual pleasures, leaving government to his ministers. In that state was Whidah in the year 1727, when the King of Dahomay requested access to the sea for trade, offering to purchase the privilege with a yearly tribute. A haughty denial furnished a pretext for war. The King of Dahomay invaded the territories of his enemy with a disciplined army, and pierced to the capital without resistance. The King of Whidah, with his women, had fled to an island, and his people were all dispersed. It amazed the conqueror, that a whole nation, without striking a blow, had thus deserted their wives, their chil-<306>dren, their gods, their possessions, and all that was dear to them. The Japanese became warlike during long and bloody civil wars, which terminated about the end of the sixteenth century, in rendering their Emperor despotic. From that period, no opportunity has occurred for exercising their military spirit, except in the education of their youth: heroism, with contempt of death, are inculcated; and the histories of their illustrious heroes are the only books that boys at school are taught to read. But, the profound tranquility that the empire now enjoys, in a strict and regular government, will in time render that warlike people effeminate and cowardly: human nature cannot resist the poison of perpetual peace and security. In the war between the Turks and Venetians, *anno* 1715, the latter put great confidence in Napoli di Romania, a city in the Morea, strongly fortified, and provided with every necessary for an obstinate defence. They had not the least doubt of being able to draw their whole force together, before the Turks could make any progress in the siege. But, to their astonishment, the taking of that city, and of every other fortified place <307> in the Morea, was the work of but a single campaign. So much had the Venetians degenerated by long peace, from the courage and patriotism of their forefathers who conquered that country from the Turks. In some late accounts from China, we are told, that the King of Bengala or Bracma, having invaded Yunnan, an opulent province of China, obtained a complete victory over the Emperor's army, commanded by his son-in-law: the

inhabitants of that province were struck with such a panic, that multitudes, for fear of the conqueror, hanged and drowned themselves. To what a torpid state, by this time, would Europe have been reduced, had the plan for a perpetual peace, projected by Henry IV. of France, been carried into execution? Conquest, in a retrograde motion, would have directed its progress from the east to the west. Our situation in an island, among several advantages, is so far unlucky, that it puts us off our guard, and renders us negligent in providing for defence: we never were invaded without being subdued.*
<308>

Montesquieu, in a warm panegyric on the English constitution, has overlooked one particular, in which it is superior to every other monarchy; and that is, the frequent opportunities it affords to exert mental powers and talents. What agitation among the candidates, and their electors, on the approach of a new parliament: what freedom of speech and eloquence in parliament! ministers and their measures laid open to the world, the nation kept alive, and inspired with a vigour of mind that tends to heroism! This government, it is true, generates factions, which sometimes generate revolutions: but the golden age, so lusciously described by poets, would to man be worse than an iron age. At any rate, better to have a government liable to <309> storms, than to seek for quiet in the dead calm of despotism.†
<310>

---

* The situation of the King of Sardinia, environed on all sides with powerful monarchs, obliges him to act with the greatest circumspection; which circumstance seems to have formed the character of the princes of that house. These princes have exerted more sagacity in steering their political vessel, and more dexterity in availing themselves of every wind, than any other race of sovereigns that figure in history; *Robertson's History of the Emperor Charles V.*

† On n'entend parler dans les auteurs que des divisions qui perdirent Rome; mais on ne voit pas que ces divisions y étoient nécessaires, qu'elles y avoient toujours été, et qu'elles y devoient toujours être. Ce fut uniquement la grandeur de la republique qui fit le mal, et qui changea en guerres civiles les tumultes populaires. Il falloit bien qu'il y eut à Rome des divisions: et ces guerriers si fiers, si audacieux, si terribles au dehors, ne pouvoient pas être bien modérés au dedans. Demander dans un état libre des gens hardis dans la guerre, et timides dans la paix, c'est vouloir des choses impossibles: et pour regle générale, toutes les fois qu'on verra tout le monde tranquille dans un état qui se donne le nom de republique, on peut être assuré que la liberté n'y est pas; *Montesquieu, grandeur des Romains, ch. 9.* [*In English thus:* "Many writers have said a great deal on those factions

Law-suits within a state, like war between different states, accustom people to opposition, and prevent too great softness and facility of manners. In a free government, a degree of stubbornness in the people is requisite for resisting encroachments on their liberties. The fondness of the French for their sovereign, and the easiness and politeness of their manners, have corrupted a good constitution. The British constitution has been preserved entire, by a people jealous of their prince, and resolute against every encroachment of regal power.

There is another advantage of war, that ought not to be overlooked, though not capital. It serves to drain the country of idlers, few of whom are innocent, and many not a little mischievous. In the years 1759 and 1760, when we were at war with France, there were but twenty-nine criminals condemned at the Old Bailey. In the years 1770 and 1771, when we were at peace with all the world, the <311> criminals condemned there amounted to one hundred and fifty-one.

But, though I declare against perpetual peace, perpetual war is still more my aversion. The condition of Europe was deplorable in the dark ages, when vassals assumed the privilege of waging war without consent of the sovereign. Deadly feuds prevailed universally, and threatened dissolution of all government: the human race never were in a more woful condition. But anarchy never fails, soon or late, to rectify itself, which effeminacy produced by long peace never does. Revenge and cruelty, it is true, are the fruits of war: but so are likewise firmness of mind, and undaunted courage; which are exerted with better will in behalf of virtue than of revenge. The crusades were what first gave a turn to the fierce manners of our ancestors. A religious enterprise, uniting numbers formerly at variance, enlarged the sphere of

---

which destroyed Rome; but they want the penetration to see, that those factions were necessary, that they had always subsisted, and ever must have subsisted. It was the grandeur of the state which alone occasioned the evil, and changed into civil wars the tumults of the people. There must of necessity have been factions in Rome; for, how was it possible, that those who abroad subdued all by their undaunted bravery, and by the terror of their arms, should live in peace and moderation at home? To look for a people, in a free state, who are intrepid in war, and, at the same time, timid in peace, is to look for an impossibility; and we may hold it as a general rule, that, in a state which professes a republican form of government, if the people are quiet and peaceable, there is no real liberty."]

social affection, and sweetened the manners of Christians to one another. These crusades filled Europe with heroes, who, at home, were ready for any new enterprise that promised laurels. Mo-<312>ved with the horror of deadly feuds, they joined in bonds of chivalry for succouring the distressed, for redressing wrongs, and for protecting widows and orphans. Such heroism inflamed every one who was fond of glory and warlike atchievements: chivalry was relished by men of birth; and even kings were proud to be of the order. An institution, blending together valour, religion, and gallantry, was wonderfully agreeable to a martial people; and humanity and gentleness could not but prevail in a society, whose profession it was to succour every person in distress. As glory and honour were the only wished-for recompense, chivalry was esteemed the school of honour, of truth, and of fidelity. Thus, truth without disguise, and a scrupulous adherence to promises, became the distinguishing virtues of a gentleman. It is true, that the enthusiasm of protecting widows and orphans, degenerated sometimes into extravagance; witness knights who wandered about in quest of adventures. But it would be unfair to condemn the whole order, because a few of their number were extravagant. The true spirit of chivalry <313> produced a single reformation in the manners of Europe. To what other cause can we so justly ascribe the point of honour, and that humanity in war, which characterize modern manners (*a*)? Are peace, luxury, and selfishness, capable of producing such effects?

That man should be the only animal that makes war upon his own kind, may appear strange and unaccountable. Did men listen to cool reason, they never would make war. Hear the celebrated Rousseau on that subject.

> Un prince, qui pour reculer ses frontieres, perd autant de ses anciens sujets qu'il en acquiert de nouveaux, s' affoiblit en s' agrandissant; parce qu'avec un plus grand espace à defendre, il n'a pas plus de défenseurs. Or on ne peut ignorer, que par la maniere dont la guerre se fait aujourd'hui, la moindre dépopulation qu'elle produit est celle qui se fait dans les armées: c'est bien-là la perte apparente et sensible: mais il s'en fait en même tems dans tout l'état une plus grave et plus irreparable que celle des hommes qui meurent, par ceux qui ne naissent pas, <314> par l'augmentation des im-

(*a*) Dr. Robertson's history of the Emperor Charles V.

pôts, par l'interruption du commerce, par la désertion des campagnes, par l'abandon de l'agriculture; ce mal qu'on n'apparçoit point d'abord, se fait sentir cruellement dans la suite: et c'est alors qu'on est étonné d'être si foible, pour s'être rendu si puissant. Ce qui rend encore les conquêtes moins intéressantes, c'est qu'on fait maintenant par quels moyens on peut doubler et tripler sa puissance, non seulement sans étendre son territoire, mais quelquefois en le resserrant, comme fit très sagement l'Empereur Adrien. On fait que ce sont les hommes seuls qui sont la force des Rois; et c'est une proposition qui découle de ce que je viens de dire, que de deux étas qui nourrissent le même nombre d'habitans, celui qui occupe une moindre étendue de terre, est réellement le plus puissant. C'est donc par de bonnes loix, par une sage police, par de grandes vues économiques, qu'un souverain judicieux est sùr d'augmenter ses forces, sans rien donner au hazard.*

But war is ne-<315>cessary for man, being a school for improving every manly virtue; and Providence renders kings blind to their true in-<316>terest, in order that war may sometimes take place. To rely upon Providence in the government of this world, is the wisdom of man.

---

* "A prince, who in extending his territories sustains the loss of as many of his old subjects as he acquires new, weakens in fact his power while he aims at strengthening it: he increases the territory to be defended, while the number of defenders is not increased. Who does not know, that in the modern manner of making war, the greatest depopulation is not from the havock made in the armies? That indeed is the obvious and apparent destruction; but there is, at the same time, in the state a loss much more severe and irreparable, not that thousands are cut off, but that thousands are not born: population is wounded by the increase of taxes, by the interruption of commerce, by the desertion of the country, and by the stagnation of agriculture: the misfortune which is overlooked at first, is severely felt in the event; and it is then that we are astonished to find we have been growing weak, while increasing our power. What renders every new conquest still the less valuable, is the consideration of the possibility of doubling and tripling a nation's power, without extending its territory, nay, even by diminishing it. The Emperor Adrian knew this, and wisely practised it. The numbers of the subjects are the strength of the prince: and a consequence of what I have said is this proposition, That of two states equal in the number of inhabitants, that is in reality the more powerful which occupies the smaller territory. It is by good laws, by a salutary police, and great oeconomical schemes, that a wise sovereign gains a sure augmentation of strength, without trusting any thing to the fortune of his arms."

Upon the whole, perpetual war is bad, because it converts men into beasts of prey: perpetual peace is worse, because it converts men into beasts of burden. To prevent such woful degeneracy on both hands, war and peace alternately are the only effectual means; and these means are adopted by Providence. <317>

SKETCH VII

Rise and Fall of Patriotism

The members of a tribe in their original state of hunting and fishing, being little united but by a common language, have no notion of a *patria;* and scarce any notion of society, unless when they join in an expedition against an enemy, or against wild beasts. The shepherd-state, where flocks and herds are possessed in common, gives a clear notion of a common interest; but still none of a *patria.* The sense of a *patria* begins to unfold itself, when a people leave off wandering, to settle upon a territory that they call their own. Agriculture connects them together; and government still more: they become fellow-citizens; and the territory is termed the *patria* of every person born in it. It is so ordered by Providence, that a man's country and his countrymen, are to him in conjunction an object of a peculiar affection, termed *amor patriae,* or <318> *patriotism;* an affection that rises high among a people intimately connected by regular government, by husbandry, by commerce, and by a common interest. "Cari sunt parentes, cari liberi, propinqui, familiares; sed omnes omnium caritates patria una complexa est: pro qua quis bonus dubitet mortem oppetere?"*

In a man of a solitary disposition who avoids society, patriotism cannot abound. He may possibly have no hatred to his countrymen; but, were he desirous to see them happy, he would live among them, and put himself in the way of doing good.

The affection a man has for the place where he was bred, ought to be

---

* "Our parents are dear to us; so are our children, our relations, and our friends: all these our country comprehends; and shall we fear to die for our country?" [[The quotation is from Cicero's *De officiis,* bk. I, sec. 57.]]

distinguished from patriotism, being a passion far inferior, and chiefly visible in the low people. A rustic has few ideas but of external sense: his hut, his wife, his children, the hills, trees, and rivulets around him, <319> compose the train of his ideas. Remove him from these objects, and he finds a dismal vacuity in his mind. History, poetry, and other subjects of literature, have no relation to time nor place. Horace is relished in a foreign country as at home: the pleasures of conversation depend on persons, not on place.[1]

Social passions and affections, beside being much more agreeable than selfish, are those only which command our esteem (*a*). Patriotism stands at the head of social affections; and stands so high in our esteem, that no actions but what proceed from it are termed grand or heroic. When that affection appears so agreeable in contemplation, how glowing, how elevating, must it be in those whom it inspires! Like vigorous health, it beats constantly with an equal pulse: like the vestal fire, it never is extinguished. No source of enjoyment is more plentiful than patriotism, where it is the ruling passion: it triumphs over every selfish motive, and is a firm support to every virtue. In fact, where-ever it prevails, the morals <320> of the people are found to be pure and correct.*

These are illustrious effects of patriotism with respect to private happiness and virtue; and yet its effects with respect to the public are still more illustrious. A nation in no other period of its progress is so flourishing, as when patriotism is the ruling passion of every member: during that period, it is invincible. Atheneus remarks, that the Athenians were the only people in the world, who, though clothed in purple, put formidable armies to flight at Marathon, Salamine, and Platea. But at that period patriotism was their ruling passion; and success attended them in every undertaking. Where

---

* I know of but one bad effect of patriotism, that it is apt to inspire too great partiality for our countrymen. Excusable in the vulgar, but unbecoming in men of rank and figure. The Duke de Montmorenci, after a victory, treated his prisoners with great humanity. He yielded his bed to Don Martin of Arragon, sent his surgeon to dress his wounds, and visited him daily. That Lord, amazed at so great humanity, said one day to the Duke, "Sir, were you a Spaniard, you would be the greatest man in the universe." It grieves me to hear it objected to the English, that they have too much of the Spaniard in their sentiments.

(*a*) Elements of Criticism, vol. 1. p. 113. edit. 5.

1. This and the previous paragraph added in 2nd edition.

patriotism rules, <321> men perform wonders, whatever garb they wear. The fall of Saguntum is a grand scene; a people exerting the utmost powers of nature, in defence of their country. The city was indeed destroyed; but the citizens were not subdued. The last effort of the remaining heroes was, to burn themselves with their wives and children in one great funeral pile. Numantia affords a scene no less grand. The citizens, such as were able to bear arms, did not exceed 8000; and yet braved all the efforts of 60,000 disciplined soldiers, commanded by Scipio Nasica. So high was their character for intrepidity, that even when but a few of them were left alive, the Romans durst not attempt to storm the town. And they stood firm, till subdued by famine they were no longer able to crawl. While the Portuguese were eminent for patriotism, Lopez Carasco, one of their sea-captains, in a single ship with but forty men, fell in among the King of Achin's fleet of twenty gallies, as many junks, and a multitude of small vessels. Resolute to perish rather than yield, he maintained the fight for three days, till his ship was pierced through <322> and through with cannon-shot, and not a single man left unwounded. And yet, after all, the King's fleet found it convenient to sheer off.

Patriotism at the same time is the great bulwark of civil liberty; equally abhorrent of despotism on the one hand, and of licentiousness on the other. While the despotic government of the Tudor family subsisted, the English were too much depressed to have any affection for their country. But when manufactures and commerce began to flourish in the latter end of Elisabeth's reign, a national spirit broke forth, and patriotism made some figure. That change of disposition was perhaps the chief cause, though not the most visible, of the national struggles for liberty, which were frequent during the government of the Stewart family, and which ended in a free government at the Revolution.

Patriotism is too much cramped in a very small state, and too much relaxed in an extensive monarchy. But that topic has already been discussed in the first sketch of this book.

Patriotism is enflamed by a struggle for <323> liberty, by a civil war, by resisting a potent invader, or by any incident that forcibly draws the members of a state into strict union for the common interest. The resolute opposition of the Dutch to Philip II. of Spain, in the cause of liberty, is an illustrious instance of the patriotic spirit rising to a degree of enthusiasm. Patriotism, roused among the Corsicans by the oppression of the Genoese, exerted itself upon every proper object. Even during the heat of the war, they erected an university for arts and sciences, a national bank, and a national library; improvements that would not have been thought of in their torpid state. Alas! they have fallen a victim to thirst of power, not to superior valour. Had Providence favoured them with success, their figure would have been considerable in peace as in war.* <324>

But violent commotions cannot be perpetual: one party prevails, and prosperity follows. What effect may this have on patriotism? I answer, that nothing is more animating than success after a violent struggle: a nation in that state resembles a comet, which, in passing near the sun, has been much heated, and continues full of motion. Patriotism made a capital figure among the Athenians, when they became a free people, after expelling the tyrant Pisistratus. Every man exerted himself for his country: every man endeavoured to excell those who went before him: and hence a Miltiades, an Aristides, a Themistocles, names that for ever will figure in the annals of time. While the Roman republic was confined within nar-<325>row bounds, austerity of manners, and disinterested love to their country, formed the national character. The elevation of the Patricians above the Plebeians, a source of endless discord, was at last remedied by placing all the citizens on a level. This signal revolution excited an animating emulation between the Patricians and Plebeians; the former, by heroic actions, labouring to maintain their superiority; the latter straining every nerve to equal them: the republic never at any other period produced so great men in the art of war.

It has been often remarked, that a nation is never so great as after a civil

---

* The elevation of sentiment that a struggle for liberty inspires, is conspicuous in the following incident. A Corsican being condemned to die for an atrocious crime, his nephew with deep concern addressed Paoli in the following terms. "Sir, if you pardon my uncle, his relations will give to the state a thousand zechins, beside furnishing fifty soldiers during the siege of Furiali. Let him be banished, and he shall never return." Paoli, knowing the virtue of the young man, said, "You are acquainted with the circumstances of that case: I will consent to a pardon, if you can say as an honest man, that it will be just or honourable for Corsica." The young man, hiding his face, burst into tears, saying, "I would not have the honour of our country sold for a thousand zechins."

war. The good of the state is commonly the object; and patriotism is the ruling passion of both sides, though not always well directed. The good of the state was not the object in the civil wars of Rome; and instead of advancing patriotism, they annihilated the small portion that remained of it. Power and riches were the objects, which the grandees were violently bent to acquire *per fas aut nefas,* without the least regard to the public. Every joint of the commonwealth was relaxed, when the power-<326>ful became greedy of more power; and it was shaken to pieces by continual struggles among the powerful. Patriotism vanished with the commonwealth: power and riches became the sole objects of pursuit; and with these every man tempted and was tempted: corruption of every sort spread wide, and venality above all. How depraved must the morals of Rome have been, when Cicero, esteemed its greatest patriot, requested Lucceius to write his history, and to set his conduct in the most advantageous light, without regard to truth. "I will venture," says he, "to entreat you, not to confine yourself to the strict laws of history; but to give a latitude to your encomiums, greater possibly than you think my actions deserve. Let me hope you will not reject the generous partiality of friendship; but give somewhat more to affection than to rigorous truth" (*a*). Yet this was the same Cicero who wrote an excellent book of morals. So little connection is there in some men between the heart and the head.[2] <327>

The tyranny exercised by the Archdukes of Austria upon their subjects of Switzerland, united all the Cantons in a common cause for liberty and independence, and inspired every individual with an uncommon degree of patriotism. They succeeded, and became the most warlike nation in Europe. Every prince was fond to have numbers of them in his pay; and the barrenness of their soil induced them to hire out their troops for gain. Avarice crept in among them, and became the ruling passion. Guicchardin, who wrote his history of Italy the beginning of the sixteenth century, reports of that nation, that formerly famous for valour and military reputation, they had in his time lost all desire of glory and zeal for their country, and had become insatiably covetous, even so far as to raise the demand for

---

(*a*) Cicero's letters, b. 1. letter 22.
2. Paragraph added in 2nd edition.

hiring their troops to the utmost that could be procured. From the time of our author the reputation of their troops gradually declined; and at present there is not a nation in Europe but can cope with them.³

There is great intricacy in human actions: tho' men are indebted to emulation <328> for their heroic actions, yet such actions never fail to suppress emulation in those who follow. An observation is made above (*a*), that a person of superior genius who damps emulation in others, is a fatal obstruction to the progress of an art: witness the celebrated Newton, to whom the decay of mathematical knowledge in Britain is justly attributed. The observation holds equally with respect to action. Those actions only that flow from patriotism are deemed grand and heroic; and such actions, above all others, rouse a national spirit. But beware of a Newton in heroism: instead of exciting emulation, he will damp it: despair to equal the great men who are the admiration of all men, puts an end to emulation. After the illustrious atchievements of Miltiades, and after the eminent patriotism of Aristides, we hear no more in Greece of emulation or of patriotism. Pericles was a man of parts, but he sacrificed Athens to his ambition. The Athenians sunk lower and lower under the Archons, who had neither parts nor patriotism; and were reduced at last <329> to slavery, first by the Macedonians, and next by the Romans. The Romans run the same course, from the highest exertions of patriotic emulation, down to the most abject selfishness and effeminacy.

And this leads to other causes that extinguish patriotism, or relax it. Factious disorders in a state never fail to relax it; for there the citizen is lost, and every person is beheld in the narrow view of a friend or an enemy. In the contests between the Patricians and Plebeians of Rome, the public was totally disregarded: the Plebeians could have no heart-affection for a country where they were oppressed; and the Patricians might be fond of their own order, but they could not sincerely love their country, while they were enemies to the bulk of their countrymen. Patriotism did not shine forth in Rome, till all equally became citizens. Between the union of the two crowns of England and Scotland and that of the kingdoms, Scotland was

(*a*) Book 1. sketch 5. § 1.
3. Paragraph added in 3rd edition.

greatly depressed: it was governed by a foreign king; the nobility, tyrants, and the low people, poor and dispirited. There was no patriotism among the former; and <330> as little among the latter. Hence it appears, that the opposition in Scotland to the union of the two kingdoms, was absurdly impolitic. The opposition ought to have been against the union of the two crowns, in order to prevent the government of a foreign prince. After being reduced to dependence on another nation, the only remedy was to become one people by an union of the kingdoms.[4]

To support patriotism, it is necessary that a people be in a train of prosperity: when a nation becomes stationary, patriotism subsides. The ancient Romans upon a small foundation erected a great empire; so great indeed, that it fell to pieces by its unwieldiness. But the plurality of nations, whether from their situation, from the temper of their people, or from the nature of their government, are confined within narrower limits; beyond which their utmost exertions avail little, unless they happen to be extraordinary favourites of fortune. When a nation becomes thus stationary, its pushing genius is at an end: its plan is to preserve, not to acquire: the members, even without any example of heroism to damp emulation, <331> are infected with the languid tone of the state: patriotism subsides; and we hear no more of bold or heroic actions. The Venetians are a pregnant instance of the observation. Their trade with Aleppo and Alexandria did for centuries introduce into Europe the commodities of Syria, Egypt, Arabia, Persia, and India. The cities of Nuremberg and Augsburg in particular, were supplied from Venice with these commodities; and by that traffick became populous and opulent. Venice, in a word, was for centuries the capital trading town of Europe, and powerful above all its neighbours, both at sea and land. A passage to the East Indies by the Cape of Good Hope was indeed an animating discovery to the Portuguese; but it did not entitle them to exclude the Venetians. The greater distance of Venice from the Cape, a trifle in itself, is more than balanced by its proximity to Greece, Germany, Hungary, Poland, and to the rest of Italy. But the Portuguese at that period were in the spring of prosperity; and patriotism envigorated them to make durable establishments on the Indian coast, overpowering every nation in opposition.

---

4. "Between the union . . . of the kingdoms": added in 2nd edition.

<332> The Venetians, on the contrary, being a nation of merchants, and having been long successful in commerce, were become stationary, and unqualified for bold adventures. Being cut out of their wonted commerce to India, and not having resolution to carry on commerce in a new channel, they sunk under the good fortune of their rivals, and abandoned the trade altogether. The Russians became a new people under Peter the Great, and are growing daily more and more powerful. The Turks, on the contrary, have been long in a declining state, and are at present a very degenerate people. Is it wonderful, that during the late war the Turks were no match for the Russians?[5]

No cause hitherto mentioned hath such influence in depressing patriotism, as inequality of rank and of riches in an opulent monarchy. A continual influx of wealth into the capital, generates show, luxury, avarice, which are all selfish vices; and selfishness, enslaving the mind, eradicates every fibre of patriotism.* Asiatic <333> luxury, flowing into Rome in a plentiful stream, produced an universal corruption of manners, and metamorphosed into voluptuousness the warlike genius of that great city. The dominions of Rome were now too extensive for a republican government, and its generals too powerful to be disinterested. Passion for glory wore out of fashion, as austerity of manners had done formerly: power and riches were now the only objects of ambition: virtue seemed a farce; honour, a chimera; and fame, mere vanity: every Roman, abandoning himself to sensuality, flattered himself, that he, more wise than his forefathers, was pursuing the cunning road to happiness. Corruption and venality became general, and maintained their usurpation in the provinces as well as in the capital, without ever losing a foot of ground. Pyrrhus attempted by presents to corrupt the Roman senators, but made not the slightest impression. Deplorable was the change of manners in the days of Jugurtha:—"Pity it is," said he, "that <334> there should not be a man so opulent as to purchase a people so willing to be sold." Cicero, mentioning an oracle of Apollo that Sparta would never be destroyed but by avarice, justly observes, that the

---

* France is not an exception. The French are vain of their country, because they are vain of themselves. But such vanity must be distinguished from patriotism, which consists in loving our country independent of ourselves.

5. "The Russians became . . . for the Russians": added in 2nd edition.

prediction holds in every nation as well as in Sparta. The Greek empire, sunk in voluptuousness without a remaining spark of patriotism, was no match for the Turks, enflamed with a new religion, that promised paradise to those who should die fighting for their prophet. How many nations, like those mentioned, illustrious formerly for vigour of mind and love to their country, are now sunk by contemptible vices as much below brutes as they ought to be elevated above them: brutes seldom deviate from the perfection of their nature, men frequently.

Successful commerce is not more advantageous by the wealth and power it immediately bestows, than it is hurtful ultimately by introducing luxury and voluptuousness, which eradicate patriotism. In the capital of a great monarchy, the poison of opulence is sudden; because opulence there is seldom acquired by reputable means: the poison of commercial <335> opulence is slow, because commerce seldom enriches without industry, sagacity, and fair dealing. But by whatever means acquired, opulence never fails soon or late to smother patriotism under sensuality and selfishness. We learn from Plutarch and other writers, that the Athenians, who had long enjoyed the sunshine of commerce, were extremely corrupt in the days of Philip, and of his son Alexander. Even their chief patriot and orator, a professed champion for independence, was not proof against bribes. While Alexander was prosecuting his conquests in India, Harpalus, to whom his immense treasure was intrusted, fled with the whole to Athens. Demosthenes advised his fellow-citizens to expell him, that they might not incur Alexander's displeasure. Among other things of value, there was the King's cup of massy gold, curiously engraved. Demosthenes, surveying it with a greedy eye, asked Harpalus what it weighed. To you, said Harpalus smiling, it shall weigh twenty talents; and that very night he sent privately to Demosthenes twenty talents with the cup. Demosthenes next day came into the assembly with a cloth <336> rolled about his neck; and his opinion being demanded about Harpalus, he made signs that he had lost his voice. The Capuans, the Tarentines, and other Greek colonies in the lower parts of Italy, when invaded by the Romans, were no less degenerate than their brethren in Greece when invaded by Philip of Macedon; the same depravation of manners, the same luxury, the same passion for feasts and spectacles, the same intestine factions, the same indifference about their country, and the same contempt of its laws. The Portuguese, enflamed with love to their country, having discovered a passage to the Indies by the Cape of Good Hope, made great and important settlements in that very distant part of the globe; and of their immense commerce there is no parallel in any age or country. Prodigious riches in gold, precious stones, spices, perfumes, drugs, and manufactures, were annually imported into Lisbon from their settlements on the coasts of Malabar and Coromandel, from the kingdoms of Camboya, Decan, Malacca, Patana, Siam, China, &c. from the islands of Ceylon, Sumatra, Java, Borneo, Moluccas, and Japan: and <337> to Lisbon all the nations in Europe resorted for these valuable commodities. But the downfal of the Portuguese was no less rapid than their exaltation; unbounded power, and immense wealth, having produced a total corruption of manners. If sincere piety, exalted courage, and indefatigable industry, made the original adventurers more than men; indolence, sensuality, and effeminacy, rendered their successors less than women. Unhappy it was for them to be attacked at that critical time by the Dutch, who, in defence of liberty against the tyranny of Spain, were inflamed with love to their country, as the Portuguese had been formerly.* The Dutch, originally from their situation a <338> temperate and industrious people, became heroes in the cause of liberty; and patriotism was their ruling passion. Prosperous commerce diffused wealth through every corner; and yet such was the inherent virtue of that people, that their patriotism resisted very long the contagion of wealth. But, as appetite for riches increases with their quantity, patriotism sunk in proportion, till it was totally extinguished; and now the Dutch never think of their country, unless as subservient to private interest. With respect to the Dutch East India company in particular, it was indebted for its prosperity to the fidelity and frugality of its servants, and to the patriotism of all. But these virtues were undermined, and at last eradicated,

---

* While patriotism was the ruling passion of the Portuguese, their illustrious General, Don Alphonso d'Albuquerque, carried all before him in the Indies. He adhered to the ancient frugality of his countrymen, and, notwithstanding his great power and wealth, remained uncorrupted. Though liberal in praising his officers, he never preferred any who attempted to gain his favour by flattery. In private life he was of the strictest honour; but, as justice is little regarded between nations, it was no obstruction to his ambitious views of extending the dominions of Portugal.

by luxury, which Europeans seldom resist in a hot climate. People go from Europe in the service of the company, bent beforehand to make their fortune *per fas aut nefas;* and their distance from their masters renders every check abortive. The company, eaten up by its servants, is rendered so feeble, as to be incapable of maintaining its ground against any extraordinary shock. A war of any continuance with the Indian poten-<339>tates, or with the English company, would reduce it to bankruptcy. Is the English East-India company in a much better condition? Such is the rise and fall of patriotism among the nations mentioned; and such will be its rise and fall among all nations in like circumstances.

It grieves me, that the epidemic distempers of luxury and selfishness are spreading wide in Britain. It is fruitless to dissemble, that profligate manners must, in Britain, be a consequence of great opulence, as they have been in every other part of the globe. Our late distractions leave no room for a doubt.[6] Listen to a man of figure, thoroughly acquainted with every machination for court-preferment.

> Very little attachment is discoverable in the body of our people to our excellent constitution: no reverence for the customs nor for the opinions of our ancestors; no attachment but to private interest, nor any zeal but for selfish gratifications. While party-distinctions of Whig and Tory, high church and low church, court and country, subsisted, the nation was indeed divided, but each side held an opinion, for which they would <340> have hazarded every thing; for both acted from principle: if there were some who sought to alter the constitution, there were many who would have spilt their blood to preserve it from violation: If divine hereditary right had its partisans, there were multitudes to stand up for the superior sanctity of a title, founded on an act of parliament, and the consent of a free people. But, the abolition of party-names hath destroyed all public principles. The power of the crown was indeed never more visibly extensive over the great men of the nation; but then these men have lost their influence over the lower orders: even parliament has lost much of its authority; and the voice of the multitude is set up against the sense of the

---

6. Kames may be alluding to the disturbances caused by supporters of the radical John Wilkes, who was elected to a Middlesex parliamentary seat in the general election of 1768.

legislature: an impoverished and heavily burdened public, a people luxurious and licentious, impatient of rule, and despising all authority, government relaxed in every sinew, and a corrupt selfish spirit pervading the whole (*a*).* <341>

It is a common observation, that, when the belly is full, the mind is at ease. That observation, it would appear, holds not in <342> London; for never, in any other place, did riot and licentiousness rise to such a height, without a cause, and without even a plausible pretext.†

It is deplorable that, in English public schools, patriotism makes no branch of education: young men, on the contrary, are trained up to selfishness. *Keep what you get, and get what you can,* is a lesson that boys learn

---

* Philip of Macedon, a Prince of great ambition, had unhappily for his neighbours great power and great talents to put his designs in execution. During the whole course of his reign, it was his favourite object to bring the Greek states under subjection, particularly that of Athens, which he the most dreaded. Athens was in a perilous situation, standing on the very brink of ruin; and yet, at that very time, a number of its citizens, men of rank, were so insensible to the distresses of their country, as to form themselves into a club, for feasting, drinking, gaming, and for every sort of sensual pleasure. It was made a rule, that nothing ought to disturb the mirth or jollity of the society. They saw, with indifference, their countrymen arming for battle; and, with the same indifference, they heard every day of the death or captivity of their fellow-citizens. Did there ever exist such wretches in human shape? Reader, spare thy indignation, to vent it on wretches still more detestable. They are at hand: they are in sight. Behold men, who term themselves Britons, fomenting a dangerous rebellion in our colonies, and sacrificing their native country to a feverish desire of power and opulence. How virtuous, in comparison, the Athenian club! But reader, banish such wretches from thy thoughts; they will sour thy temper. Deliver them over to self-condemnation: if they have any conscience left, the punishment will be severe. Wish them repentance. Extend that wish to the arch traitor, now on death-bed, torn to pieces with bodily diseases, and still more with those of the mind.

> Lord C—— if thou think'st on heaven's bliss,
> Hold up thy hand, make signal of thy hope.
> He dies, and makes no sign!

(*This was composed August* 1775.) [[Kames quotes from Shakespeare's *Henry VI, Part Two*, III.iii, lines 29–31. The "arch traitor" is presumably William Pitt the elder (1708–78), who, as earl of Chatham, proved willing to accept some of the terms of the American colonists in the early 1770s. Note added in 2nd edition.]]

† This was composed in the year 1770.

(*a*) The Honourable George Greenville.

early at Westminster, Winchester, and Eaton; and it is the lesson that perhaps takes the fastest hold of them. Students put themselves in the way of receiving vails from strangers; and that dirty practice continues, though far more poisonous to manners than the giving vails to menial servants, which the nation is now ashamed of. The Eaton scholars are at times sent to the highway to rob passengers. The strong, without controul, tyranize over the weak, subjecting them to <343> every servile office, wiping shoes not excepted. They are permitted to trick and deceive one another; and the finest fellow is he who is the most artful. Friendship indeed is cultivated, but such as we find among robbers: a boy would be run down, if he had no associate. I do not say, and am far from thinking, that such manners are inculcated by the masters; but I say, and am sorry to say, that nothing is done to prevent or correct them.⁷

When a nation, formerly warlike and public spirited, is depressed by luxury and selfishness, doth nature afford no means for restoring it to its former state? The Emperor Hadrian declared the Greeks a free people; not doubting, but that a change so animating, would restore the fine arts to their pristine lustre.—A vain attempt: for the genius of the Greeks vanished with their patriotism; and liberty to them was no blessing. With respect to the Portuguese, the decay of their power and of their commerce, hath reduced them to a much lower state, than when they rose as it were out of nothing. At that time they were poor, but innocent: at present they are poor, but corrupted with many vices. <344> Their pride, in particular, swells as high as when masters of the Indies. The following ridiculous instance is a pregnant proof: shoes and stocking are prohibited to their Indian subjects; though many of them would pay handsomely for the privilege. There is one obvious measure for reviving the Portuguese trade in India: but they have not so much vigour of mind remaining, as even to think of it. They still possess, in that country, the town and territory of Goa, the town and territory of Diu, with some other ports, all admirably situated for trade. What stands in the way but indolence merely, against declaring the places mentioned free ports, with liberty of conscience to traders of whatever re-

---

7. "I do not . . . or correct them": added in 2nd edition. In the 1st edition the paragraph ends: "In a word, the most determined selfishness is the capital lesson" [1:450].

ligion? Free traders flocking there, under protection of the Portuguese, would undermine the Dutch and English companies, which cannot trade upon an equal footing with private merchants; and by that means the Portuguese trade might again flourish. But that people are not yet brought so low, as to be compelled to change their manners, though reduced to depend on their neighbours even for common necessaries: the gold and diamonds <345> of Brasil, are a plague that corrupts all. Spain and Portugal afford instructive political lessons: the latter has been ruined by opulence; the former, as will be seen afterward, by taxes no less impolitic than oppressive. To enable these nations to recommence their former course, or any nation in the same condition, I can discover no means but pinching poverty. Commerce and manufactures taking wing, may leave a country in a very distressed condition: but a people may be very distressed, and yet very vitious; for vices generated by opulence are not soon eradicated. And, though other vices should at last vanish with the temptations that promoted them, indolence and pusillanimity will remain for ever, unless by some powerful cause the opposite virtues be introduced. A very poor man, however indolent, will be tempted, for bread, to exert some activity; and he may be trained gradually from less to more by the same means. Activity, at the same time, produces bodily strength; which will restore courage and boldness. By such means a nation may be put in motion with the same advantages it had originally; and its second progress may <346> prove as successful as the first. Thus nations go round in a circle: the first part of the progress is verified in a thousand instances; but the world has not subsisted long enough to afford any clear instance of the other.*<347>

---

* The following letter I had from a gentleman, who, though at Lisbon for the sake of health, neglects no opportunity to increase his stock of knowledge. "Nothing but ocular demonstration could have convinced me that the human species may be depraved to the degree that is exemplified in this country. Whether with regard to politics, morals, arts, or social intercourse, it is equally defective. In short, excepting the mere elementary benefits of earth and air, this country is in the lowest state. Will you believe that I found not a single man who could inform me of the price of land, very few who had any notion to what value the product of their country extends, or of its colonies. No one able to point out the means of reviving Portugal from its present desponding condition. With respect to a general plan of legislation, there is none; unless the caprices of an ignorant despot may be called such, or the projects of a designing minister, constantly endeav-

I close this Sketch with two illustrious examples of patriotism; one ancient, one modern; one among the whites, one among the blacks. Aristides the Athenian is famed above all the ancients for love to his country. Its safety and honour were the only objects of his ambition; and his signal disinterestedness made it the same to him, whether these ends were accomplished by himself, or by others, by his friends <348> or his foes. One conspicuous instance occurred before the battle of Marathon. Of the ten generals chosen to command the Athenian army, he was one: but, sensible that a divided command is subjected to manifold inconveniencies, he exerted all his influence for Miltiades; and, at the same time, zealously supported a proposal of Miltiades to meet the Persians in the field. His disinterestedness was still more conspicuous with regard to Themistocles, his bitter enemy. Suspending all enmity, he cordially agreed with him in every operation of the war; assisting him with his counsel and credit, and yet suffering him to ingross all the honour. In peace he was the same, yielding to Themistocles in the administration of government, and contenting himself with a subordinate place. In the senate, and in the assembly of the people, he made many proposals in a borrowed name, to prevent envy and opposition. He retired from public business at the latter part of his life, passing his time in training young men for serving the state, instilling into them principles of honour

---

ouring to depress the nobility, and to beggar the other orders of the state. This the Marquis Pombal has at length completed. He has left the crown possessed of a third part of the land-property, the church enjoying another third, the remainder left to an indigent nobility and their vassals. He has subjected every branch of commerce to ministerial emoluments, and fixed judicial proceedings, both civil and criminal, on the fluctuating basis of his own interest or inclination. Take an instance of their law. A small proprietor having land adjoining to, or intermixed with, the land of a great proprietor, is obliged to sell his possession, if the other wishes to have it. In the case of several competitors to the succession of land, it is the endeavour of each to seize the possession, well knowing that possession is commonly held the best title; and, at any rate, that there is no claim for rents during the time of litigation. All the corn growing in Estremadura must be sold at Lisbon. A tenth of all sales, rents, wages, &c. goes to the King. These instances are, I think, sufficient to give a notion of the present state of the kingdom, and of the merits of Pombal, who has long had the reins in his hands as first minister, who may justly boast of having freed his countrymen from the dread of becoming more wretched than they are at present. It gave me satisfaction to find the doctrines of the Sketches finely illustrated in the history of this singular kingdom. I am," &c. [[Note added in 2nd edition.]]

and virtue, and inspiring them with love to their country. His death unfold-<349>ed a signal proof of the contempt he had for riches: he who had been treasurer of Greece during the lavishment of war, did not leave money sufficient to defray the expence of his funerals: a British commissary, in like circumstances, acquires the riches of Croesus.

The scene of the other example is Fouli, a negro kingdom in Africa. Such regard is paid there to royal blood, that no man can succeed to the crown, but who is connected with the first monarch, by an uninterrupted chain of females: a connection by males would give no security, as the women of that country are prone to gallantry. In the last century, the Prince of Sambaboa, the King's nephew by his sister, was invested with the dignity of Kamalingo, a dignity appropriated to the presumptive heir. A liberal and generous mind, with undaunted courage, rivetted him in the affections of the nobility and people. They rejoiced in the expectation of having him for their King. But their expectation was blasted. The King, fond of his children, ventured a bold measure, which was, to invest his eldest son with <350> the dignity of Kamalingo, and to declare him heir to the crown. Though the Prince of Sambaboa had for him the laws of the kingdom, and the hearts of the people, yet he retired in silence to avoid a civil war. He could not, however, prevent men of rank from flocking to him; which, being interpreted a rebellion, the King raised an army, vowing to put them all to the sword. As the King advanced, the Prince retired, resolving not to draw his sword against an uncle, whom he was accustomed to call father. But, finding that the command of the army was bestowed on his rival, he made ready for battle. The Prince obtained a complete victory: but his heart was not elated. The horrors of a civil war stared him in the face: he bid farewell to his friends, dismissed his army, and retired into a neighbouring kingdom; relying on the affections of the people to be placed on the throne after his uncle's death. During banishment, which continued thirty tedious years, frequent attempts upon his life put his temper to a severe trial; for, while he existed, the King had no hopes that his son would <351> reign in peace. He had the fortitude to surmount every trial; when, in the year 1702, beginning to yield to age and misfortunes, his uncle died. His cousin was deposed; and he was called, by the unanimous voice of the nobles, to reign over a people who adored him. <352>

SKETCH VIII

Finances

PREFACE

In the following slight Essay, intended for novices only, it satisfies my ambition, to rival certain pains-taking authors, who teach history in the perspicuous mode of question and answer. Among novices, it would be unpardonable to rank such of my fellow-citizens as are ambitious of a seat in parliament; many of whom sacrifice the inheritance of their ancestors, for an opportunity to exert their patriotism in that august assembly. Can such a sacrifice permit me to doubt of their being adepts in the mysteries of government, and of taxes in particular? They ought at least to be initiated in these mysteries.

It is of importance, that taxes, and their effects, be understood, not only by the members of our parliament, but by their electors: a re-<353>presentative will not readily vote for a destructive tax, when he cannot hope to disguise his conduct. The intention of the present sketch, is to unfold the principles upon which taxes ought to be founded, and to point out what are beneficial, what noxious. I have endeavoured to introduce some light into a subject involved in Egyptian darkness; and if that end be attained, I shall die in the faith that I have not been an unprofitable servant to my country. <354>

Finances.

This subject consists of many parts, not a little intricate. A proper distribution will tend to perspicuity; and I think it may be fitly divided into the following sections. 1st, General considerations on taxes. 2d, Power of imposing taxes. 3d, Different sorts of taxes, with their advantages and disadvantages. 4th, Manner of levying taxes. 5th, Rules to be observed in taxing. 6th, Taxes examined with respect to their effects. 7th, Taxes for advancing industry and commerce.[1]

SECTION I

General Considerations on Taxes.

As opulence is not friendly to study and knowledge, the men best qualified for being generals, admirals, judges, or <355> ministers of state, are seldom opulent; and to make such men serve without pay, would be in effect to ease the rich at the expence of the poor. With respect to the military branch in particular, the bulk of those who compose an army, if withdrawn from daily labour, must starve, unless the public which they serve afford them maintenance. A republican government, during peace, may indeed be supported at a very small charge, among a temperate and patriotic people. In a monarchy, a public fund is indispensable, even during peace: and in war it is indispensable, whatever be the government. The Spartans carried all before them in Greece, but were forced to quit their hold, having no fund for a standing army; and the other Greek states were obliged to confederate with the Athenians, who had a public fund, and who after the Persian war became masters at sea. A defect so obvious in the Spartan government, did assuredly not escape Lycurgus, the most profound of all legislators. Foreseeing that conquest would be destructive to his countrymen, his sole purpose was to guard them from being conquered; which in Sparta <356> required no public fund, as all the citizens were equal, and equally bound to

---

1. In 1st edition: "6th, Examination of British taxes. 7th, Regulations for advancing industry and commerce" [1:456].

defend themselves and their country. A state, it is true, without a public fund, is ill qualified to oppose a standing army, regularly disciplined, and regularly paid. But in political matters, experience is our only sure guide; and the history of nations, at that early period, was too barren to afford instruction. Lycurgus may well be excused, considering how little progress political knowledge had made in a much later period. Charles VII. of France, was the first in modern times who established a fund for a standing army. Against that dangerous innovation, the crown-vassals had no resource but to imitate their sovereign; and yet, without even dreaming of a resource, they suffered themselves to be undermined, and at last overturned, by the King, their superior. Thus, on the one hand, a nation however warlike that has not a public fund, is no match for a standing army enured to war: extensive commerce, on the other hand, enables a nation to support a standing army; but by introducing luxury it eradicates manhood, and renders that army an <357> unfit match for any poor and warlike intruder. Hard may seem the fate of nations, laid thus open to destruction from every quarter. All that can be said is, that such vicissitudes seem to enter into the scheme of Providence.

The stability of land fits it, above all other subjects, for a public patrimony. But as crown-lands lie open to the rapacity of favourites, it becomes necessary, when these are dissipated, to introduce taxes; which have the following properties, that they unite in one common interest the sovereign and his subjects, and that they can be augmented or diminished according to exigencies.

The art of levying money by taxes was so little understood in the sixteenth century, that after the famous battle of Pavia, in which the French King was made prisoner, Charles V. was obliged to disband his victorious army, tho' consisting but of 24,000 men, because he had not the art to levy, in his extensive dominions, a sum necessary to keep it on foot. So little knowledge was there in England of political arithmetic in the days of Edward III. that L. 1: 2: 4 on each parish was com-<358>puted to be sufficient for raising a subsidy of L. 50,000. It being found, that there were but 8700 parishes, exclusive of Wales, the parliament, in order to raise the said subsidy, assessed on each parish L. 5, 16 s.

In imposing taxes, ought not the expence of living to be deducted, and to consider the remainder as the only taxable subject? This mode was adopted in the state of Athens. A rent of 500 measures of corn, burdened the landlord with the yearly contribution of a talent: a rent of 300, burdened him with half a talent: a rent of 200, burdened him with the sixth part of a talent; and land under that rent paid no tax. Here the tax was not in proportion to the estate, but to what could be spared out of it; or, in other words, in proportion to the ability of the proprietor. At the same time, ability must not be estimated by what a man actually saves, which would exempt the profuse and profligate from paying taxes, but by what a man can pay who lives with oeconomy according to his rank. This rule is founded on the very nature of government: to tax a man's food, or the subject that affords him bare necessaries, is worse than <359> the denying him protection: it starves him. Hence the following proposition may be laid down as the corner stone of taxation-building, "That every man ought to contribute to the public revenue, not in proportion to his substance, but to his ability." I am sorry to observe, that this rule is little regarded in British taxes; though nothing would contribute more to sweeten the minds of the people, and to make them fond of their government, than a regulation fraught with so much equity.

Taxes were long in use before it was discovered, that they could be made subservient to other purposes, beside that of supporting government. In the fifteenth century, the states of Burgundy rejected with indignation a demand made by the Duke, of a duty on salt; tho' they found no other objection, but that it would oppress the poor people, who lived mostly on salt meat and salt fish. It did not occur to them, that such a tax might hurt their manufactures, by raising the price of labour. A tax of two shillings on every hearth, known by the name of *hearth-money,* was granted to Charles II. his heirs <360> and successors, for ever. It was abrogated by an act of William and Mary, *anno* 1688, on the following preamble, "That it is not only a great oppression upon the poorer sort, but a badge of slavery upon the whole people, exposing every man's house to be entered into and searched at pleasure, by persons unknown to him." Had the harm done by such a tax to our manufactures been at that time understood, it would have been urged as the capital reason against it. Our late improvements in commercial politics have unfolded an important doctrine, That taxes are seldom indifferent to the public good; that frequently they are more oppressive to the people, than beneficial to the sovereign; and, on the other hand, that they may be so contrived, as to rival bounties in promoting industry, manufactures, and commerce. These different effects of taxes, have rendered the subject not a little intricate.

It is an article of importance in government, to have it ascertained, what proportion of the annual income of a nation may be drawn from the people by taxes, without impoverishing them. An eighth part <361> is held to be too much; husbandry, commerce, and population, would suffer. Davenant says, that the Dutch pay to the public annually, the fourth part of the income of their country; and he adds, that their strict oeconomy enables them to bear that immense load, without raising the price of labour so high as to cut them out of the foreign market. It was probably so in the days of Davenant; but, of late, matters are much altered: the dearness of living and of labour, has excluded all the Dutch manufactures from the foreign market. Till the French war in King William's reign, England paid in taxes but about a twentieth part of its annual income.

SECTION II

Power of imposing Taxes.

That to impose taxes belongs to the sovereign, and to him only, is undoubted. But it has been doubted, whether even King and parliament, who pos-<362>sess the sovereign authority in Britain, can legally impose a tax without consent of the people. The celebrated Locke, in his essay on Government (*a*), lays down the following proposition as fundamental. " 'Tis true, governments cannot be supported without great charge; and 'tis fit every one who enjoys his share of protection should pay out of his estate his proportion for the maintenance of it. But still it must be with his own consent, *i.e.* the consent of the majority, giving it either by themselves, or their representatives chosen by them; for if any one shall claim a power to lay and levy taxes on the people by his own authority, and without such

---

(*a*) Chap. II. § 140.

consent of the people, he thereby invades the fundamental law of property, and subverts the end of government. For what property have I in that which another may by right take when he pleases to himself?" No author has reflected more honour on his native country, and on mankind, than Mr. Locke. Yet no name is above truth; and I am obliged to observe, tho' with regret, that in the forego-<363>ing reasoning the right of imposing taxes is laid upon a very crazy foundation. It may indeed be said with some colour, that the freeholders virtually impower their representatives to tax them. But their vassals and tenants, who have no vote in electing members of parliament, empower none to tax them: yet they are taxed like others; and so are the vassals and tenants of peers. Add to these an immense number of artisans, manufacturers, day-labourers, domestics, &c. &c. with the whole female sex; and it will appear, that those who are represented in parliament, make not the hundreth part of the taxable people. But further, it is acknowledged by our author, that the majority of the Lords and Commons must bind the minority. This circumstance might have opened his eyes: for surely the minority in this case are bound without their consent; nay, against their consent. That a state cannot tax its subjects without their consent, is a rash proposition, totally subversive of government. Locke himself has suggested the solid foundation of taxes, tho' inadvertently he lays no weight on it. I borrow his own words: "That every <364> one who enjoys his share of protection, should pay out of his estate his proportion for the maintenance of the government." The duties of sovereign and of subject are reciprocal; and common justice requires, that a subject, or any person who is protected by a government, ought to pay for that protection. Similar instances without number of such reciprocal duties, occur in the laws of every civilized nation. A man calls for meat and drink in a tavern: is he not bound to pay, tho' he made no agreement beforehand? A man wafted over a river in a ferry-boat, must pay the common fare, though he made no promise. Nay, it is every man's interest to pay for protection: government cannot subsist without a public fund: and what will become of individuals, when left open to every rapacious invader? Thus taxes are implied in the very nature of government; and the interposition of sovereign authority is only necessary for determining the expediency of a tax; and the quota, if found expedient.

Many writers, misled by the respectable authority of Locke, boldly maintain, that a British parliament cannot legally tax the <365> American colonies, who are not represented in parliament. This proposition, which has drawn the attention of the public of late years has led me to be more explicit on the power of imposing taxes, than otherwise would be necessary. Those who favour the independence of our colonies urge, "That a man ought to have the disposal of what he acquires by honest industry, subject to no control: whence the necessity of a parliament for imposing taxes, where every individual is either personally present, or by a representative of his own election. The aid accordingly given to a British sovereign, is not a tribute, but a free and voluntary gift." What is said above will bring the dispute within a very narrow compass. If our colonists be British subjects, which hitherto has not been controverted, they are subjected to the British legislature in every article of government; and as from the beginning they have been protected by Britain, they ought, like other subjects, to pay for that protection. There never was a time less favourable to their claim of freedom from taxes, than the close of the late war with France.[2] Had <366> not Britain seasonably interposed, they would have been swallowed up by France, and become slaves to despotism.

If it be questioned, By what acts is a man understood to claim protection of a government; I answer, By setting his foot within the territory. If, upon landing at Dover, a foreigner be robbed, the law interposes for him as for a native. And as he is thus protected, he pays for protection when he purchases a pair of shoes, or a bottle of beer. The case is clear, with respect to a man who can chuse the place of his residence. But what shall be said of children, who are not capable of choice, nor of consent? They are protected; and protection implies the reciprocal duty of paying taxes. As soon as a young man is capable of acting for himself, he is at liberty to chuse other protectors, if those who have hitherto protected him be not to his taste.

If a legal power to impose taxes without consent of the people, did necessarily imply a legal power to impose taxes at pleasure, without limitation, Locke's argument would be invincible, in a country of freedom at least. A

---

2. Kames is presumably referring to the Seven Years' War, which ended in 1763.

power to impose taxes <367> at pleasure, would indeed be an invasion of the fundamental law of property; because, under pretext of taxing, it would subject every man's property to the arbitrary will of the sovereign. But the argument has no weight, where the sovereign's power is limited. The reciprocal duties between sovereign and subject imply, that the people ought to contribute what sums are necessary for the support of government, and that the sovereign ought not to demand more. It is true, that there is no regular check against him, when he transgresses his duty in this particular: but there is an effectual check in the nature of every government that is not legally despotic, viz. a general concert among all ranks, to vindicate their liberty against a course of violence and oppression; and multiplied acts of that kind have more than once brought about such a concert.

As every member of the body-politic is under protection of the government, every one of them, as observed above, ought to pay for being protected; and yet this proposition has been controverted by an author of some note (*a*); who maintains, <368> "That the food and raiment furnished to the society by husbandmen and manufacturers, are all that these good people are bound to contribute: and supposing them bound to contribute more, it is not till others have done as much for the public." At that rate, lawyers and physicians ought also to be exempted from contributing; especially those who draw the greatest sums, because they are supposed to do the most good. That argument, the suggestion of a benevolent heart, is no proof of an enlightened understanding. The labours of the farmer, of the lawyer, of the physician, contribute not a mite to the public fund, nor tend to defray the expence of government. The luxurious proprietor of a great estate has a still better title to be exempted than the husbandman; because he is a great benefactor to the public, by giving bread to a variety of industrious people. In a word, every man ought to contribute for being protected; and if a husbandman be protected in working for himself one-and-fifty weeks yearly, he ought thankfully to work one week more, for defraying the expence of that protection. <369>

(*a*) L'ami des hommes [[i.e., Mirabeau]].

SECTION III

Different Sorts of Taxes, with their Advantages and Disadvantages.

All taxes are laid upon persons; but in different respects: a tax laid on a man personally, for himself and family, is termed a *capitation-tax;* a tax laid on him for his property, is termed a *tax on goods.* The latter is the only rational tax, because it may be proportioned to the ability of the proprietor. It has only one inconvenience, that his debts must be overlooked; because to take these into the account, would lead to endless intricacies. But there is an obvious remedy for that inconvenience: let the man who complains free himself of debt, by selling land or moveables; which will so far relieve him of the tax. Nor ought this measure to be considered as a hardship: it is seldom the interest of a landholder to be in debt; and with respect to the public, the measure <370> not only promotes the circulation of property, but is favourable to creditors, by procuring them payment. A capitation-tax goes upon an erroneous principle, as if all men were of equal ability. What prompts it is, that many men, rich in bonds and other moveables that can easily be hid from public inspection, cannot be reached otherwise than by a capitation-tax. But as, by the very supposition, such men cannot be distinguished from the mass of the people, that mode of taxing, miserably unequal, is rarely practised among enlightened nations. Russia labours under a capitation-tax.[3] Some years ago, a capitation-tax was imposed in Denmark, obliging even day-labourers to pay for their wives and children. Upon the same absurd plan, a tax was imposed on marriage. One would be tempted to think, that population was intended to be discouraged. The Danish ministry have been sensible of the impropriety of such taxes; for a tax imposed on those who obtain titles of honour from the crown, is applied for relieving husbandmen of their capitation-tax. But a tax of this kind lies open to many other objections. It cannot fail to raise <371> the price of labour, a poisonous effect in a country of industry; for the labourer will relieve himself of the tax, by heightening his wages: more

---

3. "Russia labours under a capitation-tax": added in 2nd edition.

prudent it would be to lay the tax directly on the employer, which would remove the pretext for heightening wages. The taxing of day-labourers, whether by capitation or in any other manner, has beside an effect contrary to what is intended: instead of increasing the public revenue, it virtually lessens it, by raising the pay of soldiers, sailors, and of every workman employed by government.

Taxes upon goods are of two kinds, viz. upon things consumable, and upon things not consumable. I begin with the latter. The land-tax in Britain, paid by the proprietor according to an invariable rule, and levied with very little expence, is of all taxes the most just, and the most effectual. The proprietor, knowing beforehand the sum he is subjected to, prepares accordingly: and as each proprietor contributes in proportion to his estate, the tax makes no variation in their relative opulence. The only improvement it is susceptible of, is the Athenian regulation, of exempting small estates that are no more than sufficient <372> to afford bread to the frugal proprietor. In France, the land-tax seems to have been established on a very false foundation, viz. That the clergy perform their duty to the state by praying and instructing, that the noblesse fight for the state; and consequently, that the only duty left to the farmer, is to defray the charges of government. This argument would hold, if the clergy were not paid for praying, nor the noblesse for fighting. Such a load upon the poorest members of the state, is an absurdity in politics. And to render it still more absurd, the tax on the farmer is not imposed by an invariable rule: every one is taxed in proportion to his apparent circumstances, which in effect is to tax industry. Nor is this all. Under pretext of preventing famine, the exporting of corn, even from province to province, is frequently interrupted; by which it happens, that the corn of a plentiful year is destroyed by insects, and in a year of scarcity is engrossed by merchants. Suppose a plan were desiderated for discouraging agriculture, here is one actually put in execution, the success of which is infallible. "Were it related," observes a French <373> writer, "in some foreign history, that there is a country extremely fertile, in a fine climate, enjoying navigable rivers, with every advantage for the commerce of corn; and yet that the product is not sufficient for the inhabitants: would not one conclude the people to be stupid and barbarous? And yet this is the case of France." He adds the true reason, which is, the discouragement husbandry lies under by oppressive taxes. We have Diodorus Siculus for our authority, that the husbandman was greatly respected in Hindostan. Among other nations, says he, the land during war lies untilled; but in Hindostan, husbandmen are sacred, and no soldier ventures to lay a hand on them. They are considered as servants of the public, who cannot be dispensed with.

It is a gross error to maintain, that a tax on land is the same with a tax on the product of land. The former, which is the English mode, is no discouragement to industry and improvements: on the contrary, the higher the value of land is raised, the less will the tax be in proportion. The latter, which is the French <374> mode, is a great discouragement to industry and improvements; because the more a man improves, the deeper he is taxed. The tenth part of the product of land, is the only tax that is paid in China. This tax, of the same nature with the tithe paid among us to the clergy, yields to the British mode of taxing the land itself, and not its product; but is less exceptionable than the land-tax in France, because it is not arbitrary. The Chinese tax, paid in kind, is stored in magazines, and sold from time to time for maintaining the magistrates and the army, the surplus being remitted to the treasury. In case of famine, it is sold to the poor people at a moderate price. In Tonquin, there is a land-tax, which, like that in France, is laid upon the peasants, exempting people of condition, and the literati in particular. Many grounds that bear not corn, contribute hay for the king's elephants and cavalry: which the poor peasants are obliged to carry to the capital, even from the greatest distance; a regulation no less injudicious than slavish.

The window-tax, the coach-tax, and the plate-tax, come under the present head, being taxes upon things not consumable. <375> In Holland horses are taxed; and there is a tax on domestic servants, which deserves well to be imitated. Vanity in Britain, and love of show, have multiplied domestics, far beyond necessity, and even beyond convenience. A number of idlers collected in a luxurious family, become vitious and debauched; and many useful hands are withdrawn from husbandry and manufactures. In order that the tax may reach none but the vain and splendid, those who have but one servant pay nothing: two domestics subject the master to five shillings for each, three to ten shillings for each, four to twenty shillings, five to forty shillings, and so on in a geometrical progression. In Denmark, a farmer is taxed for every plough he uses. If the tax be intended for discouraging extensive farms, it is a happy contrivance, agreeable to sound policy; for small farms increase the number of temperate and robust people, fit for every sort of labour.

Next of taxes upon things consumable. The taxes that appear the least oppressive, because disguised, are what are laid on our manufactures: the tax is advanced by the manufacturer, and drawn from the pur-<376>chaser as part of the price. In Rome, a tax was laid upon every man who purchased a slave. It is reported by some authors, that the tax was remitted by the Emperor Nero; and yet no alteration was made, but to oblige the vender to advance the tax. Hear Tacitus on that subject (*a*). "Vectigal quintae et vicesimae venalium mancipiorum remissum, specie magis quam vi; quia cum venditor pendere juberetur, in partem pretii emptoribus accrescebat."* Thus, with respect to our taxes on soap, shoes, candles, and other things consumable, the purchaser thinks he is only paying the price, and never dreams that he is paying a tax. To support the illusion, the duty ought to be moderate: to impose a tax twenty times the value of the commodity, as is done in France with respect to salt, raises more disgust in the people as an attempt to deceive them, than when laid on without disguise. Such exorbitant taxes, which <377> are paid with the utmost reluctance, cannot be made effectual but by severe penalties, equal to what are inflicted on the most atrocious criminals; which, at the same time, has a bad effect with respect to morals, as it blends great and small crimes together, and tends to lessen the horror one naturally conceives at the former.

Such taxes are attended with another signal advantage: they bear a proportion to the ability of the contributors, the opulent being commonly the greatest consumers. The taxes on coaches and on plate are paid by men of fortune, without loading the industrious poor; and, on that account, are excellent; being imposed, however, without disguise, they are paid with more reluctance by the rich, than taxes on consumption are by the poor.

---

* "The tax of a twenty fifth upon slaves to be sold was remitted more in appearance than in reality; because when the seller was ordered to pay it, he laid it upon the price to the buyer."

(*a*) Annal. lib. 13.

I add one other advantage of taxes on consumption. They are finely contrived to connect the interest of the sovereign with that of his subjects; for his profit arises from their prosperity.

Such are the advantages of a tax on consumption; but it must not be praised, as attended with no inconvenience. The retailer, under pretext of the tax, raises the <378> price higher than barely to indemnify himself; by which means the tax is commonly doubled on the consumer. The inconvenience, however, is but temporary. "Such extortion," says Davenant, "cannot last long; for every commodity in common use finds in the market its true value and price."

There is another inconvenience much more distressing, because it admits not a remedy, and because it affects the state itself. Taxes on consumption, being commonly laid on things of the greatest use, raise a great sum to the public, without much burdening individuals; the duty on coal, for example, on candle, on leather, on soap, on salt, on malt, and on malt-liquor. These duties, however, carry in their bosom a slow poison, by raising the price of labour and of manufactures. De Wit observes, that the Dutch taxes upon consumption have raised the price of their broad cloth forty *per cent.;* and our manufactures, by the same means, are raised at least thirty *per cent.* Britain has long laboured under this chronical distemper; which, by excluding her from foreign markets, will not only put an end to her <379> own manufactures, but will open a wide door to the foreign, as smuggling cannot be prevented where commodities imported are much cheaper than our own. The Dutch taxes on consumption are exceedingly high; and yet necessary, not only for defraying the expence of government, but for guarding their frontier, and, above all, for keeping out the sea! The industry, however, and frugality of the people, enable them to bear that heavy burden without murmuring. But other European nations have now acquired a share of the immense commerce formerly carried on by the Dutch alone. Their trade, accordingly, is on the decline; and, when it sinks a little lower, the heavy taxes will undoubtedly depopulate their country.[4]

Nor ought it to be overlooked, that taxes on consumption are not equally proper in every case. They are proper in a populous country, like Holland;

---

4. "The Dutch taxes ... depopulate their country": added in 2nd edition.

because the expence of collecting is but a trifle, compared with the sums collected. But, in a country thinly peopled, such taxes are improper; because the expence of collecting makes too great a proportion of the sums collected: in the highlands of <380> Scotland, the excise on ale and spirits defrays not the expence of levying; the people are burdened, and the government is not supported. I suspect that the window-tax in Scotland lies open to the same objection.[5]

A lottery is a sort of tax different from any that have been mentioned. It is a tax, of all, the most agreeable, being entirely voluntary. An appetite for gaming, inherent even in savages, prompts multitudes to venture their money in hopes of a high prize; though they cannot altogether hide from themselves the inequality of the play. But it is well, that the selfish passions of men can be made subservient to the public good. Lotteries, however, produce one unhappy effect. They blunt the edge of industry, by directing the attention to a more compendious mode of gain. At the same time, the money acquired by a lottery, seldom turns to account; for what comes without trouble, goes commonly without thought. <381>

SECTION IV

Manner of levying Taxes.

To avoid the rapacity of farmers, a mild government will, in most cases, prefer management; i.e. it will levy taxes by officers appointed for that purpose. Montesquieu (*a*) has handled that point with his usual sprightly elegance.

Importation-duties are commonly laid upon the importer before the cargo is landed, leaving him to add the duty to the price of the goods; and the facility of levying, is the motive for preferring that mode. But, is it not hard that the importer should be obliged to advance a great sum in name of duty, before drawing a shilling by the sale of his goods? It is not only hard, but grossly unjust; for, if the goods perish without being sold, the

---

(*a*) L'Esprit des loix, liv. 13. ch. 19.
5. "I suspect that . . . the same objection": added in 2nd edition.

duty is lost to the importer: he has no claim against the public for restitution. This has <382> more the air of despotism, than of a free government. Would it not be more equitable, that the goods should be lodged in a public warehouse, under custody of revenue-officers, the importer paying the duty as goods are sold? According to the present mode, the duty remains with the collector three years, in order to be repaid to the importer, if the goods be exported within that time: but, by the mode proposed, the duty would be paid to the treasury as goods are sold, which might be within a month from the time of importation, perhaps a week; and the treasury would profit, as well as the fair trader. There are public warehouses adjoining to the customhouse of Bourdeaux, where the sugars of the French colonies are deposited, till the importer finds a market; and he pays the duty gradually as sales are made. It rejoices me, that the same mode is adopted in this island with respect to some foreign articles necessary in our trade with Africa: the duty is not demanded, till the goods be shipped for that continent. It is also adopted with respect to foreign salt, and with respect to rum imported from our sugar-colonies. <383>

Beside the equity of what is here proposed, which relieves the importer from advance of money, and from risk, many other advantages would be derived from it. In the first place, the merchant, having no occasion to reserve any portion of his capital for answering the duty, would be enabled to commence trade with a small stock, or to increase his trade, if his stock be large: trade would flourish, and the public revenue would increase in proportion. Secondly, It would lessen smuggling: many who commence trade with upright intention, are tempted to smuggle for want of ready money to pay the duty. Thirdly, This manner of levying the duty would not only lessen the number of officers, but remove every reason for claiming discount on pretext of leakage, samples, and the drying or shrinking of goods. In the present manner of levying, that discount must be left to the discretion of the officer: a private understanding is thus opened between him and the merchant, hurtful to the revenue, and destructive to morals. Fourthly, The merchant would be enabled to lower his prices, and be forced to lower them, by having many ri-<384>vals; which at the same time would give access to heighten importation-duties, without raising the price of foreign commodities, above what it is at present. But the capital advantage of all would be, to render, in effect, every port in Britain a free port, enabling English merchants, many of whom have great capitals, to outstrip foreigners in what is termed a *commerce of speculation*. This island is well situated for such commerce; and, were our ports free, the productions of all climates would be stored up in them, ready for exportation, when a market offers; an excellent plan for increasing our shipping, and for producing boundless wealth.

SECTION V

Rules to be observed in Taxing.

The different objects of taxes, and the intricacy thereby occasioned, require general rules, not only for directing the legislature in imposing them, but for ena-<385>bling others to judge what are beneficial, and what hurtful.

The first rule I shall suggest is, That, wherever there is an opportunity of smuggling, taxes ought to be moderate; for smuggling can never effectually be restrained, where the cheapness of imported goods is in effect an insurance against the risk; in which view, Swift humorously observes, that two and two do not always make four. A duty of 15 per cent. upon printed linen imported into France, encourages smuggling: a lower duty would produce a greater sum to the public, and be more beneficial to the French manufacturer. Bone-lace imported into France is charged with a duty of 20 per cent. in order to favour that manufacture at home: but in vain; for bone-lace is easily smuggled, and the price is little higher than before. The high duty on *succus liquoritiae*[6] imported into Britain, being L. 7: 2: 6 per hundred weight, was a great encouragement for smuggling; for which reason it is reduced to 30 shillings per hundred weight (*a*). <386>

Smuggling of tea, which draws great sums from Britain, is much encouraged by its high price at home. As far as I can judge, it would be profitable, both to the public, and to individuals, to lay aside the importation-duty, and to substitute in its stead a duty on the consumer. Freedom of

---

(*a*) 7th Geo. III. cap. 47.
6. Licorice juice; still used for the treatment of ulcers.

importation would enable the East India company to sell so cheap, as effectually to banish smuggling; and the low price of tea would enable the consumer to pay a pretty smart duty, without being much out of pocket. The following mode is proposed, as a hint merely that may lead to improvements. Let every man who uses tea be subjected to a moderate tax, proportioned to his mode of living. Absolute precision cannot be expected in proportioning the tax on families; but gross inequality may easily be prevented. For instance, let the mode of living be determined by the equipage that is kept. A coach or chaise with two horses shall subject a family to a yearly tax of L. 10; heightening the tax in proportion to the number of horses and carriages; two servants in livery, without a carriage, to a tax of 40 s.; every other family paying 20 s. Every <387> family where tea is used must be entered in the collector's books, with its mode of living, under a heavy penalty; which would regulate the coach-tax, as well as that on tea. Such a tax, little expensive in levying, would undoubtedly be effectual: a master of a family is imprudent indeed, if he put it in the power of the vender, of a malicious neighbour, or of a disgusted servant, to subject him to a heavy penalty. This tax, at the same time, would be the least disagreeable of any that is levied without disguise; being in effect a voluntary tax, as the mode of living is voluntary. Nor would it be difficult to temper the tax, so as to afford a greater sum to the public than it receives at present from the importation-duty, and yet to cost our people no more for tea than they pay at present, considering the high price of the commodity.*

To favour our own cambric manufacture, the importation of it is prohibited. The unhappy circumstance is, that fine cambric is easily smuggled: the price is <388> great, and the bulk small. Would it not be more politic, to admit importation under a duty so moderate as not to encourage smuggling. The duty applied for promoting our own cambric-manufacture, would in time so improve it, as to put us above the hazard of rivalship, with respect at least to our own consumption. It is pleasant to trace the progressive effects of such a plan. The importation-duties would at first be considerable; and yet no higher than necessary for nursing an infant man-

---

* In Holland, a person is prohibited from drinking tea without license, for which he pays a yearly sum. [[Note added in 3rd edition.]]

ufacture. As the manufacture improves, more and more of it would be consumed at home; and the duty would fall in proportion. But then this small duty would be sufficient to encourage a manufacture, now approaching to perfection.[7]

High duties on importation are immoral, as well as impolitic; for, is it not unjustifiable in a legislature, first to tempt, and then to punish for yielding to the temptation.

As an Appendix to the rule for preventing smuggling, I add, that a tax upon a fashion, which can be laid aside at pleasure, can little be depended on. In the year 1767, a duty was laid on chip-hats, worn <389> at that time by women of fashion. They were instantly laid aside, and the tax produced nothing.

A second rule is, That taxes expensive in the levying ought to be avoided; being heavy on the people, without a proportional benefit to the revenue. Our land-tax is admirable: it affords a great sum, levied with very little expence. The duties on coaches, and on gold and silver-plate, are similar; and so would be the tax on tea above proposed. The taxes that are the most hurtful to trade and manufactures, such as the duties on soap, candle, leather, are expensive in levying.[8]

A third rule is, To avoid arbitrary taxes. They are disgustful to all, not excepting those who are favourably treated; because self-partiality seldom permits a man to think that justice is done him. A tax laid on persons, in proportion to their trade, or their prudence, must be arbitrary, even where strict justice is intended; because it depends on vague opinion or conjecture: every man thinks himself injured; and the sum levied does not balance the discontent it occasions. The tax laid on the French farmer in proportion to his <390> substance, is an intolerable grievance, and a great engine of oppression; if the farmer exert any activity in meliorating his land, he is sure to be doubly taxed. Hamburgh affords the only instance of a tax on trade and riches, that is willingly paid, and that consequently is levied without oppression. Every merchant puts privately into the public chest the sum that, in his own opinion, he ought to contribute; a singular example of

---

7. Paragraph added in 2nd edition.
8. Paragraph added in 3rd edition.

integrity in a great trading town, for there is no suspicion of wrong in that tacit contribution. But this state is not yet corrupted by luxury.

Because many vices that poison a nation, arise from inequality of fortune, I propose it as a fourth rule, to remedy that inequality as much as possible, by relieving the poor, and burdening the rich. Heavy taxes are lightly born by men of overgrown estates. Those proprietors especially, who wound the public by converting much land from profit to pleasure, ought not to be spared. Would it not contribute greatly to the public good, that a tax of L. 50 should be laid on every house that has 50 windows; L. 150 on houses of 100 windows; and L. 400 on houses of <391> 200 windows? By the same principle, every deer-park of 200 acres ought to pay L. 50; of 500 acres L. 200; and of 1000 acres L. 600. Fifty acres of pleasure-ground to pay L. 30; 100 such acres L. 80; 150 acres L. 200; and 200 acres L. 300. Such a tax would have a collateral good effect: it would probably move high-minded men to leave out more ground for maintaining the poor, than they are commonly inclined to do.

A fifth rule of capital importance, as it regards the interest of the state in general, is, That every tax which tends to impoverish the nation ought to be rejected with indignation. Such taxes contradict the very nature of government, which is to protect, not to oppress. And, supposing the interest of the governing power to be only regarded, a state is not measured by the extent of its territory, but by what the subjects are able to pay annually without end. A sovereign, however regardless of his duty as a father of his people, will regard that rule for his own sake: a nation impoverished by oppressive taxes will reduce the sovereign at last to the same poverty; for he cannot levy what they cannot pay. <392>

Whether taxes imposed on common necessaries, which fall heavy upon the labouring poor, be of the kind now mentioned, deserves the most serious deliberation. Where they tend to promote industry, they are highly salutary: where they deprive us of foreign markets, by raising the price of labour and of manufactures, they are highly noxious. In some cases, industry may be promoted by taxes, without raising the price of labour and of manufactures. Tobolski in Siberia is a populous town, the price of provisions is extremely low, and the people on that account are extremely idle. While they are masters of a farthing, they work none: when they are pinched with hunger, they gain in a day what maintains them a week: they never think of to-morrow, nor of providing against want. A tax there upon necessaries would probably excite some degree of industry. Such a tax, renewed from time to time, and augmented gradually, would promote industry more and more, so as to squeeze out of that lazy people three, four, or even five days labour weekly, without raising their wages, or the price of their work. But beware of a <393> general rule. The effect would be very different in Britain, where moderate labour without much relaxation is requisite for living comfortably: in every such case, a permanent tax upon necessaries fails not in time to raise the price of labour. It is true, that, in a single year of scarcity, there is commonly more labour than in plentiful years. But, suppose scarcity to continue many years successively, or suppose a permanent tax on necessaries, wages must rise till the labourer find comfortable living; if the employer obstinately stand out, the labourer will in despair abandon the work altogether, and commence beggar; or will retire to a country less burdened with taxes. Hence a salutary doctrine, That, where expence of living equals, or nearly equals, what is gained by bodily labour, moderate taxes renewed from time to time after considerable intervals, will promote industry, without raising the price of labour; but that permanent taxes will unavoidably raise the price of labour, and of manufactures. In Holland, the high price of provisions and of labour, occasioned by permanent taxes, have excluded from the foreign market every one of their manufactures that can be supplied <394> by other nations. Heavy taxes have annihilated their once flourishing manufactures of wool, of silk, of gold and silver, and many others. The prices of labour and of manufactures have in England been immoderately raised by the same means.

To prevent a total downfall of our manufactures, several political writers hold, that the labouring poor ought to be disburdened of all taxes. The royal tithe proposed for France, instead of all other taxes, published in the name of Mareschal Vaubhan, or such a tax laid upon land in England, early imposed, might have produced wonders. But the expedient would now come too late, at least in England: such profligacy have the poor-rates produced among the lower ranks, that to relieve them from taxes, would probably make them work less, but assuredly would not make them work cheaper. It is vain therefore to think of a remedy against idleness and high wages, while the poor-rates subsist in their present form. Davenant pronounces, that the English poor-rates will in time be the bane of their manufactures. He computes, that the persons receiving alms in England amounted to one million and two hundred thousand; the half of <395> whom at least would have continued to work, had they not relied on parish-charity. But of this more at large in a separate sketch.[9]

Were the poor-rates abolished, a general act of naturalization would not only augment the strength of Britain, by adding to the number of its people, but would compel the natives to work cheaper, and consequently to be more industrious.

If these expedients be not relished, the only one that remains for preserving our manufactures, is, to encourage their exportation by a bounty, such as may enable us to cope with our rivals in foreign markets. But, where is the fund for a bounty so extensive? It may be raised out of land, like the Athenian tax above mentioned, burdening great proprietors in a geometrical proportion, and freeing those who have not above L. 100 of land-rent. That tax would raise a great sum to the public, without any real loss to those who are burdened; for comparative riches would remain the same as formerly. Nay, such a tax would in time prove highly beneficial to land-proprietors; for, by promoting industry and commerce, it would <396> raise the rent of land much above the contribution. The sums contributed, laid out upon interest at five *per cent.* would not produce so great profit.[10] To make landholders embrace the tax, may it not be thought sufficient, that, unless for some bounty, our foreign commerce must vanish, and land be reduced to its original low value? Can any man hesitate about paying a shilling, when it prevents the loss of a pound?

I shall close with a rule of deeper concern than all that have been mentioned, which is, To avoid taxes that require the oath of party. They are destructive to morals, as being a temptation to perjury. Few there are so wicked, as to hurt others by perjury: at the same time, not many of the lower ranks scruple much at perjury, when it prevents hurt to themselves.

---

9. See book II, sketch X ("Public Police with respect to the Poor").
10. "The sums contributed . . . so great profit": added in 2nd edition.

Consider the duty on candle: those only who brew for sale, pay the duty on malt-liquor; and to avoid the brewer's oath, the quantity is ascertained by officers who attend the process: but the duty on candle is oppressive, as comprehending poor people who make no candle for sale; and is subversive of morals, by requiring their oath <397> upon the quantity they make for their own use. Figure a poor widow, burdened with five or six children: she is not permitted to make ready a little food for her infants by the light of a rag dipped in grease, without paying what she has not to pay, or being guilty of perjury. However upright originally, poverty and anxiety about her infants, will tempt her to conceal the truth, and to deny upon oath—a sad lesson to her poor children: ought they to be punished for copying after their mother, whom they loved and revered? Whatever she did appears right in their eyes. The manner of levying the salt-tax in France is indeed arbitrary; but it has not an immoral tendency: an oath is avoided; and every master of a family pays for the quantity he is presumed to consume. French wine is often imported into Britain as Spanish, which pays less duty. To check that fraud, the importer's oath is required; and, if perjury be suspected, a jury is set upon him in exchequer. This is horrid: the importer is tempted by a high duty on French wine to commit perjury; for which he is prosecuted in a sovereign court, open to all the world: he turns <398> desperate, and loses all sense of honour. Thus custom-house oaths have become a proverb, as meriting no regard; and corruption creeping on, will become universal. Some goods imported pay a duty *ad valorem;* and to ascertain the value, the importer's oath is required. In China, the books of the merchants are trusted, without an oath. Why not imitate so laudable a practice? If our people be more corrupted, perjury may be avoided, by ordaining the merchant to deliver his goods to any who will demand them, at the rate stated in his books; with the addition of ten *per cent.* as a sufficient profit to himself. Oaths have been greatly multiplied in Britain since the Revolution, without reserve, and contrary to sound policy. New oaths have been invented against those who are disaffected to the government; against fictitious titles in electing parliament-members; against defrauding the revenue, &c. &c. They have been so hackneyed, and have become so familiar, as to be held a matter of form merely. Perjury has dwindled into a venial transgression, and is scarce held an imputation on any man's character. Lamentable indeed has <399> been the conduct of our legislature: instead of laws for reforming or improving morals, the imprudent multiplication of oaths has not only spread corruption through every rank, but, by annihilating the authority of an oath over conscience, has rendered it entirely ineffectual.

SECTION VI

Taxes examined with respect to their effects.[11]

No other political subject is of greater importance to Britain than the present: a whole life might be profitably bestowed on it, and a large volume; but hints only are my task. Considering taxes with regard to their effects, they may be commodiously distinguished into five kinds. First, Taxes that increase the public revenue, without producing any other effect, good or bad. Second, Taxes that increase the public revenue; and are also beneficial to manufactures and commerce. Third, Taxes that increase the public revenue; but are hurtful to manufactures and com-<400>merce. Fourth, Taxes that are hurtful to manufactures and commerce, without increasing the public revenue. Fifth, Taxes that are hurtful to manufactures and commerce; and also lessen the public revenue. I proceed to instances of each kind, drawn chiefly from British taxes.

Our land-tax is an illustrious instance of the first kind: it produces a revenue to the public, levied with very little expence: and it hurts no mortal; for a landholder who pays for having himself and his estate protected, cannot be said to be hurt. The duty on coaches is of the same kind. Both taxes, at the same time, are agreeable to sound principles. Men ought to contribute to the public revenue, as far as they are benefited by being protected: a rich man requires protection for his possessions, as well as for his person, and therefore ought to contribute largely: a poor man requires protection for his person only, and therefore ought to contribute little.

A tax on foreign luxuries is an instance of the second kind. It increases the public revenue: and it greatly benefits individuals: not only by restrain-

---

11. In 1st edition: "Examination of British Taxes."

ing the consumption of foreign luxuries, but by en-<401>couraging our own manufactures. Britain enjoys a monopoly of coal exported to Holland; and the duty on exportation is agreeable to sound policy, being paid by the Dutch. This duty is another instance of the second kind: it raises a considerable revenue to the public; and it enables us to cope with the Dutch in every manufacture that employs coal, such as dying, distilling, works of glass and of iron. And these manufactures in Britain, by the dearness of labour, are entitled to some aid. A tax on horses, to prevent their increase, would be a tax of the same kind. The incredible number of horses used in coaches and other wheel-carriages, has raised the price of labour, by doubling the price of oat-meal, the food of the labouring poor in many parts of Britain. The price of wheat is also raised by the same means; because the vast quantity of land employed in producing oats, lessens the quantity for wheat. I would not exempt even plough-horses from the tax; because in every view it is more advantageous to use oxen.* So little regard is paid to <402> these considerations, that a coach, whether drawn by two horses or by six, pays the same duty.

As to the third kind, our forefathers seem to have had no notion of taxes but for <403> increasing the public revenue, without once thinking of the hurt that may be done to individuals. In the reign of Edward VI. a poll-tax was laid on sheep. And so late as the reign of William III. marriage was

---

* They are preferable for husbandry in several respects. They are cheaper than horses: their food, their harness, their shoes, the attendance on them, much less expensive; and their dung much better for land. Horses are more subject to diseases; and when diseased or old are totally useless: a stock for a farm must be renewed at least every ten years; whereas a stock of oxen may be kept entire forever without any new expence, as they will always draw a full price when fatted for food. Nor is a horse more docile than an ox: a couple of oxen in a plough require not a driver more than a couple of horses. The Dutch at the Cape of Good Hope plough with oxen; and exercise them early to a quick pace, so as to equal horses both in the plough and in the waggon. The people of Malabar use no other animal for the plough nor for burdens. About Pondicherry no beasts of burden are to be seen but oxen. The Greeks and Romans anciently used no beasts in the plough but oxen. The vast increase of horses of late years for luxury as well as for draught, makes a great consumption of oats. If in husbandry oxen only were used, which require no oats, many thousand acres would be saved for wheat and barley. But the advantages of oxen would not be confined to the farmer. Beef would be much cheaper to the manufacturer, by the vast addition of fat oxen sent to market; and the price of leather and tallow would fall; a national benefit, as every one uses shoes and candles.

taxed.¹² I am grieved to observe, that even to this day we have many taxes detrimental to the state, as being more oppressive upon the people than gainful to the public revenue. Multiplied taxes on the necessaries of life, candle, soap, leather, ale, salt, &c. raise the price of labour, and consequently of manufactures. If they shall have the effect to deprive us of foreign markets, which we have reason to dread, depopulation and poverty must ensue. The salt-tax in particular is eminently detrimental. With respect to the other taxes mentioned, the rich bear the greatest burden, being the greatest consumers; but the share they pay of the salt-tax is very little, because they reject salt provisions. The salt-tax is still more absurd in another respect, salt being a choice manure for land. One would be amazed to hear of a law prohibiting the use of lime as a manure: he would be still more amazed to hear of the prohibition being extended to salt, which is a manure much superior, and <404> yet a heavy tax on salt, which renders it too dear for a manure, surprises no man. But the mental eye resembles that of the body: it seldom perceives but what is directly before it: consequences lie far out of sight. Many thousand quarters of good wheat have been annually with-held from Britain by the salt-tax. What the treasury has gained, will not compensate the fiftieth part of that loss. The absurdity of with-holding from us a manure so profitable, has at last been discovered; and remedied in part, by permitting English foul salt to be used for manure, on paying four-pence of duty per bushel (*a*). Why was not Scotland permitted to taste of that bounty? Our candidates, it would appear, are more solicitous of a seat in parliament, than of serving their country when they have obtained that honour. What pretext would there have been even for murmuring, had every one of them been rejected with indignation, in the choice of representatives for a new parliament?¹³

The window-tax is more detrimental to the people, than advantageous to the revenue. In the first place, it promotes large farms in order to save houses and <405> windows; whereas small farms tend to multiply a hardy and frugal race, useful for every purpose. In the next place, it is a discour-

---

(*a*) 8° Geo. III. cap. 25.

12. "our forefathers seem . . . marriage was taxed": added in 3rd edition.
13. "What pretext would . . . a new parliament": added in 2nd edition.

agement to manufactures, by taxing the houses in which they are carried on. Manufacturers, in order to relieve themselves as much as possible from the tax, make a side of their house but one window; and there are instances, where in three stories there are but three windows. But what chiefly raises my aversion to that tax, is that it burdens the poor more than the rich: a house in a paultry village that affords not five pounds of yearly rent, may have a greater number of windows than one in London rented at fifty. The plate-tax is not indeed hurtful to manufactures and commerce: but it is hurtful to the common interest; because plate converted into money may be the means of saving the nation at a crisis, and therefore ought to be encouraged, instead of being loaded with a tax. On pictures imported into Britain, a duty is laid in proportion to the size. Was there no intelligent person at hand, to inform our legislature, that the only means to rouse a genius for painting, is to give our youth ready access to good pictures? Till these <406> be multiplied in Britain, we never shall have the reputation of producing a good painter. So far indeed it is lucky, that the most valuable pictures are not loaded with a greater duty than the most paultry. Fish, both salt and fresh, brought to Paris, pay a duty of 48 *per cent.* by an arbitrary estimation of the value. This tax is an irreparable injury to France, by discouraging the multiplication of seamen. It is beneficial indeed in one view, as it tends to check the growing population of that great city.

Without waiting to rummage the British taxes for instances of the fourth kind, I shall present my reader with a foreign instance. In the Austrian Netherlands, there are inexhaustible mines of coal, the exportation of which would make a considerable article of commerce, were it not absolutely barred by an exorbitant duty. This absurd duty is a great injury to proprietors of coal, without yielding a farthing to the revenue. The Dutch, many years ago, offered to confine themselves to that country for coal, on condition of being relieved from the duty; which would have brought down the price below that of British coal. Is it not wonderful, that <407> the proposal was rejected? But ministers seldom regard what is beneficial to the nation, unless it produce an immediate benefit to their sovereign or to themselves. The coal-mines in the Austrian Netherlands being thus shut up, and the art of working them lost, the British enjoy the monopoly of exporting coal to Holland. And it is likely to be a very beneficial monopoly.

The Dutch turf is wearing out. The woods are cut down every where near the sea; and the expence of carrying wood for fewel from a distance, turns greater and greater every day.[14]

The duty on coal water-born is an instance of the fifth kind. A great obstruction it is to many useful manufactures that require coal; and indeed to manufactures in general, by increasing the expence of coal, an essential article in a cold country. Nay, one would imagine, that it has been intended to check population; as poor wretches benummed with cold, have little of the carnal appetite. It has not even the merit of adding much to the public revenue; for, laying aside London, it produces but a mere trifle. But the peculiarity of this tax, which entitles it to a conspicuous place in the fifth class, is, that it is not less <408> detrimental to the public revenue, than to individuals. No sedentary art nor occupation, can succeed in a cold climate without plenty of fewel. One may at the first glance distinguish the coal-countries from the rest of England, by the industry of the inhabitants, and by plenty of manufacturing towns and villages. Where there is scarcity of fewel, some hours are lost every morning; because people cannot work till the place be sufficiently warmed, which is especially the case in manufactures that require a soft and delicate finger. Now, in many parts of Britain that might be provided with coal by water, the labouring poor are deprived of that comfort by the tax. Had cheap firing encouraged these people to prosecute arts and manufactures, it is more than probable, that at this day they would be contributing to the public revenue by other duties, much greater sums than are drawn from them by the duty on coal. At the same time, if coal must pay a duty, why not at the pit, where it is cheapest? Is it not an egregious blunder, to lay a great duty on those who pay a high price for coal, and no duty on those who have it cheap? If there must be a <409> coal-duty, let water-born coal at any rate be exempted; not only because even without duty it comes dear to the consumer, but also for the encouragement of seamen. For the honour of Britain this duty ought to be expunged from our statute-book, never again to show its face. Great reason indeed there is for continuing the duty on coal consumed in London; because every artifice should be practised, to prevent the increase of a capital,

---

14. "And it is . . . greater every day": added in 2nd edition.

that is already too large for this or for any other kingdom. Towns are unhealthy in proportion to their size; and a great town, like London, is a greater enemy to population than war or famine.

SECTION VII

Taxes for advancing Industry and Commerce.[15]

Of all sciences, that of politics is the most intricate; and its progress toward maturity is slow in proportion. In the present section, taxes on exportation of native commodities take the lead; and <410> nothing can set in a stronger light the gross ignorance of former ages, than a maxim universally adopted, That to tax exportation, or to prohibit it altogether, is the best means for having plenty at home. In Scotland, we were not satisfied with prohibiting the exportation of corn, of fish, and of horses: the prohibition was extended to manufactures, linen cloth, candle, butter, cheese, barked hides, shoes (*a*).*

Duties on exportation are in great favour, from a notion that they are paid by foreigners. This holds sometimes, as in the above mentioned case of coal exported to Holland: but it fails in every case where the foreign market can be supplied by others; for, whatever be the duty, the merchant must regulate his price by the <411> market. And, even supposing the market-price at present to be sufficient for the duty, with a reasonable profit to the exporter; those who pay no duty will strain every nerve of rivalship, till they cut us out by low prices. The duty on French wine exported from France, is in effect a bounty to the wines of neighbouring countries. The duty is unskilfully imposed, being the same upon all wines exported, without regard to flavour or strength; which bars the commerce of small wines,

---

* Oil was the only commodity that by the laws of Solon was permitted to be exported from Africa. The figs of that country, which are delicious, came to be produced in such plenty, that there was not consumpt for them at home; and yet the law prohibiting exportation was not abrogated. Sycophant denotes a person who informs against the exporter of figs: but the prohibition appearing absurd, sycophant became a term of reproach.

(*a*) Act 59. parl. 1573.

15. In 1st edition: "Regulations for advancing Industry and Commerce."

tho' they far exceed the strong in quantity. A moderate duty on exportation, such as small wines can bear, would add a greater sum to the revenue, and also be more beneficial to commerce. To improve the commerce of wine in France, the exportation ought to be free, or at most charged with a moderate duty *ad valorem*. In Spain an excessive duty is laid upon the plant barrile when exported; from an opinion, that it will not grow in any other country. It is not considered, that this tax, by lessening the demand, is a discouragement to its culture. A moderate duty would raise more money to the public, would employ more hands, <412> and would make that plant a permanent article of commerce. The excessive duty has set invention at work, for some material in place of that plant. If such a material shall be discovered, the Spanish ministry will be convinced of a salutary maxim, That it is not always safe to interrupt by high duties the free course of commerce. Formerly in Britain, the exportation of manufactured copper was prohibited. That blunder in commercial politics was corrected by a statute in the reign of King William, permitting such copper to be exported, on paying a duty of four shillings the hundred weight. The exportation ought to have been declared free; which was done by a statute of Queen Anne. But, as the heat of improvement tends naturally to excess, this statute permits even unwrought copper, a raw material, to be exported. This probably was done to favour copper-mines: but did it not also favour foreign copper-manufactures? Goods and merchandise of the product or manufacture of Great Britain, may be exported duty-free (*a*). A few years ago, the East India Company <413> procured an act of parliament, prohibiting the exportation of cannon to the East Indies; which was very short sighted: the Dutch and Danes purchase cannon here, of which they make a profitable trade by exporting them to the East Indies. A cannon is purchased in Scotland for about L. 14 per ton, and sold to the Nabobs of Hindostan for between L. 50 and L. 70 per ton. And the only effect of the act of parliament, is to cut the British out of that profitable branch of commerce.[16] Allum, lead, and some other commodities specified in the statute, are excepted; and a duty formerly paid on exportation is continued, for

---

(*a*) George I. cap. 14. act 8.

16. "A few years . . . branch of commerce": added in 2nd edition.

encouraging such of our own manufactures as employ any of the articles specified. In Ireland, to this day, goods exported are loaded with a high duty, without even distinguishing made work from raw materials; corn, for example, fish, hops, butter, horned cattle, wrought iron, leather and every thing made of it, &c. &c. And, that nothing may escape, all goods exported that are not contained in the book of rates, pay five *per cent. ad valorem.*

When Sully entered on the administra-<414>tion of the French finances, corn in France was at an exorbitant price, occasioned by neglect of husbandry during the civil war. That sagacious minister discovered the secret of re-establishing agriculture, and of reducing the price of corn, which is, to allow a free exportation. So rapid was the success of that bold but politic measure, that in a few years France became the granary of Europe; and, what at present may appear wonderful, we find in the English records, *anno* 1621, bitter complaints of the French underselling them in their own markets. Colbert, who, fortunately for us, had imbibed the common error, renewed the ancient prohibition of exporting corn, hoping to have it cheap at home for his manufacturers. But he was in a gross mistake; for that prohibition has been the chief cause of many famines in France since that time. The corn-trade in France, by that means, lay long under great discouragements; and the French ministry continued long blind to the interest of their country. At last, edicts were issued, authorising the commerce of corn to be absolutely free, whether sold within the kingdom or exported. The genera-<415>lity, however, continued blind. In the year 1768, the badness of the harvest having occasioned a famine, the distresses of the people were excessive, and their complaints universal. Overlooking altogether the bad harvest, they attributed their misery to the new law. It was in vain urged, that freedom in the corn-trade encourages acriculture: the popular opinion was adopted, even by most of the parliaments: so difficult it is to eradicate established prejudices. In Turky, about thirty years ago, a grand vizir permitted corn to be exported more freely than had been done formerly, a bushel of wheat being sold at that time under seventeen pence. Every nation flocked to Turky for corn; and, in particular, no fewer than three hundred French vessels, from twenty to two hundred tons, entered Smyrna bay in one day. The Janissaries and populace took the alarm, fearing that all the corn would be exported, and that a famine would ensue. In Constantinople they grew mutinous, and were not appeased till the vizir was strangled, and his body thrown out to them. His successor, cautious of splitting on the same rock, prohibited <416> exportation absolutely. In that country, rent is paid in proportion to the product; and the farmers, who saw no demand, neglected tillage. In less than three years, the bushel of wheat rose to six shillings; and the distresses of the people became intolerable. To this day, the fate of the good visir is lamented.

We have improved upon Sully's discovery, by a bounty on corn exported, which has answered our most sanguine expectations. A great increase of gold and silver subsequent to the said bounty, which has raised the price of many other commodities, must have also raised that of corn, had not a still greater increase of corn, occasioned by the bounty, reduced its price even below what it was formerly; and, by that means, our manufactures have profited by the bounty, no less than our husbandry. The bounty is still more important in another respect: our wheat can be afforded in the French markets cheaper than their own; by which agriculture in France is in a languishing state. And it is in our power, during a war, to dash all the French schemes for conquest, by depriving <417> them of bread.* This bounty, therefore, is our palladium, which we ought religiously to guard, if we would avoid being a province of France. Some sage politicians have begun of late to mutter against it, as feeding our rival manufacturers cheaper than our own; which is doubtful, as the expence of exportation commonly equals the bounty. But, supposing it true, will the evil be remedied by withdrawing the bounty? On the contrary, it will discourage manufacturers, by raising the price of wheat at home. It will beside encourage French husbandry, so as in all probability to reduce the price of their wheat below what we afford it to them. In France, labour is cheaper than in England, the people are more frugal, they possess a better soil and climate: what have we to balance these signal advantages but our bounty? and were that bounty <418> withdrawn, I should not be surprised to see French corn poured in

* Between the years 1715 and 1755, there was of wheat exported from England to France twenty-one millions of *septiers,* estimated at two hundred millions of livres. The bounty for exporting corn has sometimes amounted to L. 150,000 for a single year. But this sum is not all lost to the revenue; for frequently our corn is exchanged with goods that pay a high duty on importation.

upon us, at a lower price than it can be furnished at home; the very evil that was felt during Sully's administration.*

The exportation of British manufactures to our American colonies, ought to meet with such encouragement as to prevent them from rivalling us: it would be a gross blunder to encourage their manufactures, by imposing a duty on what we export to them. We ought rather to give a bounty on exportation; which, by underselling them in their own markets, would quash every attempt to rivalship.

As the duty on foreign linen imported into Britain is drawn back when exported to America, our legislature gave a bounty on our coarse linen exported to that country, which enables us to cope with the Germans in the American markets. The staining or printing linen cloth has of late become a considerable article in the ma-<419>nufactures of Britain: and there is no sort of linen more proper for that manufacture than our own. The duty of foreign linen is drawn back when exported to America, whether plain or stamped: and, as we lose the bounty on our coarse linen when stamped, none but foreign linen is employed in the stamping manufacture. This is an oversight, such as our legislature is guilty of sometimes.†

It is not always true policy to discourage the exportation of our own rude materials: liberty of exportation gives an encouragement to produce them in greater plenty at home; which consequently low-<420>ers the price to our manufacturers. Upon that principle, the exporting corn is permitted,

---

* Public granaries, which rest on a principle contrary to that of exportation, are hurtful in a fertile and extensive country like Britain, being a discouragement to agriculture; but are beneficial in great towns, which have no corn of their own. Swisserland could not exist without granaries. [[Note added in 3rd edition.]]

† Early in the year 1774, an application was made to parliament for supporting the linen manufacture, at that time in a declining state; praying in particular that stamped linen should be comprehended under the bounty for coarse linen exported to America: in order that his Majesty's loyal subjects might have the same favour that is bestowed on foreigners. From an ill-grounded jealousy, that this application might be of some prejudice to the English woolen manufactures, the bill, in a peevish fit, was rejected by the House of Commons. With respect, at least, to the prayer concerning stamped linen, I may boldly affirm, that it was doing wrong, without even a pretext. There is nothing perfect of human invention. Where the legislature consists of a single person, arbitrary and oppressive measures always prevail; where it consists of a great number, passion and prejudice cannot always be prevented. [[Note added in 2nd edition.]]

and in Britain even encouraged with a bounty. But, where exportation of a rude material will not increase its quantity, the prohibition is good policy. For example, the exporting of rags for paper may be prohibited; because liberty of exporting will not occasion one yard more of linen cloth to be consumed.

Lyons is the city of Europe where the greatest quantity of silk stuffs is made: it is at the same time the greatest staple of raw silk; the silk of Italy, of Spain, of the Levant, and of the south of France, being there collected. The exportation of raw silk is prohibited in France, with a view to lessen its price at home, and to obstruct the silk manufacture among foreigners. The first is a gross error; the prohibition of exportation producing scarcity, not plenty: and, with respect to the other view, it seems to have been overlooked, that the commerce of the silks of Italy, of Spain, and of the Levant, is open to all trading nations. This prohibition is indeed so injudicious, that, without any benefit to France, it has done irreparable <421> mischief to the city of Lyons: while the commerce of raw silk, both buying and selling, was monopolized by the merchants of that city, they had it in their power to regulate the price; but to compel foreigners to go to the fountainhead, not only raises the price by concurrence of purchasers, but deprives Lyons of a lucrative monopoly. The same blunder is repeated with respect to raw silk spun and dyed. In Lyons, silk is prepared for the loom with more art than any where else; and, to secure the silk manufacture, the exportation of spun silk is prohibited; which must rouse foreigners to bestow their utmost attention upon improving the spinning and dressing of silk: and who knows whether reiterated trials by persons of genius may not, in England, for example, bring these branches of the manufacture to greater perfection than they are even in Lyons?

Whether we have not committed a blunder of the same kind in prohibiting exportation of our wool, is a very serious question, which I proceed to examine. A spirit for husbandry, and for every sort of improvement, is in France turning more and more general. In several provinces <422> there are societies, who have command of public money for promoting agriculture; and about no other article are these societies more solicitous, than about improving their wool. A book lately published in Sweden, and translated into French, has inspired them with sanguine hopes of success; as it contains an account of the Swedish wool being greatly improved in quality, as well as in quantity, by importing Spanish and English sheep for breed. Now, as France is an extensive country, situated between Spain and England, two excellent wool countries, it would be strange, if there should not be found a single corner in all France that can produce good wool. Britain may be justly apprehensive of these attempts; for, if France can cope with us under the disadvantage of procuring our wool by smuggling, how far will they exceed us with good wool of their own! The woollen cloth of England has always been esteemed its capital manufacture; and patriotism calls on every one to prevent, if possible, the loss of that valuable branch. Till something better be discovered, I venture to propose what at first may be thought a strange measure; and <423> that is, to permit the exportation of our wool upon a moderate duty, such as will raise the price to the French, but not such as to encourage smuggling. The opportunity of procuring wool in the neighbourhood at a moderate price, joined with several unsuccessful attempts to improve their own wool, would soon make the French abandon thoughts of that improvement.

Experience has unfolded the advantages of liberty to export corn: that liberty has greatly encouraged agriculture, and, by increasing the quantity of corn, has made it even cheaper at home than formerly. Have we not reason to expect a similar consequence, from the same measure, with respect to wool? A new vent for that commodity would improve the breed of our sheep, increase their number, meliorate the land by their dung, and probably bring down the price of our wool at home. It would be proper indeed to prohibit the exportation of wool, as of corn, when the price rises above a certain sum. This measure would give us the command of that valuable commodity: it would secure plenty to ourselves, and distress our rivals, <424> at critical times, when the commodity is scarce.

There is one reason that should influence our legislature to permit the exportation of wool, even supposing the foregoing arguments to be inconclusive: very long experience may teach us, if we can be taught by experience, that vain are our endeavours to prevent wool from being exported: it holds true with respect to all prohibitions, that smuggling will always prevail, where the profit rises above the risk. Why not then make a virtue of necessity, by permitting exportation under a duty? The sum yearly expended for preventing the exportation of wool is above L. 20,000. The fourth part of that sum would be sufficient to make effectual a moderate duty.[17] Let the remainder, with the duty, be applied as a premium for exporting our woollen manufactures: such a premium would make them flourish more than ever. Were that measure adopted, the liberty of exporting wool would prove a singular blessing to England.

I close this branch with a commercial lesson, to which every other consideration <425> ought to yield. The trade of a nation depends, for the most part, on very delicate circumstances, and requires to be carefully nursed. Foreigners, in particular, ought to be flattered and encouraged, that they may prefer us before others. Nor ought we ever to rely entirely on our natural advantages; for it is not easy to foresee what may occur to overbalance them. As this reflection is no less obvious than weighty, facts will be more effectual than argument for making a deep impression. Before the time of the famous Colbert, Holland was the chief market for French manufactures. That minister, in order to monopolize every article of commerce, laid a high duty on Dutch goods brought into France. The Dutch, resenting this measure, prohibited totally some French manufactures, and laid a high duty on others; which had the effect to encourage these manufactures at home. The revocation of the edict of Nantz, drove a vast number of French manufacturers into Holland; and perfected various manufactures formerly brought from France. In a word, this measure intended by Colbert to turn the balance of trade entirely on the side of his <426> country, had the effect of turning it more for the Dutch than formerly.[18] The Swiss, some years ago, imported all their wines from the King of Sardinia's dominions. The King laid a high duty on these wines, knowing that the Swiss had not ready access to any other wine-country. He did not foresee, that this high duty was equal to a premium for cultivating the vine at home. They succeeded; and now are provided with wine of their own growth. The city of Lyons, by making silver-thread in perfection, had maintained a monopoly of that article against foreigners, as well as natives. But a high duty on its exportation, in order to monopolize also the manufacture of silver-lace, will

---

17. "The sum yearly . . . a moderate duty": added in 3rd edition.
18. "Before the time . . . Dutch than formerly": added in 2nd edition.

probably excite foreigners to improve their own silver-thread and silver-lace; and France will be deprived of both monopolies, by the very means employed for securing both. English goods, purchased by Spaniards for the American market, pay to the King of Spain on exportation a duty equal to their value. This impolitic measure opens a wide door to smuggling; as English goods can be furnished *50 per cent.* cheaper from Jamaica. The Spanish go-<427>vernor of Mexico joins under-hand in the smuggling; which is commonly carried on in the following manner. The governor, to whom early notice is given, gives notice to others by a proclamation, that a foreign ship, with English goods on board, every article being specified, is hovering on the coast; and prohibiting, under severe penalties, any person to be a purchaser, that public proclamation has the desired effect: all flock to the shore, and purchase in perfect tranquility.

Beside heavy duties, commerce with foreigners has been distressed by many unwary regulations. The herring-fishery, which is now an article of immense commerce, was ingrossed originally by the Scots. But, grasping at all advantages, the royal boroughs of Scotland, in the reign of the second James, prohibited their fishermen to sell herrings at sea to foreigners; ordering, that they should be first landed, in order that they themselves might be first provided. Such was the policy of those times. But behold the consequence. The Netherlanders and people of the Hanse towns, being prohibited to purchase as formerly, became fishers themselves, and <428> cut the Scots out of that profitable branch of trade. The tar-company of Sweden, taking it for granted that the English could not be otherwise supplied, refused to let them have any pitch or tar, even for ready money, unless permitted to be imported into England in Swedish bottoms; and consequently in such quantities only as the company should be pleased to furnish. This hardship moved the parliament to give a bounty for pitch and tar made in our own colonies. And, if we be not already, we shall soon be altogether independent of Sweden. The Dutch, excited by the profitable trade of Portugal with the East Indies, attempted a northeast passage to China; and that proving abortive, they set on foot a trade with Lisbon for East-India commodities. Portugal was at that time subject to the King of Spain; and the Dutch, though at war with Spain, did not doubt of their being well received in Portugal, with which kingdom they had no cause of quarrel. But the

King of Spain, overlooking not only the law of nations, but even his own interest as King of Portugal, confiscated at short-hand the Dutch ships and their car-<429>goes, in the harbour of Lisbon. That unjust and impolitic treatment provoked the Dutch to attempt an East-India trade, which probably they would not otherwise have thought of; and they were so successful, as to supplant the Portuguese in every quarter. Thus the King of Spain, by a gross error in policy, exalted his enemies to be a powerful maritime state. Had he encouraged the Dutch to trade with Lisbon, other nations must have resorted to the same market. Portugal would have been raised to such a height of maritime power as to be afraid of no rival: the Dutch would not have thought of coping with it, nor would any other nation.

We proceed to foreign commodities. The measures laid down for regulating their importation, have different views. One is, to keep down a rival power; in which view, it is prudent to prohibit importation from one country, and to encourage it from another. It is judicious in the British legislature to load French wines with a higher duty than those of Portugal; and in France it would be a proper measure to prefer the beef of Holstein, or of Russia, before that of Ireland; and <430> the tobacco of the Ukraine or of the Palatinate, before that of Virginia. But such measures of government ought to be sparingly exercised, for fear of retaliation.

There is no cause more cogent for regulating importation, than an unfavourable balance, by permitting French goods to be imported free of duty, the balance against England was computed to be a million Sterling yearly. In the year 1678, that importation was regulated; which, with a prohibition of wearing East-India manufactures, did in twenty years turn the balance of trade in favour of England.

Most of the British regulations concerning goods imported, are contrived for promoting our own manufactures, or those of our Colonies. A statute, 3° Edward IV. cap. 4. entitled, "Certain merchandises not lawful to be brought ready wrought into the kingdom," contains a large list of such merchandises; indicating the good sense of the English in an early period, intent on promoting their own manufactures. To favour a new manufacture of our own, it is proper to lay a duty on the same manufacture imported. To encourage the art of throwing silk, the duty on <431> raw silk imported is reduced, and that on thrown silk is heightened. But such a measure ought to be taken with precaution, lest it recoil against ourselves. The Swedes, some years ago, intent on raising manufactures at home, prohibited at once foreign manufactures, without due preparation. Smuggling ensued; for people must import what they cannot find at home; and the home manufactures were not benefited. But the consequences were still more severe. Foreign manufactures were formerly purchased with their copper, iron, timber, pitch, tar, &c.: but now, as foreigners cannot procure these commodities but with ready money, they resort to Russia and Norway, where commodities of the same kind are procured by barter. The Swedish government, perceiving their error, permit several foreign manufactures to be imported as formerly. But it is now too late; for the trade flows into another channel: and at present, the Swedish copper and iron works are far from flourishing as they once did. In the year 1768, an ordinance was issued by the court of Spain, prohibiting printed or painted linen and cotton to be imported; intended for encouraging a manufacture of <432> printed cottons projected in Catalonia and Arragon. The Spanish ministry have been ever singularly unlucky in their commercial regulations. It is easy to foresee, that such a prohibition will have no effect, but to raise the price on the subjects of Spain; for the prohibited goods will be smuggled, discouraging as much as ever the intended manufacture. The prudent measure would have been, to lay a duty upon printed cottons and linens imported, so small as not to encourage smuggling; and to apply that duty for nursing the infant manufacture. A foreign manufacture ought never to be totally prohibited, till that at home be in such plenty, as nearly to supply the wants of the natives. During ignorance of political principles, a new manufacture was commonly encouraged with an exclusive privilege for a certain number of years. Thus in Scotland, an exclusive privilege of exporting woollen and linen manufactures, was given to some private societies (*a*). Such a monopoly is ruinous to a nation; and frequently to the manufacture itself (*b*). I know no <433> monopoly that in sound policy can be justified, except that given to authors of books for fourteen years by

---

(*a*) Act 42. parl. 1661.
(*b*) See Elemens du Commerce [[by Forbonnais]], tom. 1. p. 334.

an act of Queen Anne.* Exemption from duty, <434> premiums to the best workmen, a bounty on exportation, joined with a duty on goods of the same kind imported, and at last a total prohibition, are the proper encouragements to a new manufacture.

The importation of raw materials ought to be encouraged in every manufacturing country, permitting only a moderate duty for encouraging our own rude materials of the same kind. By a French edict 1654, for encouraging ship-building, ship-timber imported pays no duty. But perhaps a moderate duty would have been better, in order to encourage such timber of the growth of France. Deal timber accordingly, and other timber, imported into Britain from any part of Europe, Ireland excepted, pays a moderate duty. And oak-bark imported pays a duty, which is <435> an encouragement to propagate oak at home. The importation of lean cattle from Ireland, which in effect are raw materials, is, by a statute of Charles

---

* That act is judiciously contrived, not only for the benefit of authors, but for that of learning in general. It encourages men of genius to write, and multiplies books, both of instruction and amusement; which, by concurrence of many editors, after the monopoly is at an end, are sold at the cheapest rate. Many well disposed persons complain, that the exclusive privilege bestowed by the statute upon authors, is too short, and that it ought to be perpetual. Nay, it is asserted, that authors have a perpetual privilege at common law; and it was so determined lately in the court of king's bench. Nothing more frequently happens, than by grasping at the shadow, to lose the substance; for I have no difficulty to maintain, that a perpetual monopoly of books would prove more destructive to learning, and even to authors, than a second irruption of Goths and vandals. It is the nature of a monopoly to raise the price of commodities; and by a perpetual monopoly in the commerce of books, the price of good books would be raised far beyond the reach of most readers; they would be sold like pictures of the great masters. The works of Shakespeare, for example, or of Milton, would be seen in very few libraries. In short, the only purchasers of good books would be a few learned men, such as have money to spare, and a few rich men, who buy out of vanity, as they buy a diamond, or a fine coat. Fashions at the same time are variable; and books, even the most splendid, would wear out of fashion with men of opulence, and be despised as antiquated furniture. And, with respect to men of taste, their number is so small, as not to afford encouragement even for the most frugal edition. Thus booksellers, by grasping too much, would put an end to their trade altogether. At the same time, our present authors and booksellers would not be much benefited by such a monopoly. Not many books have so long a run as fourteen years; and the success of a book on the first publication is so uncertain, that a bookseller will give little more for a perpetuity, than for the temporary privilege of the statute. This was foreseen by the legislature; and the privilege was wisely confined to fourteen years, equally beneficial to the public and to authors.

II. declared a public nuisance. What gross ignorance! Is it not evident, that, to feed cattle, is more profitable than to breed them? The chief promoter of that notable statute was Sir John Knight, famous, or rather infamous, for an insolent speech in King William's reign against naturalizing foreign Protestants, and proposing to kick out of the kingdom those already settled. Experience hath made evident the advantage of importing lean cattle into England; witness the vast quantities imported yearly from Scotland. Diamonds, pearls, and jewels of every kind, paid formerly, upon importation, a duty of ten *per cent. ad valorem;* which, by act 6° George II. cap. 7. was taken off, upon the following preamble, "That London is now become a great mart for diamonds and other precious stones, from whence most foreign countries are supplied; that great numbers of rough diamonds are sent here to be cut and <436> polished; and that a free importation would increase the trade."

Sorry I am to observe, that several of our duties on importation are far from being conformable to the foregoing rule; many raw materials necessary for our manufactures being loaded with a duty on importation, and some with a heavy duty. Barilla, for example, is a raw material used in the glass-manufacture: the exportation from Spain is loaded with a very high duty: and to raise the price still higher, we add a duty on importation; without having the pretext of encouraging a raw material of our own growth, for barilla grows not in this island. Hair is a raw material employed in several manufactures; and yet every kind of it, human hair, horse hair, goat's hair, &c. pays a duty on importation; which consequently raises the price of our own hair, as well as of what is imported. Nor has this duty, more than the former, the pretext of being an encouragement to our own product; for surely there will not on that account be reared one child more, or foal, or kid. The same objection lies against the duty on foreign kelp, which is <437> very high. Rancid oil of olives, fit for soap and woollen manufactures, pays upon importation a high duty: were it free of duty, we should be able to serve ourselves with Castile soap of home manufacture; and likewise our colonies, which are partly supplied by the French. Each of the following raw materials ought in sound policy to be free of duty on importation; and yet they are loaded with a duty, some with a high duty; pot-ashes, elephant's teeth, raw-silk from the East Indies, lamp-black, bristles dressed or undressed, horns of beeves. Undressed skins, though a rude material, pay a duty on importation; and French kid-skins are honoured above others with a high duty: to reject a great benefit to ourselves rather than afford a small benefit to a rival nation, savours more of peevishness than of prudence.

For encouraging our colonies, coffee is permitted to be imported from the plantations free of duty, while other coffee pays sixpence *per* pound. The heavy duty on whale-bone and whale-oil imported, which was laid on for encouraging our own whale-fishing, is taken off with respect to <438> the importation from our American colonies (*a*). This may put an end to our own whale-fishery: but it will enable the Americans to cope with the Dutch; and who knows whether they may not at last prevail? For encouraging the culture of hemp and flax in America, there is a bounty given upon what is imported into Britain. One would imagine, that our legislature intended to enable the colonies to rival us in a staple manufacture, contrary to the fundamental principle of colonization. But we did not see so far: we only foresaw a benefit to Britain, in being supplied with hemp and flax from our colonies, rather than from Russia and the Low Countries. But, even abstracting from rivalship, was it not obvious, that a bounty for encouraging the culture of hemp and flax at home, would be more successful, than for encouraging the culture in America, where the price of labour is excessively high, not to talk of the freight?* <439>

(*a*) 4° Geo. III. Cap. 29.

* Between the mother-country and her colonies the following rule ought to be sacred, That with respect to commodities wanted, each of them should prefer the other before all other nations. Britain should take from her colonies whatever they can furnish for her use; and they should take from Britain whatever she can furnish for their use. In a word, every thing regarding commerce ought to be reciprocal, and equal between them. To bar a colony from access to the fountain head for commodities that cannot be furnished by the mother-country but at second hand, is oppression: it is so far degrading the colonists from being free subjects to be slaves. What right, for example, has Britain to prohibit her colonies from purchasing tea or porcelane at Canton, if they can procure it cheaper there than in London? It is equally oppressive to bar them from resorting to the best markets with their own product. No connection between two nations can be so intimate, as to excuse such a restraint. Our legislature, however, have acted like a stepmother to her American colonies, by prohibiting them to have any commerce but with Britain only. They must first land in Britain all their commodities, even what are not intended to be

The encouragement given to foreign <440> linen-yarn, by taking off the duty on importation, is a measure that greatly concerns Britain; and how far salutary, shall be strictly examined, after stating some preliminary observations. The first is, That our own commodities will never draw a greater price in a market, than imported commodities of the same goodness. Therefore, the price of imported linen, must regulate the price of home-made linen. The next is, That though the duty on importation is paid by the merchant at the first instance, he relieves himself of it, by raising the price on the purchaser; which of course raises the price of the same sort of goods made at home; and accordingly a duty on importation is in effect a bounty to our own manufacturers. A third observation is, That the market-price of our linen-cloth ought to be divided between the spinner and the weaver, in such proportion as to afford bread to both. If the yarn be too high, the weaver is undone: if too low, the spinner is undone. This was not attended to, when, for encouraging our spinners, a duty of three pence was laid on every pound of imported linen-yarn; which had the effect to raise the price of our own yarn beyond <441> what the weaver could afford. This mystery being unvailed, the duty was first lowered to two pence, and then to a penny: our spinners had tolerable bread, and our weavers were not oppressed with paying too high a price for yarn.

Some patriotic gentlemen, who had more zeal than knowledge, finding the linen-manufacture benefited by the several reductions of the duty, rashly concluded, that it would be still more benefited by a total abolition of the duty. The penny accordingly was taken off (*a*), and linen yarn was

---

sold there; and they must take from Britain, not only its own product, but every foreign commodity that is wanted. This regulation is not only unjust but impolitic; as by it the interest of a whole nation is sacrificed to that of a few London merchants. Our legislature have of late so far opened their eyes, as to give a partial relief. Some articles are permitted to be carried directly to the place of destination, without being first entered in Britain, wheat, for example, rice, &c. The Dutch deal more liberally with their colonists in Guiana. They are bound, indeed, to carry their sugar, coffee, cotton, and cocoa, to the mother-country, where there is a ready market for such commodities; but they are permitted to carry their other products, such as rum, melasses, timber, where they can find the best market; and, in return, to import without duty whatever they want. [["The Dutch deal . . . whatever they want": added in 3rd edition.]]

(*a*) 29° George II.

permitted to be imported duty free. Had matters continued as at the date of the act, this impolitic measure would have left us not a single spinner by profession; because it would have reduced the price of our yarn below what could afford bread to them. Lucky it has been for our linen-manufacture, that the German war,[19] which soon followed, suspended all their manufactures, and spinning in particular; which proved to us a favourable opportunity for diffusing widely the art of spinning, and for making our spin-<442>ners more and more dextrous. And yet, now that the war is at an end, it is far from being certain, that our yarn can be afforded as cheap as what is imported from Silesia. We have good authority for asserting, that the English spinners have suffered by that statute: from the books of many parishes it appears, that soon after the statute, a number of women, who had lived by spinning, became a burden upon the parish. One thing is evident, that as spinning is the occupation of females who cannot otherwise be so usefully employed, and as more hands are required for spinning than for weaving, the former is the more valuable branch of the manufacture. Very little attention however seems to have been given to that branch, in passing the act under consideration. Why was it not inquired into, whether the intended reduction of the price of yarn, would leave bread to the British spinner? The result of that inquiry would have been fatal to the intended act; for it would have been clearly seen, that the Scotch spinner could not make bread by her work, far less the English. Other particulars ought also to have <443> been suggested to the legislature; that flax-spinning is of all occupations the fittest for women of a certain class, confined within small houses; that a flax-wheel requires less space than a wheel for wool; and that the toughness of British flax makes it excel for sail-cloth, dowlas, ticking, and sheeting. The British spinner might, in a British statute, have expected the cast of the scale, had it been but a halfpenny *per* pound on importation.

At the same time, it is a national reproach that there should be any inconsistency in our commercial regulations, when the wisest heads of the nation are employed about them. Flax rough or undressed, being a rude material, is imported duty-free, but dressed flax pays a high duty; both of

19. The Seven Years' War (1756–63).

them calculated for encouraging our own manufacturers. Behold now a glaring inconsistency: though dressed flax, for the reason given, pays a high duty; yet when by additional labour it is converted into yarn, it pays no duty. Further, foreign yarn is not only made welcome duty-free, but even receives a bounty when converted into linen, and exported to our plantations. What absurdities are <444> here! Have we no reason to be afraid, that such indulgence to foreign yarn will deprive us of foreign rough flax? The difference of bulk and freight will determine the Germans to send us nothing but their yarn, and equally determine our importers to commission that commodity only.

Goods imported, if subjected to a duty, are generally of the best kind; because the duty bears a less proportion to such than to meaner sorts. The best French wines are imported into Britain, where the duty is higher than in any other country. For that reason, the best linen-yarn was imported while the duty subsisted; but now the German yarn is sorted into different kinds, of which the worst is reserved for the English market.

Regulations concerning the exportation of commodities formerly imported, come next in order. And for encouraging such exportation, one method practised with success, is, to restore to the merchant the whole or part of the duty paid at importation; which is termed a *drawback*. This in particular is done with respect to tobacco the product of our own colonies; <445> which by that means can be afforded to foreigners at two pence halfpenny *per* pound, when the price at home is eight pence halfpenny. By this regulation, luxury is repressed at home, and at the same time our colonies are encouraged. But by an omission in the act of parliament, a drawback is only given for raw tobacco; which bars the exportation of snuff or manufactured tobacco, as foreigners can undersell us five-and-thirty *per cent*. Tobacco being an article of luxury, it was well judged to lay a heavier duty on what is consumed at home, than on what is exported. Upon the same principle, the duty that is paid on the importation of coffee and cocoa from our American plantations, is wholly drawn back when exported (*a*). But as China earthen ware is not entitled to any encouragement from us, and as it is an article of luxury, it gets no drawback even when exported to

(*a*) 7° George III cap. 46.

America (*a*). The exporter of rice from Britain, first imported from America, is entitled to draw back but half the duty paid on importation. Rice imported duty-free might rival our wheat-crop. But the <446> whole duty ought to be drawn back on exportation: it ought to be afforded to our neighbours at the lowest rate, partly to rival their wheat-crop, and partly to encourage our rice-colonies.

Tobacco is an article of luxury; and it is well ordered, that it should come dearer to us than to foreigners. But every wise administration will take the opposite side, with respect to articles that concern our manufactures. Quicksilver pays upon importation a duty of about 8 d. *per* pound; 7 d. of which is drawn back upon exportation. The intention of the drawback was to encourage the commerce of quicksilver; without adverting, that to afford quicksilver to foreign manufacturers cheaper than to our own, is a gross blunder in commercial politics. Again, when quicksilver is manufactured into vermilion or sublimate, no drawback is allowed; which effectually bars their exportation: we ought to be ashamed of such a regulation. In the reign of Queen Elizabeth, dyers were prohibited to use logwood, which was ordered to be openly burnt. But the English dyers having acquired the art of fixing colours made of <447> logwood, it was permitted to be imported (*b*), every ton paying on importation L. 5; L. 4 of which was to be drawn back upon exportation. That law, made in the days of ignorance, was intended to encourage the commerce of logwood; and had that effect: but the blunder of discouraging our own manufactures, by furnishing logwood cheaper to our rivals, was overlooked. Both articles were put upon a better footing (*c*), giving a greater encouragement to the commerce of logwood, by allowing it to be imported duty-free; and by giving an advantage to our own manufactures, by laying a duty of 40 s. upon every hundred weight exported. Lastly, Still more to encourage the commerce of logwood (*d*), the duty upon exportation is discontinued. It will have the

---

(*a*) Ibid.
(*b*) Act 13. and 14. Cha. II. cap. 11.§ 26. 27.
(*c*) Act 8° George I. cap. 14.
(*d*) 7° George III. cap. 47.

effect proposed: but will not that benefit be more than balanced by the encouragement it gives to foreign manufactures? By the late peace,[20] we have obtained the <448> monopoly of gum-senega; and proper measures have been taken for turning it to the best account: the exportation from Africa is confined to Great Britain; and the duty on importation is only six pence *per* hundred weight: but the duty on exportation from Britain is thirty shillings *per* hundred weight (*a*); which, with freight, commission, and insurance, makes it come dear to foreigners. Formerly, every beaver's skin paid upon importation seven pence of duty; and the exporter received a drawback of four pence; as if it had been the purpose of the legislature, to make our own people pay more for that useful commodity than foreigners. Upon obtaining a monopoly of beaver-skins by the late peace, that absurd regulation was altered: a penny *per* skin of duty is laid on importation, and seven pence on exportation (*b*). By that means beaver-skins are cheaper here than in any other country of Europe. A similar regulation is established with respect to gum-arabic. A hundred weight pays on importation six <449> pence, and on exportation L. 1, 10 s. (*c*). As the foregoing articles are used in various manufactures, their cheapness in Britain, by means of these regulations, will probably balance the high price of labour, so as to keep open to us the foreign market.

James I. of England issued a proclamation, prohibiting the exportation of gold and silver whether in coin or plate, of goldsmith's work, or of bullion. Not to mention the unconstitutional step of an English King usurping the legislative power, it was a glaring absurdity to prohibit manufactured work from being exported. Gold and silver, coined or uncoined, are to this day prohibited to be exported from France; a ridiculous prohibition: a merchant will never willingly export gold and silver; but if the balance be against him, the exportation is unavoidable. The only effect of the prohibition is, to swell the merchant's debt; for he must bribe a smuggler to undertake the exportation. It is still more absurd that in Spain, which

(*a*) 5° George III. cap. 37.
(*b*) 4° George III. cap. 9.
(*c*) 5° George III. cap. 37.
20. The Treaty of Paris (1763).

has the command of more <450> silver mines than any other nation, silver is prohibited to be exported under the pain of death. Necessity forces it to be exported; and the absurdity of the prohibition prevails to make it be exported even in open day.[21]

A French author remarks, that in no country are commercial regulations better contrived than in Britain; and instances the following particulars. 1st, Foreign commodities, such as may rival their own, are prohibited, or burdened with duties. 2d, Their manufactures are encouraged by a free exportation. 3d, Raw materials which cannot be produced at home, cochineal, for example, indigo, &c. are imported free of duty. 4th, Raw materials of their own growth, such as wool, fuller's earth, &c. are prohibited to be exported. 5th, Every commodity has a free course through the kingdom, without duty. And lastly, Duties paid on importation, are repaid on exportation. This remark is for the most part well founded: and yet the facts above set forth will not permit us to say, that the English commercial laws have as yet arrived at perfection. <451>

Having thus gone through the several articles that enter into the present sketch, I shall close with some general reflections. The management of the finances is a most important branch of government; and no less delicate than important. Taxes may be so contrived as to promote in a high degree the prosperity of a state; and unless well contrived, they may do much mischief. The latter, by rendering the sovereign odious and the people miserable, effectually eradicate patriotism: no other cause is more fruitful of rebellion; and no other cause reduces a country to be a more easy prey to an invader. To that cause were the Mahometans chiefly indebted for their conquest of the Greek empire. The people were glad to change their master; because, instead of multiplied, intricate, and vexatious duties, they found themselves subjected to a simple tribute, easily collected, and easily paid. Had the art of oppressive taxes been known to the Romans, when the utmost perfidy and cruelty were practised against the Carthaginians, to make them abandon their city, the sober method of high duties on exportation

---

21. "It is still . . . in open day": added in 3rd edition.

and im-<452>portation would have been chosen. This method, beside gratifying Roman avarice, would infallibly have ruined Carthage.²²

From the union of the different Spanish kingdoms under one monarch, there was reason to expect an exertion of spirit, similar to that of the Romans when peace was restored under Augustus. Spain was at that period the most potent kingdom in Europe, or perhaps in the world; and yet, instead of flourishing in that advantageous condition, it was by oppressive taxes reduced to poverty and depopulation. The political history of that kingdom with respect to its finances, ought to be kept in perpetual remembrance; that kings, and their ministers, may shun the destructive rock upon which Spain hath been wrecked. The cortes of Spain had once as extensive powers as ever were enjoyed by an English parliament; but at the time of the union their power being sunk to a shadow, the king and his ministers governed without much control. Britain cannot be too thankful to Providence for her parliament. From the history of every modern European nation, an instructive lesson may be gathered, that the three <453> estates, or in our language a parliament, are the only proper check to the ignorance and rapacity of ministers. The fertility of the Spanish soil is well known. Notwithstanding frequent droughts to which it is liable, it would produce greatly with diligent culture; and in fact, during the time of the Roman domination, produced corn sufficient for its numerous inhabitants, and a great surplus, which was annually exported to Italy. During the domination of the Moors, Arabian authors agree, that Spain was extremely populous. An author of that nation, who wrote in the tenth century, reports, that in his time there were in Spain 80 capital cities, 300 of the second and third orders, beside villages so frequent, that one could not go a mile without meeting one or more of them. In Cordova alone, the capital of the Moorish empire, he reckons 200,000 houses,* 600 mosques, and 900 public baths. In the eleventh century, another author mentions no fewer than 12,000 villages in the plain of Seville. High must have been the <454> perfection

---

* Dwelling houses at that time were not so large, nor so expensive, as they came to be in later times.

22. In the 1st edition the next paragraph begins: "But such taxes require not the aid of external force to subdue a nation: they alone will reduce it to the most contemptible weakness" [1:511].

of agriculture in Spain, when it could feed such multitudes. What was the extent of their internal commerce, is not recorded; but all authors agree, that their foreign commerce was immense. Beside many articles of smaller value, they exported raw silk, oil, sugar, a sort of cochineal, quicksilver, iron wrought and unwrought, manufactures of silk, of wool, &c. The annual revenue of Abdoulrahman III. one of the Spanish califs, was in money 12,045,000 dinares, above five millions Sterling, beside large quantities of corn, wine, oil, and other fruits. That prince's revenue must indeed have been immense, to supply the sums expended by him. Beside the annual charges of government, fleets, and armies, he laid out great sums on his private amusements. Though engaged continually in war, he had money to spare for building a new town three miles from Cordova, named *Zehra* after his favourite mistress. In that town he erected a magnificent palace, sufficiently capacious for his whole seraglio of 6300 persons. There were in it 1400 columns of African and Spanish marble, 19 of Italian marble, and 140 of the finest <455> kind, a present from the Greek Emperor. In the middle of the great saloon, were many images of birds and beasts in pure gold adorned with precious stones, pouring water into a large marble bason. That prince must have had immense stables for horses, when he entertained for his constant guard no fewer than 12,000 horsemen, having sabres and belts enriched with gold. Upon the city of Zehra alone, including the palace and gardens, were expended annually 300,000 dinares, which make above L. 100,000 Sterling; and it required twenty-five years to complete these works.*

---

* A present made to Abdoulrahman by Abdoulmelik, when chosen prime vizir, is a specimen of the riches of Spain at that period. 1st, 408 pounds of virgin gold. 2d, The value of 420,000 sequins in silver ingots. 3d, 400 pounds of the wood of aloes, one piece of which weighed 180 pounds. 4th, 500 ounces of ambergrease, of which there was one piece that weighed 100 ounces. 5th, 300 ounces of the finest camphire. 6th, 300 pieces of gold-stuff, such as were prohibited to be worn but by the Caliph himself. 7th, A quantity of fine fur. 8th, Horse furniture of gold and silk, Bagdad fabric, for 48 horses. 9th, 4000 pounds of raw silk. 10th, 30 pieces Persian tapestry of surprising beauty. 11th, Complete armour for 800 war-horses. 12th, 1000 bucklers, and 100,000 arrows. 13th, Fifteen Arabian horses, with most sumptuous furniture; and a hundred other Arabian horses for the King's attendants. 14th, Twenty mules, with suitable furniture. 15th, Forty young men, and twenty young women, complete beauties, all of them dressed in superb habits.

The great fertility of the soil, the industry of the Moors, and their advantage-<456>ous situation for trade, carried on the prosperity of Spain down to the time that they were subdued by Ferdinand of Aragon. Of this we have undoubted evidence, from the condition of Spain in the days of Charles V. and of his son Philip, being esteemed at that period the richest country in the universe. We have the authority of Ustariz, that the town of Seville, in the period mentioned, contained 60,000 silk looms. During the sixteenth century, the woollen cloth of Segovia was esteemed the finest in Europe; and that of Catalonia long maintained its preference in the Levant, in Italy, and in the adjacent islands. In a memorial addressed to the second Philip, Louis Valle de la Cerda reports, that in the fair of Medina he had negotiated bills of exchange to the extent of one hundred and fifty-five millions of crowns; <457> and in Spain at that time there were several other fairs, no less frequented.

The expulsion of the Moors deprived Spain of six or seven hundred thousand frugal and industrious inhabitants; a wound that touched its vitals, but not mortal: tender care, with proper remedies, would have restored Spain to its former vigour. But unhappily for that kingdom, its political physicians were not skilled in the method of cure: instead of applying healing medicines, they enflamed the disease, and rendered it incurable. The ministry, instigated by the clergy, had prevailed on the King to banish the Moors. Dreading loss of favour if the King's revenues should fall, they were forced in self-defence to heighten the taxes upon the remaining inhabitants. And what could be expected from that fatal measure, but utter ruin; when the poor Christians, who were too proud to be industrious, had scarce been able to crawl under the load of former taxes?

But a matter that affords a lesson so instructive, merits a more particular detail. The extensive plantations of sugar in the kingdom of Granada, were, upon the oc-<458>casion mentioned, deeply taxed, so as that the duty amounted to 36 *per cent.* of the value. This branch of husbandry, which could not fail to languish under such oppression, was in a deep consumption when the first American sugars were imported into Europe, and was totally extinguished by the lower price of these sugars. Spain once enjoyed a most extensive commerce of spirits manufactured at home, perhaps more extensive than France does at present. But two causes concurred to ruin that manufacture; first, oppressive taxes; and next, a prohibition to the manufacturer, of vending his spirits to any but to the farmers of the revenue. Could more effectual means be invented to destroy the manufacture, root and branch? Spanish salt is superior in quality to that of Portugal, and still more to that of France: when refined in Holland, it produces 10 *per cent.* more than the former, and 20 *per cent.* more than the latter; and the making of salt, requires in Spain less labour than in Portugal or in France. Thus Spanish salt may be afforded the cheapest, as requiring less labour; and yet may draw the highest price, as superior in quality: notwithstand-<459>ing which shining advantages, scarce any salt is exported from Spain; and no wonder, for an exorbitant duty makes it come dearer to the purchaser than any other salt. A more moderate duty would bring more profit to the public; beside easing the labouring poor, and employing them in the manufacture. The superior quality of Spanish raw silk, makes it in great request; but as the duty upon it exceeds 60 *per cent.* it can find no vent in a foreign market: nor is there almost any demand for it at home, as its high price has reduced the silk-manufacture in Spain to the lowest ebb. But the greatest oppression of all, as it affects every sort of manufacture, is the famous tax, known by the name of *alcavala,* upon every thing bought and sold, which was laid on in the fifteenth century by a cortes or parliament. It was limited expressly to eight years; and yet was kept up, contrary to law, merely by the King's authority. This monstrous tax, originally 10 *per cent. ad valorem,* was by the two Philips, III. and IV. augmented to 14 *per cent.* sufficient of itself to annihilate every branch of internal commerce, <460> by the encouragement it gives to smuggling.* The difficulty of recovering payment of such oppressive taxes, heightened the brutality of the farmers; which hastened

---

* The following passage is from Ustariz, ch. 96. "After mature consideration of the duties imposed upon commodities, I have not discovered in France, England, or Holland, any duty laid upon the home-sale of their own manufactures, whether the first or any subsequent sale. As Spain alone groans under the burden of 14 *per cent.* imposed not only on the first sale of every parcel, but on each sale, I am jealous that this strange tax is the chief cause of the ruin of our manufactures." As to the ruinous consequences of this tax, see Bernardo de Ulloa upon the manufactures and commerce of Spain, part 2. ch. 3. ch. 13. And yet so blind was Philip II. of Spain, as to impose the alcavala upon the Netherlands, a country flourishing in commerce both internal and external. It must have given a violent shock to their manufactures.

the downfal of the manufactures: poverty and distress banished workmen that could find bread elsewhere; and reduced the rest to beggary. The poor husbandmen sunk under the weight of taxes: and, as if this had not been sufficient to ruin agriculture totally, the Spanish ministry superadded an absolute prohibition of exporting corn. The most amazing article of all, is a practice that has subsisted more <461> than three centuries, of setting a price on corn; which ruins the farmer when the price is low, and yet refuses him the relief of a high price. That agriculture in Spain should be in a deep consumption, is far from being a wonder: it is rather a wonder that it has not long ago died of that disease. Formerly there was plenty of corn for twenty millions of inhabitants, with a surplus for the great city of Rome; and yet at present, and for very many years back, there has not been corn for seven millions, its present inhabitants. Their only resource for procuring even the necessaries of life, were the treasures of the new world, which could not last for ever; and Spain became so miserably poor, that Philip IV. was necessitated to give a currency to his copper coin, almost equal to that of silver. Thus in Spain, the downfal of husbandry, arts, and commerce, was not occasioned by expulsion of the Moors, and far less by discovery of a new world,* of which the gold and silver <462> were favourable to husbandry at least; but by exorbitant taxes, a voracious monster, which, after swallowing up the whole riches of the kingdom, has left nothing for itself to feed on. The following picture is drawn by a writer of that nation, who may be depended on for veracity as well as knowledge (*a*). "Poverty and distress dispeople a country, by banishing all thoughts of marriage. They even destroy sucking children; for what nourishment can a woman afford to her infant, who herself is reduced to bread and water, and is overwhelmed

---

* Ustariz, in his Theory and Practice of Commerce, proves, from evident facts, that the depopulation of Spain is not occasioned by the West Indies. From Castile few go to America, and yet Castile is the worst peopled country in Spain. The northern provinces, Gallicia, Asturia, Biscay, &c. send more people to Mexico and Peru than all the other provinces; and yet of all are the most populous. He ascribes the depopulation of Spain to the ruin of the manufactures by oppressive taxes; and asserts, that the West Indies tend rather to people Spain: many return home laden with riches; and of those who do not return, many remit money to their relations, which enables them to marry, and to rear children.

(*a*) Don Gieronimo de Ustariz.

with labour and despair? A greater proportion accordingly die here in infancy, than where the labouring poor are more at <463> ease; and of those who escape by strength of constitution, the scarcity of cloathing and of nourishment makes them commonly short-lived."

So blind however are the Spaniards in the administration of their finances, that the present ministry are following out the same measures in America, that have brought their native country to the brink of ruin. Cochineal, cocoa, sugar, &c. imported into Spain duty-free, would be a vast fund of commerce with other nations: but a heavy duty on importation is an absolute bar to that commerce, by forcing the other European nations to provide themselves elsewhere. Spanish oil exported to America would be a great article of commerce, were it not barred by a heavy duty on exportation, equal almost to a prohibition: and the Spanish Americans, for want of oil, are reduced to use fat and butter, very improper for a hot climate. The prohibition of planting vines in Mexico, and the excessive duty on the importation of Spanish wines into that country, have introduced a spirit drawn from the <464> sugar-cane; which, being more destructive than a pestilence, is prohibited under severe penalties. The prohibition however has no effect, but to give the governors of the provinces a monopoly of these spirits, which, under their protection, are sold publicly.*[23]

But this subject seems to be inexhaustible. The silver and gold mines in the Spanish West Indies are, by improper taxes, rendered less profitable, both to the King and to the proprietors, than they ought to be. The King's share is the fifth part of the silver that the mines produce, and the tenth part of the gold. There is, <465> beside, a duty of eighty piasters upon every quintal of mercury employed in the mines. These heavy exactions have occasioned all mines to be given up but of the richest sort. The in-

---

* It gives me pleasure to find, for the sake of my fellow-creatures, that the Spanish ministry begin to perceive the fatal consequences of these impolitic measures. In the year 1765, the trade to the islands Cuba, Hispaniola, Porto Rico, Margarita, and Trinidad, was laid open to merchants in every province of Spain, who were released from the oppressive duties on goods exported to America, by paying only six *per cent.* on commodities sent from Spain. It is probable that the beneficial effects of this measure may open the eyes of the Spanish ministry to further improvements. The power of the Spanish inquisitors is reduced within moderate bounds. May we not indulge the hope, that Spain will again become both a learned and commercial country? [[Note added in 2nd edition.]]

23. The 1st edition adds: "a commerce no less shameful than destructive" [1:518].

habitants pay 33 *per cent.* on the goods imported to them from Spain, and they are subjected beside to the alcavala, which is 14 *per cent.* of every thing bought and sold within the country. The most provoking tax of all is what is termed *la cruciade,* being a sum paid for indulgence to eat eggs, butter, and cheese, during Lent, which is yielded by the Pope to the King of Spain. The government, it is true, obliges no person to take out such an indulgence: but the priests refuse every religious consolation to those who do not purchase; and there is not perhaps a single person in Spanish America who is bold enough to stand out against such compulsion.

There is recorded in history, another example of destructive taxes similar to that now mentioned. Augustus, on his conquest of Egypt, having brought to Rome the treasure of its kings, gold and silver overflowed in Italy; the bulk of which <466> found its way to Constantinople, when it became the seat of empire. By these means, Italy was sadly impoverished: the whole ground had been covered with gardens and villas, now deserted; and there was neither corn nor manufactures to exchange for money. Gold and silver became as rare in Italy as they had been of old; and yet the same taxes that had been paid with ease during plenty of money, were rigidly exacted, which ruined all. The duchy of Ferrara, in a narrower compass, affords a later example of the same kind. It was one of the richest and most populous districts in Italy, when governed by its own princes; but at present, under the Papal despotism, it is reduced to poverty and depopulation. There may be seen extensive meadows without a hand to cut down the grass, or a beast to eat it. The water-passages are not kept open: the stagnating waters are putrid, and infect the air with a poisonous steam. In a word, that duchy is approaching to the unwholesome state of the Compagna di Roma, and soon like it will become uninhabitable. Well may it be said, that oppressive taxation is a <467> monster, which, after devouring every other thing, devours itself at last. Bologna surrendered to the Pope upon terms, reserving many of its most valuable privileges. Bologna continues a rich and populous city; and by moderate taxes the Pope draws from it ten times the sum that can be squeezed out of Ferrara by all the engines of oppression.[24]

END of the SECOND VOLUME.

24. "The duchy of . . . engines of oppression": added in 2nd edition.

SKETCHES
OF THE
HISTORY OF MAN.

CONSIDERABLY ENLARGED
BY THE LAST ADDITIONS
AND CORRECTIONS
OF THE AUTHOR.

IN FOUR VOLUMES.

VOLUME III.

EDINBURGH:

PRINTED FOR A. STRAHAN AND T. CADELL, LONDON;
AND FOR WILLIAM CREECH, EDINBURGH.

M,DCC,LXXXVIII.

CONTENTS[1]

VOL. III. BOOK II. *Continued.*

Sk.
9. Military branch of government, 1
10. Public police with respect to the poor, 66
11. A great city considered in physical, moral, and
    political views, 120
12. Origin and progress of American nations, 138

1. The original page numbers from the 1788 edition are retained here.

BOOK II

Progress of Men in Society

⌘ SKETCH IX ⌘

Military Branch of Government

During the infancy of a nation, every member depends on his own industry for procuring the necessaries of life: he is his own mason, his own tailor, his own physician; and on himself he chiefly relies for offence as well as defence. Every savage can say, what few beggars among us can say, *Omnia mea mecum porto;*[1] and hence the apti-<2>tude of a savage for war, which makes little alteration in his manner of living. In early times accordingly, the men were all warriors, and every known art was exercised by women; which continues to be the case of American savages. And even after arts were so much improved as to be exercised by men, none who could bear arms were exempted from war. In feudal governments, the military spirit was carried to a great height: all gentlemen were soldiers by profession; and every other art was despised, as low, if not contemptible.

Even in the unnatural state of the feudal system, arts made some progress, not excepting those for amusement; and many conveniencies, formerly unknown, became necessary to comfortable living. A man accus-

---

1. "I carry everything I own with me."

tomed to manifold conveniencies, cannot bear with patience to be deprived of them: he hates war, and clings to the sweets of peace. Hence the necessity of a military establishment, hardening men by strict discipline to endure the fatigues of war. By a standing army, war is carried on more regularly and scientifically than in a feudal government; but as it is carried on with infinitely greater expence, na-<3>tions are more reserved in declaring war than formerly. Long experience has at the same time made it evident, that a nation seldom gains by war; and that agriculture, manufactures, and commerce, are the only solid foundations of power and grandeur. These arts accordingly have become the chief objects of European governments, and the only rational causes of war. Among the warlike nations of Greece and Italy, how would it have sounded, that their effeminate descendents would employ soldiers by profession to fight their battles! And yet this is unavoidable in every country where arts and manufactures flourish; which, requiring little exercise, tend to enervate the body, and of course the mind. Gain, at the same time, being the sole object of industry, advances selfishness to be the ruling passion, and brings on a timid anxiety about property and self-preservation. Cyrus, tho' enflamed with resentment against the Lydians for revolting, listened to the following advice, offered by Croesus, their former King. "O Cyrus, destroy not Sardis, an ancient city, famous for arts and arms; but, pardoning what is past, <4> demand all their arms, encourage luxury, and exhort them to instruct their children in every art of gainful commerce. You will soon see, O King, that instead of men, they will be women." The Arabians, a brave and generous people, conquered Spain; and drove into the inaccessible mountains of Biscay and Asturia, the few natives who stood out. When no longer an enemy appeared, they turned their swords into ploughshares, and became a rich and flourishing nation. The inhabitants of the mountains, hardened by poverty and situation, ventured, after a long interval, to peep out from their strong holds, and to lie in wait for straggling parties. Finding themselves now a match for a people, whom opulence had betrayed to luxury, and the arts of peace to cowardice; they took courage to display their banners in the open field; and after many military atchievements, succeeded in reconquering Spain. The Scots, inhabiting the mountainous parts of Caledonia, were an overmatch for the Picts, who occupied the fertile plains, and at last subdued them.*² <5>

Benjamin de Tudele, a Spanish Jew, who wrote in the twelfth century, observes, that by luxury and effeminacy the Greeks had contracted a degree of softness, more proper for women than for men; and that the Greek Emperor was reduced to the necessity of employing mercenary troops, to defend his country against the Turks.³ In the year 1453, the city of Constantinople, defended by a garrison not exceeding 6000 men, was besieged by the Turks, and reduced to extremity; yet <6> not a single inhabitant had courage to take arms, all waiting with torpid despondence the hour of utter extirpation. Venice, Genoa, and other small Italian states, became so effeminate by long and successful commerce, that not a citizen ever thought of serving in the army; which obliged them to employ mercenaries, officers as well as private men. These mercenaries at first, fought conscientiously for their pay; but reflecting, that the victors were no better paid than the vanquished, they learned to play booty. In a battle particularly between the Pisans and Florentines, which lasted from sun-rising to sun-setting, there was but a single man lost, who, having accidentally fallen from his horse, was trodden under foot. Men at that time fought on horseback, covered

---

* Before the time that all Scotland was brought under one king, the highlanders, divided into tribes or clans, made war upon each other; and continued the same practice irregularly many ages after they submitted to the king of Scotland. Open war was repressed, but it went on privately by depredations and reprisals. The clan-spirit was much depressed by their bad success in the rebellion 1715; and totally crushed by the like bad success in the rebellion 1745. The mildness with which the highlanders have been treated of late, and the pains that have been taken to introduce industry among them, have totally extirpated depredations and reprisals, and have rendered them the most peaceable people in Scotland; but have at the same time reduced their military spirit to a low ebb. To train them for war, military discipline has now become no less necessary than to others.

2. In the 1st edition the following paragraph begins: "Where arts, manufactures, and commerce, have arrived at perfection, a pacific spirit prevails universally: not a spark of military ardor, nor will any man be a soldier. Hence in such a state, the necessity of mercenary troops, hired among nations less effeminate, who fight for pay, not for the state they serve" [2:4].

3. Tudele's book is included in Pieter van der Aa, *Recueil de divers voyages curieux*, 1729.

with iron from head to heel. Machiavel mentions a battle between the Florentines and Venetians which lasted half a day, neither party giving ground; some horses wounded, not a man slain. He observes, that such cowardice and disorder was in the armies of those times, that the turning of a single horse either to charge or retreat, would have decided a battle.[4] <7> Charles VIII. of France, when he invaded Italy *anno* 1498, understood not such mock battles; and his men were held to be devils incarnate, who seemed to take delight in shedding human blood. The Dutch, who for many years have been reduced to mercenary troops, are more indebted to the mutual jealousy of their neighbours for their independence, than to their own army. In the year 1672, Lewis of France invaded Holland, and in forty days took forty walled towns. That country was saved, not by its army, but by being laid under water. Frost, which is usual at that season, would have put an end to the seven United Provinces.

The small principality of Palmyra is the only instance known in history, where the military spirit was not enervated by opulence. Pliny describes that country as extremely pleasant, and blessed with plenty of springs, tho' surrounded with dry and sandy deserts. The commerce of the Indies was at that time carried on by land; and the city of Palmyra was the centre of that commerce between the East and the West. Its territory being very small, little more than sufficient for villas and plea-<8>sure-grounds, the inhabitants, like those of Hamburgh, had no way to employ their riches for profit but in trade. At the same time, being situated between the two mighty empires of Rome and Parthia; it required great address and the most assiduous military discipline, to guard it from being swallowed up by the one or the other. This ticklish situation preserved the inhabitants from luxury and effeminacy, the usual concomitants of riches. Their superfluous wealth was laid out on magnificent buildings, and on embellishing their country-seats. The fine arts were among them carried to a high degree of perfection. The famous Zenobia, their Queen, being led captive to Rome after being deprived of her dominions, was admired and celebrated for spirit, for learning, and for an exquisite taste in the fine arts.

Thus, by accumulating wealth, a manufacturing and commercial people

---

4. "Men at that time . . . decided a battle": added in 2nd edition.

become a tempting object for conquest; and by effeminacy become an easy conquest. The military spirit seems to be at a low ebb in Britain: will no phantom appear, even in a dream, to disturb our downy <9> rest? Formerly, plenty of corn in the temperate regions of Europe and Asia, proved a tempting bait to northern savages who wanted bread: have we no cause to dread a similar fate from some warlike neighbour, impelled by hunger, or by ambition, to extend his dominions? The difficulty of providing for defence, consistent with industry, has produced a general opinion among political writers, that a nation, to preserve its military spirit, must give up industry; and to preserve industry, must give up a military spirit. In the former case, we are secure against any invader: in the latter, we lie open to every invader. A military plan that would secure us against enemies, without hurting our industry and manufactures, would be a rich present to Britain. That such a plan is possible, will appear from what follows; tho' I am far from hoping that it will meet with universal approbation. To prepare the reader, I shall premise an account of the different military establishments that exist, and have existed, in Europe, with the advantages and disadvantages of each. In examining these, who knows whether some hint may not <10> occur of a plan more perfect than any of them.

The most illustrious military establishment of antiquity is that of the Romans, by which they subdued almost all the known world. The citizens of Rome were all of them soldiers: they lived upon their pay when in the field; but if they happened not to be successful in plundering, they starved at home. An annual distribution of corn among them, became necessary; which in effect corresponded to the halfpay of our officers. It is believed, that such a constitution would not be adopted by any modern state. It was a forc'd constitution; contrary to nature, which gives different dispositions to men, in order to supply hands for every necessary art. It was a hazardous constitution, having no medium between universal conquest and wretched slavery. Had the Gauls who conquered Rome, entertained any view but of plunder, Rome would never have been heard of. It was on the brink of ruin in the war with Hannibal. What would have happened had Hannibal been victorious? It is easy to judge, by comparing it with Carthage. Car-<11>thage was a commercial state, the people all employ'd in arts, manufactures, and navigation. The Carthaginians were subdued; but they could not be reduced to extremity, while they had access to the sea. In fact, they prospered so much by commerce, even after they were subdued, as to raise jealousy in their masters; who thought themselves not secure while a house remained in Carthage. On the other hand, what resource for the inhabitants of Rome, had they been subdued? They must have perished by hunger; for they could not work. In a word, ancient Rome resembles a gamester who ventures all upon one decisive throw: if he lose, he is undone.

I take it for granted, that our feudal system will not have a single vote. It was a system that led to confusion and anarchy, as little fitted for war as for peace. And as for mercenary troops, it is unnecessary to bring them again into the field, after what is said of them above.

The only remaining forms that merit attention, are a standing army, and a militia; which I shall examine in their order, with the objections that lie against <12> each. The first standing army in modern times was established by Charles VII. of France, on a very imperfect plan. He began with a body of cavalry termed *companies of ordonnance.* And as for infantry, he, *anno* 1448, appointed each parish to furnish an archer: these were termed *franc-archers,* because they were exempted from all taxes. This little army was intended for restoring peace and order at home, not for disturbing neighbouring states. The King had been forc'd into many perilous wars, some of them for restraining the turbulent spirit of his vassals, and most of them for defending his crown against an ambitious adversary, Henry V. of England. As these wars were carried on in the feudal mode, the soldiers, who had no pay, could not be restrained from plundering; and inveterate practice rendered them equally licentious in peace and in war. Charles, to leave no pretext for free quarters, laid upon his subjects a small tax, no more than sufficient for regular pay to his little army.* <13>

---

* This was the first tax imposed in France without consent of the three estates: and, however unconstitutional, it occasioned not the slightest murmur, because its visible good tendency reconciled all the world to it. Charles, beside, was a favourite of his people; and justly, as he shewed by every act his affection for them. Had our first Charles been such a favourite, who knows whether the taxes he imposed without consent of parliament, would have met with any opposition? Such taxes would have become customary, as in France; and a limited monarchy would, as in France, have become absolute. Governments, like men, are liable to many revolutions: we remain, it is true, a free people; but for that blessing we are perhaps more indebted to fortune, than to patriotic vigilance.

First attempts are commonly crude and defective. The franc-archers, dispersed one by one in different villages, and never collected but in time of action, could not easily be brought under regular discipline: in the field, they display'd nothing but vicious habits, a spirit of laziness, of disorder, and of pilfering. Neither in peace were they of any use: their character of soldier made them despise agriculture, without being qualified for war: in the army they were no better than peasants: at the plough, no better than idle soldiers. But in the hands of a monarch, a standing army is an instrument of power, too valuable ever to be abandoned: if one sove-<14>reign entertain such an army, others in self-defence must follow. Standing armies are now established in every European state, and are brought to a competent degree of perfection.

This new instrument of government, has produced a surprising change in manners. We now rely on a standing army, for defence as well as offence: none but those who are trained to war, ever think of handling arms, or even of defending themselves against an enemy: our people have become altogether effeminate, terrified at the very sight of a hostile weapon. It is true, they are not the less qualified for the arts of peace; and if manufacturers be protected from being obliged to serve in the army, I discover not any incompatibility between a standing army and the highest industry. Husbandmen at the same time make the best soldiers: a military spirit in the lower classes arises from bodily strength, and from affection to their natal soil. Both are eminent in the husbandman: constant exercise in the open air renders him hardy and robust; and fondness for the place where he finds comfort and plenty, attaches him to his <15> country in general.* An artist

---

* Nunquam credo potuisse dubitari, aptiorem armis rusticam plebem, quae sub divo et in labore nutritur; solis patiens; umbrae negligens; balnearum nescia; deliciarum ignara; simplicis animi; parvo contenta; duratis ad omnem laborum tolerantiam membris: cui gestare ferrum, fossam ducere, onus ferre, consuetudo de rure est. Nec inficiandum est, post urbem conditam, Romanos ex civitate profectos semper ad bellum: sed tunc nullis voluptatibus, nullis deliciis frangebantur. Sudorem cursu et campestri exercitio collectum nando juventus abluebat in Tybere. Idem bellator, idem agricola, genera tantum mutabat armorum. *Vegetius, De re militari, l.* 1. *cap.* 3.—[*In English thus:* "I believe it was never doubted, that the country-labourers were, of all others, the best soldiers. Inured to the open air, and habitual toil, subjected to the extremes of heat and cold, ignorant of the use of the bath, or any of the luxuries of life, contented with bare nec-

or manufacturer, on the contrary, is attached to no country but where he finds the best bread; and a sedentary life, enervating his body, renders him pusillanimous. For these reasons, among many, agriculture ought to be honoured and cherished above all other arts. It is not only a fine <16> preparation for war, by breeding men who love their country, and whom labour and sobriety qualify for being soldiers; but is also the best foundation for commerce, by furnishing both food and materials to the industrious.

But several objections occur against a standing army, that call aloud for a better model than has hitherto been established, at least in Britain. The subject is interesting, and I hope for attention from every man who loves his country. During the vigour of the feudal system, which made every land-proprietor a soldier, every inch of ground was tenaciously disputed with an invader: and while a sovereign retained any part of his dominions, he never lost hopes of recovering the whole. At present, we rely entirely on a standing <17> army, for defence as well as offence; which has reduced every nation in Europe to a precarious state. If the army of a nation happen to be defeated, even at the most distant frontier, there is little resource against a total conquest. Compare the history of Charles VII. with that of Lewis XIV. Kings of France. The former, tho' driven into a corner by Henry V. of England, was however far from yielding: on the contrary, relying on the military spirit of his people, and indefatigably intent on stratagem and surprise, he recovered all he had lost. When Lewis XIV. succeeded to the crown, the military spirit of the people was contracted within the narrow span of a standing army. Behold the consequence. That ambitious monarch, having provoked his neighbours into an alliance against him, had no resource against a more numerous army, but to purchase peace by an abandon of all his conquests, upon which he had lavished much blood and

---

essaries, there was no severity in any change they could make: their limbs, accustomed to the use of the spade and plough, and habituated to burden, were capable of the utmost extremity of toil. Indeed, in the earliest ages of the commonwealth, while the city was in her infancy, the citizens marched out from the town to the field: but at that time they were not enfeebled by pleasures, nor by luxury: The military youth, returning from their exercise and martial sports, plunged into the Tyber to wash off the sweat and dust of the field. The warrior and the husbandman were the same, they changed only the nature of their arms."]

treasure (*a*). France at that period contained several millions capable of bearing arms; and yet was not in a condition <18> to make head against a disciplined army of 70,000 men. Poland, which continues upon the ancient military establishment, wearied out Charles XII. of Sweden; and had done the same to several of his predecessors. But Saxony, defended only by a standing army, could not hold out a single day against the prince now mentioned, at the head of a greater army. Mercenary troops are a defence still more feeble, against troops that fight for glory, or for their country. Unhappy was the invention of a standing army; which, without being any strong bulwark against enemies, is a grievous burden on the people; and turns daily more and more so. Listen to a first-rate author on that point. "Sitôt qu' un état augmente ce qu'il appelle ses troupes, les autres augmentent les leurs; de façon qu'on ne gagne rien par-là que la ruine commune. Chaque monarque tient sur pied toutes les armées qu'il pourroit avoir si ses peuples étoient en danger d' être exterminées; et on nomme paix cet état d'effort de tous contre tous. Nous sommes pauvres avec les richesses et le commerce de tout l'univers; et bientôt à force d'avoir <19> des soldats, nous n'aurons plus que des soldats, et nous serons comme de Tartares" (*b*).*

But with respect to Britain, and every free nation, there is an objection still more formidable; which is, that a standing army is dangerous to liberty. It avails very little to be secure against foreign enemies, supposing a standing army to afford security, if we have no security against an enemy at home. If a warlike king, heading his own troops, be ambitious to render himself absolute, there are no means to evade the impending blow; for what avail the greatest number of effeminate <20> cowards against a disciplined army, devoted to their prince, and ready implicitly to execute his commands? In a word, by relying entirely on a standing army, and by trusting the sword

---

* "As soon as one state augments the number of its troops, the neighbouring states of course do the same; so that nothing is gained, and the effect is, the general ruin. Every prince keeps as many armies in pay, as if he dreaded the extermination of his people from a foreign invasion; and this perpetual struggle, maintained by all against all, is termed *peace*. With the riches and commerce of the whole universe, we are in a state of poverty; and by thus continually augmenting our troops, we shall soon have none else but soldiers, and be reduced to the same situation as the Tartars."

(*a*) Treaty of St. Gertrudenberg.
(*b*) [[Montesquieu,]] L'esprit des loix. liv. 13. chap. 17.

in the hands of men who abhor the restraints of civil law, a solid foundation is laid for military government. Thus a standing army is dangerous to liberty, and yet no sufficient bulwark against powerful neighbours.

Deeply sensible of the foregoing objections, Harrington proposes a militia as a remedy. Every male between eighteen and thirty, is to be trained to military exercises, by frequent meetings, where the youth are excited by premiums to contend in running, wrestling, shooting at a mark, &c. &c. But Harrington did not advert, that such meetings, enflaming the military spirit, must create an aversion in the people to dull and fatiguing labour. His plan evidently is inconsistent with industry and manufactures: it would be so at least in Britain. An unexceptionable plan it would be, were defence our sole object; and not the less so by reducing Britain to such poverty as scarce to be a tempting conquest. Our late war with France is a conspicuous <21> instance of the power of a commercial state, entire in its credit; a power that amaz'd all the world, and ourselves no less than others. Politicians begin to consider Britain, and not France, to be the formidable power that threatens universal monarchy. Had Harrington's plan been adopted, Britain must have been reduced to a level with Sweden or Denmark, having no ambition but to draw subsidies from its more potent neighbours.

In Switzerland, it is true, boys are, from the age of twelve, exercised in running, wrestling, and shooting. Every male who can bear arms is regimented, and subjected to military discipline. Here is a militia in perfection upon Harrington's plan, a militia neither forc'd nor mercenary; invincible when fighting for their country. And as the Swiss are not an idle people, we learn from this instance, that the martial spirit is not an invincible obstruction to industry. But the original barrenness of Switzerland, compelled the inhabitants to be sober and industrious: and industry hath among them become a second nature; there scarcely being a child above six years of age but who is employ'd, <22> not excepting children of opulent families. England differs widely in the nature of its soil, and of its people. But there is little occasion to insist upon that difference; as Switzerland affords no clear evidence, that a spirit of industry is perfectly compatible with a militia: the Swiss, it is true, may be termed industrious; but their industry is confined to necessaries and conveniencies: they are less ambitious of wealth than of military glory; and they have few arts or manufactures, either to support foreign commerce, or to excite luxury.

Fletcher of Salton's plan of a militia, differs little from that of Harrington. Three camps are to be constantly kept up in England, and a fourth in Scotland; into one or other of which, every man must enter upon completing his one and twentieth year. In these camps, the art of war is to be acquired and practised: those who can maintain themselves must continue there two years, others but a single year. Secondly, Those who have been thus educated, shall for ever after have fifty yearly meetings, and shall exercise four hours every meeting. It is not <23> said, by what means young men are compelled to resort to the camp; nor is any exception mentioned of persons destin'd for the church, for liberal sciences, or for the fine arts. The weak and the sickly must be exempted; and yet no regulation is proposed against those who absent themselves on a false pretext. But waving these, the capital objection against Harrington's plan strikes equally against Fletcher's, That by rousing a military spirit, it would alienate the minds of our people from arts and manufactures, and from constant and uniform occupation. The author himself remarks, that the use and exercise of arms, would make the youth place their honour upon that art, and would enflame them with love of military glory; not adverting, that love of military glory, diffused through the whole mass of the people, would unqualify Britain for being a manufacturing and commercial country, rendering it of little weight or consideration in Europe.

The military branch is essential to every species of government: The Quakers are the only people who ever doubted of it. Is it not then mortifying, that a capital <24> branch of government, should to this day remain in a state so imperfect? One would suspect some inherent vice in the nature of government, that counteracts every effort of genius to produce a more perfect mode. I am not disposed to admit any such defect, especially in an article essential to the well-being of society; and rather than yield to the charge, I venture to propose the following plan, even at the hazard of being thought an idle projector. And what animates me greatly to make the attempt, is a firm conviction that a military and an industrious spirit are of equal importance to Britain; and that if either of them be lost, we are undone. To reconcile these seeming antagonists, is my chief view in the following plan; to which I shall proceed, after paving the way by some preliminary considerations.

The first is, that as military force is essential to every state, no man is exempted from bearing arms for his country: all are bound; because no person has right to be exempted more than another. Were any difference to be made, persons of figure and fortune ought first to be called to that service, as being the most interested in the <25> welfare of their country. Listen to a good soldier delivering his opinion on that subject.

> Les levées qui se sont par supercherie sont tout aussi odieuses; on met de l'argent dans la pochette d'un homme, et on lui dit qu'il est soldat. Celles qui se font par force, le sont encore plus; c'est une desolation publique, dont le bourgeois et l'habitant ne se sauvent qu'à force d'argent, et dont le fond est toujours un moyen odieux. Ne voudroit-il pas mieux établer, par une loi, que tout homme, de quelque condition qu'il fût, seroit obligé de servir son prince et sa patrie pendant cinq ans? Cette loi ne sçauroit être desapprouvée, parce qu'il est naturel et juste que les citoyens s'emploient pour la défense de l'état. Cette methode de lever des troupes seroit un fond inépuisable de belles et bonnes recrues, qui ne seroient pas sujetes a déserter. L'on se feroit même, par la suite, un honneur et un devoir de servir sa tâche. Mais, pour y parvenir, il faudroit n'en excepter aucune condition, être sévére sur ce point, et s'attacher a faire exécuter cette loi de préférence aux nobles et aux riches. <26> Personne n'en murmureroit. Alors ceux qui auroient servi leur temps, verroient avec mépris ceux qui repugneroient à cette loi, et insensiblement on se feroit un honneur de servir: le pauvre bourgeois seroit consolé par l'example du riche; et celui-ci n'oseroit se plaindre, voyant servir le noble (*a*).* <27>

(*a*) Les reveries du Comte de Saxe.
* "The method of inlisting men, by putting a trick upon them, is fully as odious. They slip a piece of money into a man's pocket, and then tell him he is a soldier. Inlisting by force is still more odious. It is a public calamity, from which the citizen has no means of saving himself but by money; and it is consequently the worst of all the resources of government. Would it not be more expedient to enact a law, obliging every man, whatever be his rank, to serve his King and country for five years? This law could not be disapproved of, because it is consistent both with nature and justice, that every citizen should be employed in the defence of the state. Here would be an inexhaustible fund of good and able soldiers, who would not be apt to desert, as every man would reckon it both his honour and his duty to have served his time. But to effect this, it must be a fixed principle, That there shall be no exception of ranks. This point must be rigorously attended to, and the law must be enforced, by way of preference, first among the nobility and the men of wealth. There would not be a single man who would complain of it. A

Take another preliminary consideration. While there were any remains among us of a martial spirit, the difficulty was not great of recruiting the army. But that task hath of late years become troublesome; and more disagreeable still than troublesome, by the necessity of using deceitful arts for trepanning the unwary youth. Nor are such arts always successful: in our late war with France, we were necessitated to give up even the appearance of voluntary service, and to recruit the army on the solid principle, that every man should fight for his country; the justices of peace being empowered to force into the service such as could be best spared from civil occupation. If a single clause had been added, limiting the service to five or seven years, the measure <28> would have been unexceptionable, even in a land of liberty. To relieve officers of the army from the necessity of practising deceitful arts, by substituting a fair and constitutional mode of recruiting the army, was a valuable improvement. It was of importance with respect to its direct intendment; but of much greater, with respect to its consequences. One of the few disadvantages of a free state, is licentiousness in the common people, who may wallow in disorder and profligacy without control, if they but refrain from gross crimes, punishable by law. Now, as it appears to me, there never was devised a plan more efficacious for restoring industry and sobriety, than that under consideration. Its salutary effects were conspicuous, even during the short time it subsisted. The dread of being forc'd into the service, rendered the populace peaceable and orderly: it did more; it rendered them industrious in order to conciliate favour. The most beneficial discoveries have been accidental: without having any view but for recruiting the army, our legislature stumbled upon an excellent plan for reclaiming the idle and the profligate; a <29> matter, in the present depravity of manners, of greater importance than any other that concerns the police of Britain. A perpetual law of that kind, by promoting industry, would prove a sovereign remedy against mobs and riots, diseases of a free

---

person who had served his time, would treat with contempt another who should show reluctance to comply with the law; and thus, by degrees, it would become a task of honour. The poor citizen would be comforted and inspirited by the example of his rich neighbour; and he again would have nothing to complain of, when he saw that the nobleman was not exempted from service."

state, full of people and of manufactures.* Why were the foregoing statutes, for there were two of them, limited to a temporary existence? There is not on record another statute better intitled to immortality.

And now to the project, which after all my efforts I produce with trepidation; not from any doubt of its solidity, but as ill suited to the present manners of this island. To hope that it will be put in practice, would indeed be highly ridiculous: this can never happen, till patriotism flourish more in Britain than it has <30> done for some time past. Supposing now an army of 60,000 men to be sufficient for Britain, a rational method for raising such an army, were there no standing forces, would be, that land-proprietors, in proportion to their valued rents, should furnish men to serve seven years, and no longer.† But as it would be no less unjust than imprudent, to disband at once our present army, we begin with moulding gradually the old army into the new, by filling up vacancies with men bound to serve seven years and no longer. And for raising proper men, a matter of much delicacy, it is proposed, that in every shire a special commission be given to certain landholders of rank and figure, to raise recruits out of the lower classes, selecting always those who are the least useful at home.

Second. Those who claim to be dismissed after serving the appointed time, shall never again be called to the service, ex-<31>cept in case of an actual invasion. They shall be intitled each of them to a premium of eight or ten pounds, for enabling them to follow a trade or calling, without being subjected to corporation-laws. The private men in France are inlisted but for six years; and that mode has never been attended with any inconvenience.‡

---

* Several late mobs in the south of England, all of them on pretext of scarcity, greatly alarmed the administration. A fact was discovered by a private person (*Six-weeks tour through the south of England* [[by Arthur Young]],) which our ministers ought to have discovered, that these mobs constantly happened where wages were high and provisions low; consequently that they were occasioned, not by want, but by wantonness.

† In Denmark, every land-proprietor of a certain rent, is obliged to furnish a militia-man, whom he can withdraw at pleasure upon substituting another; an excellent method for taming the peasants, and for rendering them industrious.

‡ Had the plan of discharging soldiers after a service of five or seven years been early adopted by the Emperors of Rome, the Pretorian bands would never have become masters of the state. It was a gross error to keep these troops always on foot without change

Third. With respect to the private men, idleness must be totally and for ever banished. Supposing three months yearly to be sufficient for military discipline; the men, during the rest of the year, ought to be employ'd upon public works, forming roads, erecting bridges, making rivers navigable, clearing harbours, &c. &c. Why not also furnish men for half-pay to private undertakers of useful works? And supposing the daily pay of a soldier to be <32> ten pence, it would greatly encourage extensive improvements, to have at command a number of stout fellows under strict discipline, at the low wages of five pence a-day. An army of 60,000 men thus employ'd, would not be so expensive to the public, as 20,000 men upon the present establishment: for beside the money contributed by private undertakers, public works carried on by soldiers would be miserably ill contrived, if not cheaply purchased with their pay.*

It has more than once been under deliberation, whether the tolls may not be added to the public revenue, after paying the expence of keeping the turnpike-roads in good order. But as ministers frequently are more intent upon serving themselves than their country, it may happen that the tolls will be levied and the roads neglected. Upon the plan here proposed of a military establishment, the reparation of the roads would contribute to keep the sol-<33>diers in constant employment. And as it would be difficult otherwise to find constant exercise for threescore thousand men, no minister surely, for the sake of his own character, will suffer men in government-pay to remain idle, when they can be employed so usefully for the public service. Now, were a law made permitting no wheel-carriages on a toll-road that require more than one horse, it would lessen wonderfully the expence of reparation. Nor would such a law be a hardship, as goods can be carried cheaper that way than in huge waggons, requiring from six to ten horses (*a*). By such a law the tolls would make a capital branch of

---

of members; which gave them a confidence in one another, to unite in one solid body, and to be actuated as it were by one mind. [[Note added in 2nd edition.]]

* Taking this for granted, I bring only into the computation the pay of the three months spent in military discipline; and the calculation is very simple, the pay of 20,000 for twelve months amounting to a greater sum than the pay of 60,000 for three months.

(*a*) [[Kames,]] Gentleman Farmer, edition second, p. 46.

the public revenue, being levied without any deduction but for carrying gravel, or stones where gravel is not to be had.⁵

The most important branch of the project, is what regards the officers. The necessity of reviving in our people of rank some military spirit, will be acknowledged by every person of reflection; and in that view, the following articles are proposed. First, That there be two classes of <34> officers, one serving for pay, one without pay. In filling up every vacant office of cornet or ensign, the latter are to be preferred; but in progressive advancement, no distinction is to be made between the classes. An officer who has served seven years without pay, may retire with honour.

Second. No man shall be privileged to represent a county in parliament, who has not served seven years without pay; and, excepting an actual burgess, none but those who have performed that service, shall be privileged to represent a borough. The same qualification shall be necessary to every one who aspires to serve the public or the King in an office of dignity; excepting only churchmen and lawyers with regard to offices in their respective professions. In old Rome, none were admitted candidates for any civil employment, till they had served ten years in the army.

Third. Officers of this class are to be exempted from the taxes imposed on land, coaches, windows, and plate; not for saving a trifling sum, but as a mark of distinction. <35>

The military spirit must in Britain be miserably low, if such regulations prove not effectual to decorate the army with officers of figure and fortune. Nor need we to apprehend any bad consequence from a number of raw officers who serve without pay: among men of birth, emulation will have a more commanding influence than pay or profit; and at any rate, there will always be a sufficiency of old and experienc'd officers receiving pay, ready to take the lead in every difficult enterprise.

To improve this army in military discipline, it is proposed, that when occasion offers, 5 or 6000 of them be maintained by Great Britain, as auxiliaries to some ally at war. And if that body be changed from time to time, knowledge and practice in war will be diffused thro' the whole army.

Officers who serve for pay, will be greatly benefited by this plan: frequent

---

5. Paragraph added in 3rd edition.

removes of those who serve without pay, make way for them; and the very nature of the plan excludes buying and selling.

I proceed to the alterations necessary for accommodating this plan to our present <36> military establishment. As a total revolution at one instant would breed confusion, the first step ought to be a specimen only, such as the levying two or three regiments on the new model; the expence of which ought not to be grudged, as the forces presently in pay, are not sufficient, even in peace, to answer the ordinary demands of government. And as the prospect of civil employments, will excite more men of rank to offer their service than can be taken in, the choice must be in the crown, not only with respect to the new regiments, but with respect to the vacant offices of cornet and ensign in the old army. But as these regulations will not instantly produce men qualified to be secretaries of state or commissioners of treasury, so numerous as to afford his Majesty a satisfactory choice; that branch of the plan may be suspended, till those who have served seven years without pay, amount to one hundred at least. The article that concerns members of parliament must be still longer suspended: it may however, after the first seven years, receive execution in part, by privileging those who have served without pay to represent a borough, <37> refusing that privilege to others, except to actual burgesses. We may proceed one step farther, That if in a county there be five gentlemen who have the qualification under consideration, over and above the ordinary legal qualifications; one of the five must be chosen, leaving the electors free as to their other representative.

With respect to the private men of the old army, a thousand of such as have served the longest may be disbanded annually, if so many be willing to retire; and in their stead an equal number may be inlisted to serve but seven years. Upon such a plan, it will not be difficult to find recruits.

The advantage of this plan, in one particular, is eminent. It will infallibly fill the army with gallant officers: Other advantages concerning the officers themselves, shall be mentioned afterward. An appetite for military glory, cannot fail to be roused in officers who serve without pay, when their service is the only passport to employments of trust and honour. And may we not hope, that officers who serve for pay, will, by force of imitation, be inspired with the same appetite? No-<38>thing ought to be more sedulously inculcated into every officer, than to despise riches, as a mercantile object below the dignity of a soldier. Often has the courage of victorious troops been blunted by the pillage of an opulent city; and may not rich captures at sea have the same effect? Some sea-commanders have been suspected, of bestowing their fire more willingly upon a merchantman, than upon a ship of war. A triumph, an ovation, a civic crown, or some such mark of honour, were in old Rome the only rewards for military atchievements.* Money, it is true, was sometimes distributed among the private men, as an addition to their pay, after a fatiguing campaign; but not as a recom-<39>pence for their good behaviour, because all shared alike. It did not escape the penetrating Romans, that wealth, the parent of luxury and selfishness, fails not to eradicate the military spirit. The soldier who to recover his baggage performed a bold action, gave an instructive lesson to all princes. Being invited by his general to try his fortune a second time; "Invite (says the soldier) one who has lost his baggage." Many a bold adventurer goes to the Indies, who, returning with a fortune, is afraid of every breeze. Britain, I suspect, is too much infected with the spirit of gain. Will it be thought ridiculous in any man of figure, to prefer reputation and respect before riches; provided only he can afford a frugal meal, and a warm garment? Let us compare an old officer, who never deserted his friend nor his country, and a wealthy merchant, who never indulged a thought but of gain: the wealth is tempting;— and yet does there exist a man of spirit, who would not be the officer rather than the merchant, even with his millions? Sultan Mechmet granted to the Janisaries a privilege of importing foreign commodities free of duty: <40> was it his intention to metamorphose soldiers into merchants, loving peace, and hating war?

In the war 1672 carried on by Lewis XIV. against the Dutch, Dupas was made governor of Naerden, recommended by the Duke of Luxembourg;

---

* A Roman triumph was finely contrived to excite heroism; and a sort of triumph no less splendid, was usual among the Fatemite Califs of Egypt. After returning from a successful expedition, the Calif pitched his camp in a spacious plain near his capital, where he was attended by all his grandees, in their finest equipages. Three days were commonly spent in all manner of rejoicings, feasting, music, fireworks, &c. He marched into the city with this great cavalcade, through roads covered with rich carpets, strewed with flowers, gums, and odoriferous plants, and lined on both sides with crouds of congratulating subjects.

who wrote to M. de Louvois, that he wished nothing more ardently, than that the Prince of Orange would besiege Naerden, being certain of a defence so skilful and vigorous, as to furnish an opportunity for another victory over the Prince. Dupas had served long in honourable poverty; but in this rich town he made a shift to amass a considerable sum. Terrified to be reduced to his former poverty, he surrendered the town on the first summons. He was degraded in a court-martial, and condemned to perpetual prison and poverty. Having obtained his liberty at the solicitation of the Viscount de Turenne, he recovered his former valour, and ventured his life freely on all occasions.[6]

But tho' I declare against large appointments beforehand, which, instead of promoting service, excite luxury and effeminacy; yet to an officer of character, who <41> has spent his younger years in serving his king and country, a government or other suitable employment that enables him to pass the remainder of his life in ease and affluence, is a proper reward for merit, reflecting equal honour on the prince who bestows, and on the subject who receives; beside affording an enlivening prospect to others, who have it at heart to do well.

With respect to the private men, the rotation proposed, aims at improvements far more important than that of making military service fall light upon individuals. It tends to unite the spirit of industry with that of war; and to form the same man to be an industrious labourer, and a good soldier. The continual exercise recommended, cannot fail to produce a spirit of industry; which will occasion a demand for the private men after their seven years service, as valuable above all other labourers, not only for regularity, but for activity. And with respect to service in war, constant exercise is the life of an army, in the literal as well as metaphorical sense. Boldness is inspired by strength and agility, to which constant motion mainly contributes. The Roman citizens, trained <42> to arms from their infancy and never allowed to rest, were invincible. To mention no other works, spacious and durable roads carried to the very extremities of that vast empire, show clearly how the soldiers were employ'd during peace;

---

6. Paragraph added in 2nd edition.

which hardened them for war, and made them orderly and submissive (*a*). So essential was labour held by the Romans for training an army, that they never ventured to face an enemy with troops debilitated with idleness. The Roman army in Spain, having been worsted in several engagements and confined within their entrenchments, were sunk in idleness and luxury. Scipio Nasica, having demolished Carthage, took the command of that army; but durst not oppose it to the enemy, till he had accustomed the soldiers to temperance and hard labour. He exercised them without relaxation, in marching and countermarching, in fortifying camps and demolishing them, in digging trenches and filling them up, in building high walls and pulling them down; he himself, from morning till evening, going about, and directing every <43> operation. Marius, before engaging the Cimbri, exercised his army in turning the course of a river. Appian relates, that Antiochus, during his winter-quarters at Calchis, having married a beautiful virgin with whom he was greatly enamoured, spent the whole winter in pleasure, abandoning his army to vice and idleness; and that when the time of action returned with the spring, he found his soldiers unfit for service. It is reported of Hannibal, that to preserve his troops from the infection of idleness, he employ'd them in making large plantations of olive trees. The Emperor Probus exercised his legions in covering with vineyards the hills of Gaul and Pannonia.⁷ The idleness of our soldiers in time of peace, promoting debauchery and licentiousness, is no less destructive to health than to discipline. Unable for the fatigues of a first campaign, our private men die in thousands, as if smitten with a pestilence.* We never read of any <44> mortality in the Roman legions, though frequently en-

---

* The idleness of British soldiers appears from a transaction of the commissioners of the annexed estates in Scotland. After the late war with France, they judged, that part of the King's rents could not be better applied, than in giving bread to the disbanded soldiers. Houses were built for them, portions of land given them to cultivate at a very low rent, and maintenance afforded them till they could reap a crop. These men could not wish to be better accommodated: but so accustomed they had been to idleness and change of place, as to be incapable of any sort of work: they deserted their farms one after another, and commenced thieves and beggars. Such as had been made serjeants must be excepted: these were sensible fellows, and prospered in their little farms.

(*a*) Bergiere histoire des grands chemins, vol. 2. p. 152.

7. "It is reported . . . Gaul and Pannonia": added in 2nd edition.

gaged in climates very different from their own. Let us listen to a judicious writer, to whom every one listens with delight:

> Nous remarquons aujourd'hui, que nos armées périssent beaucoup par le travail immodéré des soldats; et cependant c'étoit par un travail immense que les Romains se conservoient. La raison en est, je crois, que leurs fatigues étoient continuelles; au lieu que nos soldats passent sans cesse d'un travail extreme à une extreme oisivété, ce qui est la chose du monde la plus propre à les faire perir. Il faut que je rapporte ici ce que les auteurs, nous disent de l'education de soldats <45> Romains. On les accoutumoit à aller le pas militaire, c'est-a-dire, à faire en cinq heures vingt milles, et quelquefois vingt-quatre. Pendant ces marches, on leur faisoit porter de poids de soixante livres. On les entretenoit dans l'habitude de courir et de sauter tout armés; ils prenoient dans leurs exercices des epées, de javelots, de flêches, d'une pésanteur double des armes ordinaires; et ces exercices étoient continuels. Des hommes si endurcis étoient ordinairement sains; on ne remarque pas dans les auteurs que les armées Romaines, qui faisoient la guerre en tant de climats, perissoient beaucoup par les maladies; au lieu qu'il arrive presque continuellement aujourd'hui, que des armées, sans avoir combattu, se fondent, pour ainsi dire, dans une campagne (*a*).*

Our author must be here <46> understood of the early times of the Roman state. Military discipline was much sunk in the fourth century when Vegetius wrote (Lib. 3. cap. 14. 15.). The sword and pilum, these formidable

---

* "We observe now-a-days, that our armies are consumed by the fatigues and severe labour of the soldiers; and yet it was alone by labour and toil that the Romans preserved themselves from destruction. I believe the reason is, that their fatigue was continual and unremitting, while the life of our soldiers is a perpetual transition from severe labour to extreme indolence, a life the most ruinous of all others. I must here recite the account which the Roman authors give of the education of their soldiers. They were continually habituated to the military pace, which was, to march in five hours twenty, and sometimes twenty-four miles. In these marches each soldier carried sixty pounds weight. They were accustomed to run and leap in arms; and in their military exercises, their swords, javelins, and arrows, were of twice the ordinary weight. These exercises were continual, which so strengthened the constitution of the men, that they were always in health. We see no remarks in the Roman authors, that their armies, in the variety of climates where they made war, ever perished by disease; whilst now-a-days it is not unusual, that an army, without ever coming to an engagement, dwindles away by disease in one campaign."

(*a*) Montesquieu, Grandeur de Romains, chap. 2.

weapons of their forefathers, were totally laid aside for slings and bows, the weapons of effeminate people. About this time it was, that the Romans left off fortifying their camps, a work too laborious for their <47> weakly constitutions.⁸ Mareschal Saxe, a soldier, not a physician, ascribes to the use of vinegar the healthiness of the Roman legions: were vinegar so salutary, it would of all liquors be the most in request. Exercise without intermission, during peace as well as during war, produced that salutary effect; which every prince will find, who is disposed to copy the Roman discipline.* The Mareschal guesses better with respect to a horse. Discoursing of cavalry, he observes, that a horse becomes hardy and healthful by constant exercise, and that a young horse is unable to bear fatigue; for which reason he de-<48>clares against young horses for the service of an army.

That the military branch of the British government is susceptible of improvements, all the world will admit. To improve it, I have contributed my mite; which is humbly submitted to the public, a judge from which there lies no appeal. It is submitted in three views. The first is, Whether an army modelled as above, would not secure us against the boldest invader; the next, Whether such an army be as dangerous to liberty, as an army in its present form; and the last, Whether it would not be a school of industry and moderation to our people.

With respect to the first, we should, after a few years, have not only an army of sixty thousand well-disciplined troops, but the command of another army, equally numerous and equally well disciplined. It is true, that troops inured to war have an advantage over troops that have not the same experience: but with assurance it may be pronounced impracticable, to land at once in Britain an army that can stand against 100,000 British soldiers

---

* Rei militaris periti, plus quotidiana armorum exercitia ad sanitatem militum putaverunt prodesse, quam medicos. Ex quo intelligitur quanto studiosius armorum artem docendus sit semper exercitus, cum ei laboris consuetudo et in castris sanitatem, et in conflictu possit praestare victoriam. *Vegetius, De re militari, lib.* 3. *cap.* 2.—[*In English thus:* "Our masters of the art-military were of opinion, that daily exercise in arms contributed more to the health of the troops, than the skill of the physician: from which we may judge, what care should be taken, to habituate the soldiers to the exercise of arms, to which they owe both their health in the camp, and their victory in the field."]

8. "Our author must . . . their weakly constitutions": added in 2nd edition.

well disciplined, fighting, even the first time, <49> for their country, and for their wives and children.

A war with France raises a panic on every slight threatening of an invasion. The security afforded by the proposed plan, would enable us to act offensively at sea, instead of being reduced to keep our ships at home for guarding our coasts. Would Britain any longer be obliged to support her continental connections? No sooner does an European prince augment his army, or improve military discipline, than his neighbours, taking fright, must do the same. May not one hope, that by the plan proposed, or by some such, Britain would be relieved from jealousy and solicitude about its neighbours?

This is a subject that deserves deep attention, being of the utmost importance to Great Britain. The importance will clearly appear upon considering our late war with France, and our present war with France, Spain, and our American colonies, all united against us.⁹ France and Britain have made frequent attempts to distress one another by threatening an invasion. But they are not upon an equal footing: England has many good harbours, not a <50> single fortified town; France has few harbours and many fortified towns. It is provided with a standing army much greater in proportion than Britain; and above all, our capital is open to a sudden attack by sea, which the capital of France is not. Our Bank may in an instant be ruined, and public credit suffer a stupifying blow. We accordingly are terrified at the very thought of a flat-bottom'd boat; and it is acknowledged on all hands, that we have no security against an invasion but a superior fleet. This unhappy situation has, in the present war, thrown our ministers into great perplexity. Our field of action is America and the West Indies, and yet our grand fleet is locked up at home, while the French and Spaniards are at liberty to direct all their force to that part of the world. Our intelligence of the motions of our enemies must be always late, often uncertain; and in fact several capital blows have been struck before we could give any reinforcement to our fleets in those parts. Now if the military branch pro-

---

9. The "late war with France" was the Seven Years' War (1756–63). France entered the American War of Independence on the American side in 1778; Spain did the same a year later.

posed above had been adopted early during intervals of peace, our ministry would have been at liberty to employ our whole naval force <51> where it could do the greatest execution, and would soon have brought the war to an end.[10]

With respect to the second view, having long enjoy'd the sweets of a free government under a succession of mild princes, we begin to forget that our liberties ever were in danger. But drousy security is of all conditions the most dangerous; because the state may be overwhelmed before we even dream of danger. Suppose only, that a British King, accomplished in the art of war and beloved by his soldiers, heads his own troops in a war with France; and after more than one successful campaign, gives peace to his enemy, on terms advantageous to his people: what security have we for our liberties, when he returns with a victorious army, devoted to his will? I am talking of a standing army in its present form. Troops modelled as above would not be so obsequious: a number of the prime nobility and gentry serving without pay, who could be under no temptation to enslave themselves and their country, would prove a firm barrier against the ambitious views of such a prince. And even supposing <52> that army to be totally corrupted, the prince could have little hope of success against the nation, supported by a veteran army, that might be relied on as champions for their country.*

And as to the last view mentioned, the plan proposed would promote industry and virtue, not only among the soldiers, but among the working people in general. To avoid hard labour and severe discipline in the army, men would be sober and industrious at home; and such untractable spirits as cannot be reached by the mild laws of a free government, would be effectually tamed by military law. At the same time, as sobriety and innocence are constant attendants upon industry, the manners of our people would

---

* While it was a law in Rome that a man must serve ten years in the army before he could be admitted to a civil office, the republic had nothing to dread from their armies. But when by luxury the fatigues of war appeared unsupportable to men of condition, there was a necessity to fill the legions with the low and indigent, who followed their leaders implicitly, and were as ready to overturn the republic as to protect it. Hence the civil war between Marius and Sylla; and hence the overthrow of the republic by Julius Caesar. [[Note added in 3rd edition.]]

10. Paragraph added in 3rd edition.

be much purified; a <53> circumstance of infinite importance to Britain. The salutary influence of the plan, would reach persons in a higher sphere. A young gentleman, whipt at school, or falling behind at college, contracts an aversion to study; and flies to the army, where he is kept in countenance by numbers, idle and ignorant like himself. How many young men are thus daily ruined, who, but for the temptation of idleness and gaiety in the army, would have become useful subjects! In the plan under consideration, the officers who serve for pay would be so few in number, and their prospect of advancement so clear, that it would require much interest to be admitted into the army. None would be admitted but those who have been regularly educated in every branch of military knowledge; and idle boys would be remitted to their studies.

Here is display'd an agreeable scene with relation to industry. Supposing the whole threescore thousand men to be absolutely idle; yet, by doubling the industry of those who remain, I affirm, that the sum of industry would be much greater than before. And the scene becomes en-<54>chanting, when we consider, that these threescore thousand men, would not only be of all the most industrious, but be patterns of industry to others.

Upon conclusion of a foreign war, we suffer grievously by disbanded soldiers, who must plunder or starve. The present plan is an effectual remedy: men accustomed to hard labour under strict discipline, can never be in want of bread: they will be sought for every where, even at higher than ordinary wages; and they will prove excellent masters for training the peasants to hard labour.

A man indulges emulation more freely in behalf of his friend or his country, than of himself: emulation in the latter case is selfish; in the former, is social. Doth not that give us reason to hope, that the separating military officers into different classes will excite a laudable emulation, prompting individuals to exert themselves on every occasion for the honour of their class? Nor will such emulation, a virtuous passion, be any obstruction to private friendship between members of different classes. May it not be expected, that young officers of birth and fortune, zea-<55>lous to qualify themselves at their own expence for serving their country, will cling for instruction to officers of experience, who have no inheritance but personal merit? Both find their account in that connection: men of rank become adepts in military affairs, a valuable branch of education for them; and officers who serve for pay, acquire friends at court, who will embrace every opportunity of testifying their gratitude.

The advantages mentioned are great and extensive; and yet are not the only advantages. Will it be thought extravagant to hope, that the proposed plan would form a better system of education for young men of fortune, than hitherto has been known in Britain? Before pronouncing sentence against me, let the following considerations be weigh'd. Our youth go abroad to *see* the world in the literal sense; for to pierce deeper than eye-sight, cannot be expected of boys. They resort to gay courts, where nothing is found for imitation but pomp, luxury, dissembled virtues, and real vices: such scenes make an impression too deep on young men of a warm imagination. Our plan <56> would be an antidote to such poisonous education. Supposing eighteen to be the earliest time for the army; here is an object held up to our youth of fortune, for rousing their ambition: they will endeavour to make a figure, and emulation will animate them to excel: supposing a young man to have no ambition, shame however will push him on. To acquire the military art, to discipline their men, to direct the execution of public works, and to conduct other military operations, would occupy their whole time, and banish idleness. A young gentleman, thus guarded against the enticing vices and sauntering follies of youth, must be sadly deficient in genius, if, during his seven years service, reading and meditation have been totally neglected. Hoping better things from our youth of fortune, I take for granted, that during their service they have made some progress, not only in military knowledge, but in morals, and in the fine arts, so as at the age of twenty-five to be qualified for profiting, instead of being undone, by *seeing* the world.* <57>

Further, young men of birth and fortune, acquire indeed the smoothness and suppleness of a court, with respect to their superiors; but the restraint

---

* Whether hereditary nobility may not be necessary in a monarchical government to support the King against the multitude, I take not on me to pronounce: but this I pronounce with assurance, that such a constitution is unhappy with respect to education; and appears to admit no remedy, if it be not that above mentioned, or some such. In fact, few of those who received their education while they were the eldest sons of Peers, have been duly qualified to manage public affairs.

of such manners, makes their temper break out against inferiors, where there is no restraint. Insolence of rank, is not so visible in Britain as in countries of less freedom; but it is sufficiently visible to require correction. To that end, no method promises more success than military service; as command and obedience alternately, are the best discipline for acquiring temper and moderation. Can pride and insolence be more effectually stemmed, than to be under command of an inferior?

Still upon the important article of education. Where pleasure is the ruling passion in youth, interest will be the ruling passion in age: the selfish principle is the <58> foundation of both; the object only is varied. This observation is sadly verified in Britain: our young men of rank, loathing an irksome and fatiguing course of education, abandon themselves to pleasure. Trace these very men through the more settled part of life, and they will be found grasping at power and profit, by means of court-favour; with no regard to their country, and with very little to their friends. The education proposed, holding up a tempting prize to virtuous ambition, is an excellent fence against a life of indolent pleasure. A youth of fortune, engaged with many rivals in a train of public service, acquires a habit of business; and as he is constantly employ'd for the public, patriotism becomes his ruling passion.* <59>

A number of noblemen and gentlemen, led by ambition, did lately join in parliament to oppose the King's measures; and with true antipatriotic zeal stood up as champions for the American rebels.[11] Charity leads me to think, that they would have acted very differently had they been trained in

---

* The following portrait is sketched by a good hand, (Madame Pompadour); and if it have any resemblance, it sets our plan in a conspicuous light. The French noblesse, says that lady, spending their lives in dissipation and idleness, know as little of politics as of economy. A gentleman hunts all his life in the country, or perhaps comes to Paris to ruin himself with an opera-girl. Those who are ambitious to be of the ministry, have seldom any merit, if it be not in caballing and intrigue. The French noblesse have courage, but without any genius for war, the fatigue of a soldier's life being to them unsupportable. The King has been reduced to the necessity of employing two strangers for the safety of his crown: had it not been for the Counts Saxe and Louendahl, the enemies of France might have laid siege to Paris.

11. Kames is perhaps referring to the passing on February 27, 1781, of Henry Conway's motion in favor of ending the war in America, an event instrumental to the downfall of North's ministry.

the military line, and consequently been employed during a course of years in the service of their country.[12]

The advantages of a military education, such as that proposed, are not yet exhausted. Under regular government promoting the arts of peace, social intercourse refines, and fondness for company increases in proportion. And hence it is, that the capital is crowded with every person who can afford to live there. A man of fortune, who has no taste but for a city life, happens to be forc'd into the country <60> by business: finding business and the country equally insipid, he turns impatient, and flies to town, with a disgust at every rural amusement. In France, the country has been long deserted: in Britain the same fondness for a town-life is gaining ground. A stranger considering the immense sums expended in England upon country-seats, would conclude, in appearance with great certainty, that the English spend most of their time in the country. But how would it surprise him to be told, not only that people of fashion in England pass little of their time there, but that the immense sums laid out upon gardening and pleasure-grounds, are the effect of vanity more than of taste! In fact, such embellishments are beginning to wear out of fashion; appetite for society leaving neither time nor inclination for rural pleasures. If the progress of that disease can be stayed, the only means is military education. In youth lasting impressions are made; and men of fortune who take to the army, being confined mostly to the country in prime of life, contract a liking for country occupations and amusements: which withdraw them from <61> the capital, and contribute to the health of the mind, no less than of the body.

A military life is the only cure for a disease much more dangerous. Most men of rank are ambitious of shining in public. They may assume the patriot at the beginning; but it is a false appearance, for their patriotism is only a disguise to favour their ambition. A court life becomes habitual and engrosses their whole soul: the minister's nod is a law to them: they dare not disobey; for to be reduced to a private station, would to them be a cruel misfortune. This impotence of mind is in France so excessive, that to banish a courtier to his country seat, is held an adequate punishment for the highest misdemeanor. This sort of slavery is gaining ground in Britain; and it ought

---

12. Paragraph added in 3rd edition.

to be dreaded, for scarce another circumstance will more readily pave the way to absolute power, if adverse fate shall afflict us with an ambitious King. There is no effectual remedy to the servility of a court life, but the military education here recommended.[13]

A military education would contribute equally to moderation in social enjoyments. The pomp, ceremony, and ex-<62>pence, necessary to those who adhere to a court and live always in public, are not a little fatiguing and oppressive. Man is naturally moderate in his desire of enjoyment; and it requires much practice to make him bear excess without satiety and disgust. The pain of excess, prompts men of opulence to pass some part of their time in a snug retirement, where they live at ease, free from pomp and ceremony. Here is a retirement, which can be reached without any painful circuit; a port of safety and of peace, to which we are piloted by military education, avoiding every dangerous rock, and every fatiguing agitation.

Reflecting on the advantages of military education above display'd, is it foolish to think, that our plan might produce a total alteration of manners in our youth of birth and fortune? the idler, the gamester, the profligate, compared with our military men, would make a despicable figure; shame, not to talk of pride, would compel them to reform.

How conducive to good government might the proposed plan be, in the hands of a virtuous king, supported by a public-<63>spirited ministry! In the present course of advancement, a youth of quality who aspires to serve his country in a civil employment, has nothing to rely on but parliamentary interest. The military education proposed, would afford him opportunity to improve his talents, and to convince the world of his merit. Honour and applause thus acquired, would intitle him to demand preferment; and he ought to be employed, not only as deserving, but as an encouragement to others. Frequent instances of neglecting men who are patronized by the public, might perhaps prove dangerous to a British minister.

If I have not all this while been dreaming, here are display'd illustrious advantages of the military education proposed. Fondness for the subject excites me to prolong the entertainment; and I add the following reflection on the education of such men as are disposed to serve in a public station.

13. Paragraph added in 2nd edition.

The sciences are mutually connected: a man cannot be perfect in any one, without being in some degree acquainted with every one. The science of politics in particular, being not a little intricate, cannot be acquired in perfection by <64> any one whose studies have been confined to a single branch, whether relative to peace or to war. The Duke of Marlborough made an eminent figure in the cabinet, as well as in the field; and so did equally the illustrious Sully, who may serve as a model to all ministers. The great aim in modern politics is, to split government into the greatest number possible of departments, trusting nothing to genius. China affords such a government in perfection. National affairs are there so simplified by division, as to require scarce any capacity in the mandarines. These officers, having little occasion for activity either of mind or of body, sink down into sloth and sensuality: motives of ambition or of fame make no impression: they have not even the delicacy to blush when they err: and as no punishment is regarded but what touches the person or the purse, it is not unusual to see a mandarine beaten with many stripes, sometimes for a very slight transgression. Let arts be subdivided into many parts: the more subdivisions the better. But I venture to pronounce, that no man ever did, nor ever will, make a capital figure in the government of a state, <65> whether as a judge, a general, or a minister, whose education is rigidly confined to one science.*

Sensible I am that the foregoing plan is in several respects imperfect; but if it be sound at bottom, polish and improvement are easy operations. My capital aim has been, to obviate the objections that press hard against every military plan, hitherto embraced or proposed. A standing army in its present form, is dangerous to liberty; and but a feeble bulwark against superior force. On the other hand, a nation in which every subject is a soldier, must not indulge any hopes of becoming powerful by manufactures and commerce: it is indeed vigorously defended, but is scarce worthy of being defended. The golden mean of rotation and constant labour in a standing army, would discipline multitudes for peace as well as for war. And a nation so defended would be invincible. <66>

---

* Phocion is praised by ancient writers, for struggling against an abuse that had crept into his country of Attica, that of making war and politics different professions. In imitation of Aristides and of Pericles, he studied both equally.

SKETCH X

Public Police with respect to the Poor

Among the industrious nations of Europe, regulations for the poor make a considerable branch of public police. These regulations are so multiplied and so anxiously framed, as to move one to think, that there cannot remain a single person under a necessity to beg. It is however a sad truth, that the disease of poverty, instead of being eradicated, has become more and more inveterate. England in particular overflows with beggars, tho' in no other country are the indigent so amply provided for. Some radical defect there must be in these regulations, when, after endless attempts to perfect them, they prove abortive. Every writer, dissatisfied with former plans, fails not to produce one of his own; which, in its turn, meets with as little approbation as any of the foregoing.

The first regulation of the states of Hol-<67>land concerning the poor, was in the year 1614 prohibiting all begging. The next was in the year 1649. "It is enacted, That every town, village, or parish, shall maintain its poor out of the income of its charitable foundations and collections. And in case these means fall short, the magistrates shall maintain them at the general expence of the inhabitants, as can most conveniently be done: Provided always, that the poor be obliged to work either to merchants, farmers, or others, for reasonable wages, in order that they may, as far as possible, be supported that way; provided also, that they be indulged in no idleness nor insolence." The advice or instruction here given to magistrates, is sensible; but falls short of what may be termed a *law*, the execution of which can be enforc'd in a court of justice.

In France, the precarious charity of monasteries proving ineffectual, a hospital was erected in the city of Paris *anno* 1656, having different apartments; one for the innocent poor, one for putting vagabonds to hard labour, one for foundlings, and one for the sick and maimed; with cer-<68>tain funds for defraying the expence of each, which produce annually much about the same sum. In imitation of Paris, hospitals of the same kind were erected in every great town of the kingdom.

The English began more early to think of their poor; and in a country without industry, the necessity probably arose more early. The first English statute bears date in the year 1496, directing, "That every beggar unable to work, shall resort to the hundred where he last dwelt or was born; and there shall remain, upon pain of being set in the stocks three days and three nights, with only bread and water, and then shall be put out of town." This was a law against vagrants, for the sake of order. There was little occasion, at that period, to provide for the innocent poor; their maintenance being a burden upon monasteries. But monasteries being put down by Henry VIII. a statute, 22d year of his reign, cap. 12. empowered the justices of every county, to license poor aged and impotent persons to beg within a certain district; those who beg without it, to be whipt, or set in the stocks. In the <69> first year of Edward VI. cap. 3. a statute was made in favour of impotent, maimed, and aged persons, that they shall have convenient houses provided for them, in the cities or towns where they were born, or where they resided for three years, to be relieved by the *willing and charitable disposition* of the parishioners. By 2d and 3d Philip and Mary, cap. 5. the former statutes of Henry VIII. and Edward VI. were confirmed, of gathering weekly relief for the poor by charitable collections. "A man licensed to beg, shall wear a badge on his breast and back openly."

The first compulsory statute was 5° Elisab. cap. 3. empowering justices of peace to raise a weekly sum for the poor, by taxing such persons as obstinately refuse to contribute, after repeated admonitions from the pulpit. In the next statute, 14° Elisab. cap. 5. a bolder step was made, empowering justices to tax the inhabitants of every parish, in a weekly sum for their poor. And taxations for the poor being now in some degree familiar, the remarkable statutes, 39° Elisab. cap. 3. and 43° Elisab. cap. 2. were enacted, which are the ground-work of all the subsequent <70> statutes concerning the poor. By these statutes, certain householders, named by the justices, are, in conjunction with the church-wardens, appointed overseers for the poor;

and these overseers, with consent of two justices, are empowered to tax the parish in what sums they think proper, for maintaining the poor.

Among a people so tenacious of liberty as the English are, and so impatient of oppression, is it not surprising, to find a law, that without ceremony subjects individuals to be taxed at the arbitrary will of men, who seldom either by birth or education deserve that important trust; and without even providing any effectual check against embezzlement? At present, a British parliament would reject with scorn such an absurd plan; and yet, being familiarized to it, they never seriously have attempted a repeal. We have been always on the watch to prevent the sovereign's encroachments, especially with regard to taxes: but as parish-officers are low persons who inspire no dread, we submit to have our pockets pick'd by them, almost without repining. There is provided, it is true, an appeal to the general sessions <71> for redressing inequalities in taxing the parishioners. But it is no effectual remedy: artful overseers will not over-rate any man so grossly as to make it his interest to complain, considering that these overseers have the poor's money to defend themselves with. Nor will the general sessions readily listen to a complaint, that cannot be verified but with much time and trouble. If the appeal have any effect, it makes a still greater inequality, by relieving men of figure at the expence of their inferiors; who must submit, having little interest to obtain redress.

The English plan, beside being oppressive, is grossly unjust. If it should be reported of some distant nation, that the burden of maintaining the idle and profligate, is laid upon the frugal and industrious, who work hard for a maintenance to themselves; what would one think of such a nation? Yet this is literally the case of England. I say more: the plan is not only oppressive and unjust, but miserably defective in the checking of maladministration. In fact, great sums are levied beyond what the poor receive: it requires briguing to be named a church-warden; <72> the nomination, in London especially, gives him credit at once; and however meagre at the commencement of his office, he is round and plump before it ends. To wax fat and rich by robbing the poor! Let us turn our eyes from a scene so horrid.*

* In the parish of St. George, Hanover Square, a great reform was made some years

Inequality in taxing, and embezzlement of the money levied, which are notorious, poison the minds of the people; and impress them with a notion, that all taxes raised by public authority are ill managed.

These evils are great, and yet are but slight compared with what follow. As the number of poor in England, as well as <73> the expence of maintenance, are increasing daily; proprietors of land, in order to be relieved of a burden so grievous, drive the poor out of the parish, and prevent all persons from settling in it who are likely to become a burden: cottages are demolished, and marriage obstructed. Influenced by the present evil, they look not forward to depopulation, nor to the downfall of husbandry and manufactures by scarcity of hands. Every parish is in a state of war with every other parish, concerning *pauper* settlements and removals.* <74>

At an average, England by its various products can maintain more than its present inhabitants. How comes it then that it is not more populous, according to the noted observation that where-ever there is food men will be found? I can discover no cause but the poor's rates, which make the people thoughtless and idle. Idleness begets profligacy; and the profligate avoid loading themselves with wives and children.¹

The price of labour is generally the same in the different shires of Scotland, and in the different parishes. A few exceptions are occasioned by the

---

ago. Inhabitants of figure, not excepting men of the highest rank, take it in turn to be church-wardens; which has reduced the poor-rates in that parish to a trifle. But people, after acquiring a name, soon tire of drudging for others. The drudgery will be left to low people as formerly, and the tax will again rise as high in that parish as in others. The poor-rates in Dr. Davenant's time, were about L. 700,000 yearly. In the year 1764, they amounted to L. 2,200,000. In the year 1773, they amounted to L. 3,000,000, equal to six shillings in the pound land-tax.

* In an address by Mr. Greaves to both Houses of Parliament there is the following passage: "It happens to be the mistaken policy of most of our very wise parish-officers, that as soon as a young man is married, a state of life which is the most likely to make him a good member of society, to endeavour to get him removed to the place of his legal settlement, out of pretence that he may soon have a family, which may possibly bring a charge upon the parish. Young men, intimidated by frequent examples of such cruel treatment, are unwilling to marry; and this leads them frequently to debauch young women, and then leave them with child in a very helpless condition. Thus they get into an unsettled and debauched way of life, acquire a habit of idleness, and become a burden upon the public." [[Note added in 3rd edition.]]

1. Paragraph added in 3rd edition.

neighbourhood of a great town, or by some extensive manufacture that requires many hands. In Scotland, the price of labour resembles water, which always levels itself: if high in any one corner, an influx of hands brings it down. The price of labour varies in every parish of England: a labourer who has gain'd a settlement in a parish, on which he depends for bread when he inclines to be idle, dares not remove to another parish where wages are higher, fearing to be cut out of a settlement altogether. England is in the same condition <75> with respect to labour, that France lately was with respect to corn; which, however plentiful in one province, could not be exported to supply the wants of another. The pernicious effects of the latter with respect to food, are not more obvious, than of the former with respect to manufactures.

English manufactures labour under a still greater hardship than inequality of wages. In a country where there is no fund for the poor but what nature provides, the labourer must be satisfied with such wages as are customary: he has no resource; for pity is not moved by idleness. In England, the labourers command the market: if not satisfied with customary wages, they have a tempting resource; which is, to abandon work altogether, and to put themselves on the parish. Labour is much cheaper in France than in England: several plausible reasons have been assigned; but in my judgement, the difference arises from the poor-laws. In England, every man is entitled to be idle; because every idler is entitled to a maintenance. In France, the funds allotted for the poor, yield the same sum an-<76>nually: that sum is always preoccupied; and France, with respect to all but those on the list, is a nation that has no fund provided by law for the poor.

Depopulation, inequality in the price of labour, and extravagant wages, are deplorable evils. But the English poor laws are productive of evils still more deplorable: they are subversive both of morality and industry. This is a heavy charge, but no less true than heavy. Fear of want is the only effectual motive to industry with the labouring poor: remove that fear, and they cease to be industrious. The ruling passion of those who live by bodily labour, is to save a pittance for their children, and for supporting themselves in old age: stimulated by desire of accomplishing these ends, they are frugal and industrious; and the prospect of success is to them a continual feast. Now, what worse can malice invent against such a man, under colour of friendship, than to secure bread to him and his children whenever he takes a dislike to work; which effectually deadens his sole ambition, and with it his honest industry? Relying on the certainty of a provision against want, <77> he relaxes gradually till he sinks into idleness: idleness leads to profligacy: profligacy begets diseases: and the wretch becomes an object of public charity before he has run half his course. Such are the genuine effects of the English tax for the poor, under a mistaken notion of charity. There never was known in any country, a scheme for the poor more contradictory to sound policy. Might it not have been foreseen, that to a groveling creature, who has no sense of honour and scarce any of shame, the certainty of maintenance would prove an irresistible temptation to idleness and debauchery? The poor-house at Lyons contained originally but forty beds, of which twenty only were occupied. The eight hundred beds it contains at present, are not sufficient for those who demand admittance. A premium is not more successful in any case, than where given to promote idleness.* A house for the poor <78> was erected in a French village, the revenue of which by economy became considerable. Upon a representation by the curate of the parish that more beds were necessary, the proprietor undertook the <79> management. He sold the house, with the furniture; and to every proper object of charity, he ordered a moderate proportion of bread and

---

* A London alderman named *Harper,* who was cotemporary with James I. or his son Charles, bequeathed ten or twelve acres of meadow-ground in the parish of St. Andrew's, Holborn, London, for the benefit of the poor in the town of Bedford. This ground has been long covered with houses, which yield from L. 4000 to L. 5000 yearly. That sum is laid out upon charity-schools, upon defraying the expence of apprenticeships, and upon a stock to young persons when they marry; an encouragement that attracts to the town of Bedford great numbers of the lower classes. So far well: but mark the consequence. That encouragement relaxes the industry of many, and adds greatly to the number of the poor. Hence it is, that in few places of England does the poor's rate amount so high as in the town of Bedford. An extensive common in the parish of Charley, Sussex, is the chief cause of an extravagant assessment for the poor, no less than nine shillings in the pound of rack rent. Give a poor man access to a common for feeding two or three cows, you make him idle by a dependence upon what he does not labour for. The town of Largo in Fife has a small hospital, erected many years ago by a gentleman of the name of Wood; and confined by him to the poor of his own name. That name being rare in the neighbourhood, access to the hospital is easy. One man in particular is entertained there, whose father, grandfather, and great-grandfather, enjoy'd successively the same benefit; every one of whom probably would have been useful members of society, but for that temptation to idleness. [[Note added in 2nd edition.]]

beef. The poor and sick were more comfortably lodged at home, than formerly in the poor-house. And by that management, the parish-poor decreased, instead of increasing as at Lyons. How few English manufacturers labour the whole week, if the work of four or five days afford them maintenance? Is not this a demonstration, that the malady of idleness is widely spread? In Bristol, the parish-poor twenty years ago did not exceed four thousand: at present, they amount to more than ten thousand. But as a malady, when left to itself, commonly effectuates its own cure; so it will be in this case: when, by prevailing idleness, every one without shame claims parish-charity, the burden will become intolerable, and the poor will be left to their shifts.

The immoral effects of public charity are not confined to those who depend on it, but extend to their children. The constant anxiety of a labouring man to provide for his issue, endears them to him. <80> Being relieved of that anxiety by the tax for the poor, his affection cools gradually, and he turns at last indifferent about them. Their independence, on the other hand, weans them from their duty to him. And thus, affection between parent and child, which is the corner-stone of society, is in a great measure obliterated among the labouring poor. In a plan published by the Earl of Hilsborough, an article is proposed to oblige parents to maintain their indigent children, and children to maintain their indigent parents. Natural affection must be at a low ebb, where such a regulation is necessary: but it is necessary, at least in London, where it is common to see men in good business neglecting their aged and diseased parents, for no better reason than that the parish is bound to find them bread: *Proh tempora, proh mores!*

The immoral effects of public charity spread still wider. It fails not to extinguish the virtue of charity among the rich; who never think of giving charity, when the public undertakes for all. In a scheme published by Mr. Hay, one article is, to raise a stock for the poor by volun-<81>tary contributions, and to make up the deficiency by a parish-tax. Will individuals ever contribute, when it is not to relieve the poor, but to relieve the parish? Every hospital has a poor-box, which seldom produces any thing.* The

---

* One exception I am fond to mention. The poor-box of the Edinburgh Infirmary was neglected two or three years, little being expected from it. When opened, L. 74 and

great comfort of society is assistance in time of need; and its firmest cement is, the bestowing and receiving kindly offices, especially in distress. Now to unhinge or suspend the exercise of charity by rendering it unnecessary, relaxes every social virtue by supplanting the chief of them. The consequence is dismal: exercise of benevolence to the distressed is our firmest guard against the encroachments of selfishness: if that guard be withdrawn, selfishness will prevail, and become the ruling passion. In fact, the tax for the poor has contributed greatly to the growth of that groveling passion, so conspicuous at present in England.

English authors who turn their thoughts <82> to the poor, make heavy complaints of decaying charity, and increasing poverty: never once dreaming, that these are the genuine effects of a legal provision for the poor; which on the one hand eradicates the virtue of charity, and on the other is a violent temptation to idleness. Wonderfully ill contrived must the English charity-laws be, when their consequences are to sap the foundation of voluntary charity; to deprive the labouring poor of their chief comfort, that of providing for themselves and children; to relax mutual affection between parent and child; and to reward, instead of punishing, idleness and vice. Consider whether a legal provision for the poor, be sufficient to atone for so many evils.

No man had better opportunity than Fielding to be acquainted with the state of the poor: let us listen to him.

> That the poor are a very great burden, and even a nuisance to the kingdom; that the laws for relieving their distresses and restraining their vices, have not answered; and that they are at present very ill provided for and much worse governed, are truths which every one will <83> acknowledge. Every person who hath property, must feel the weight of the tax that is levied for the poor; and every person of understanding, must see how absurdly it is applied. So useless indeed is this heavy tax, and so wretched its disposition, that it is a question, whether the poor or rich are actually more dissatisfied; since the plunder of the one serves so little to the real advantage of the other; for while a million yearly is raised among the rich, many

---

a fraction was found in it; contributed probably by the lower sort, who were ashamed to give their mite publicly.

of the poor are starved; many more languish in want and misery; of the rest, numbers are found begging or pilfering in the streets to-day, and to-morrow are locked up in gaols and Bridewells. If we were to make a progress through the outskirts of the metropolis and look into the habitations of the poor, we should there behold such pictures of human misery, as must move the compassion of every heart that deserves the name of human. What indeed must be his composition, who could see whole families in want of every necessary of life, oppressed with hunger, cold, nakedness, and filth; and with <84> diseases, the certain consequence of all these! The sufferings indeed of the poor are less known than their misdeeds; and therefore we are less apt to pity them. They starve, and freeze, and rot, among themselves; but they beg, and steal, and rob, among their betters. There is not a parish in the liberty of Westminster, which doth not raise thousands annually for the poor; and there is not a street in that liberty, which doth not swarm all day with beggars, and all night with thieves.

There is not a single beggar to be seen in Pensylvania. Luxury and idleness have got no footing in that happy country; and those who suffer by misfortune, have maintenance out of the public treasury. But luxury and idleness cannot for ever be excluded; and when they prevail, this regulation will be as pernicious in Pensylvania, as the poor-rates are in Britain.

Of the many proposals that have been published for reforming the poor-laws, not one has pierced to the root of the evil. None of the authors entertain the slightest doubt of a legal provision being necessary, tho' all our distresses arise evidently from <85> that very cause. Travellers complain, of being infested with an endless number of beggars in every English town; a very different scene from what they meet with in Holland or Switzerland. How would it surprise them to be told, that this proceeds from an overflow of charity in the good people of England!

Few institutions are more ticklish than those of charity. In London, common prostitutes are treated with singular humanity: a hospital for them when pregnant, disburdens them of their load, and nurses them till they be again fit for business: another hospital cures them of the venereal disease: and a third receives them with open arms, when, instead of desire, they become objects of aversion. Would not one imagine, that these hospitals have been erected for encouraging prostitution? They undoubtedly have that effect, tho' far from being intended. Mr. Stirling, superintendant of the Edinburgh poor-house, deserves a statue for a scheme he contrived to reform common prostitutes. A number of them were confined in a house of correction, on a daily allowance of three pence; and even part of that small pittance was <86> embezzled by the servants of the house. Pinching hunger did not reform their manners; for being absolutely idle, they encouraged each other in vice, waiting impatiently for the hour of deliverance. Mr. Stirling, with consent of the magistrates, removed them to a clean house; and instead of money, which is apt to be squandered, appointed for each a pound of oat-meal daily, with salt, water, and fire for cooking. Relieved now from distress, they longed for comfort: what would they not give for milk or ale? Work, says he, will procure you plenty. To some who offered to spin, he gave flax and wheels, engaging to pay them half the price of their yarn, retaining the other half for the materials furnished. The spinners earned about nine pence weekly, a comfortable addition to what they had before. The rest undertook to spin, one after another; and before the end of the first quarter, they were all of them intent upon work. It was a branch of his plan, to set free such as merited that favour; and some of them appeared so thoroughly reformed, as to be in no danger of a relapse.

The ingenious author of *The Police of* <87> *France,* who wrote in the year 1753,[2] observes, that notwithstanding the plentiful provision for the poor in that kingdom, mentioned above, there was a general complaint of the increase of beggars and vagrants; and adds, that the French political writers, dissatisfied with their own plan, had presented several memorials to the ministry, proposing to adopt the English parochial assessments, as greatly preferable. This is a curious fact; for at that very time, people in London, no less dissatisfied with these assessments, were writing pamphlets in praise of the French hospitals. One thing is certain, that no plan hitherto invented, has given satisfaction. Whether an unexceptionable plan is at all possible, seems extremely doubtful.

In every plan for the poor that I have seen, workhouses make one article; to provide work for those who are willing, and to make those work who are unwilling. With respect to the former, men need never be idle in En-

2. Sir William Mildmay.

gland for want of employment; and they always succeed the best at the employment they chuse for themselves. With respect to the latter, <88> punishment will not compel a man to labour: he may assume the appearance, but will make no progress; and the pretext of sickness or weakness is ever at hand for an excuse. The only compulsion to make a man work seriously, is fear of want.

A hospital for the sick, for the wounded, and for the maimed, is a right establishment; being productive of good, without doing any harm. Such a hospital should depend partly on voluntary charity; to procure which, a conviction of its being well managed, is necessary. Hospitals that have a sufficient fund of their own, and that have no dependence on the good will of others, are commonly ill managed.

Lies there any objection against a workhouse, for training to labour, destitute orphans, and begging children? It is an article in Mr. Hay's plan, that the workhouse should relieve poor families of all their children above three. This has an enticing appearance, but is unsound at bottom. Children require the tenderness of a mother, during the period of infantine diseases; and are far from being safe in the hands of mercenaries, who study no- <89>thing but their own ease and interest. Would it not be better, to distribute small sums from time to time among poor families overburdened with children, so as to relieve them from famine, not from labour? And with respect to orphans and begging children, I incline to think, that it would be a more salutary measure, to encourage mechanicks, manufacturers, and farmers above all, to educate such children. A premium for each, the half in hand, and the other half when they can work for themselves, would be a proper encouragement. The best-regulated orphan-hospital I am acquainted with, is that of Edinburgh. Orphans are taken in from every corner, provided only they be not under the age of seven, nor above that of twelve: under seven, they are too tender for a hospital; above twelve their relations can find employment for them. Beside the being taught to read and write, they are carefully instructed in some art, that may afford them comfortable subsistence.

No man ever called in question the utility of the marine society; which will reflect honour on the members as long as we have a navy to protect us: they de-<90>serve a rank above that of gartered knights. That institution is the most judicious exertion of charity and patriotism, that ever existed in any country.

A sort of hospital for servants who for twenty years have faithfully adhered to the same master, would be much to my taste; with a few adjoining acres for a kitchen-garden. The fund for purchasing, building, and maintenance, must be raised by contribution; and none but the contributors should be entitled to offer servants to the house. By such encouragement, a malady would be remedied, that of wandering from master to master for better wages, or easier service; which seldom fail to corrupt servants. They ought to be comfortably provided for, adding to the allowance of the house what pot-herbs are raised by their own labour. A number of virtuous men thus associated, would end their days in comfort; and the prospect of attaining a settlement so agreeable, would form excellent servants. How advantageous would such a hospital prove to husbandry in particular! But I confine this hospital to servants who are single. Men <91> who have a family will be better provided separately.[3]

Of all the mischiefs that have been engendered by over-anxiety about the poor, none have proved more fatal than a foundling-hospital. They tend to cool affection for children, still more effectually than the English parish-charity. At every occasional pinch for food, away goes a child to the hospital; and parental affection among the lower sort turns so languid, that many who are in no pinch, relieve themselves of trouble by the same means. It is affirmed, that of the children born annually in Paris, about a third part are sent to the foundling-hospital. The Paris almanack for the year 1768, mentions, that there were baptised 18,576 infants, of whom the foundling-hospital received 6025. The same almanack for the year 1773 bears, that of 18,518 children born and baptised, 5989 were sent to the foundling-hospital.[4] The proportion originally was much less; but vice advances with a swift pace. How enormous must be the degeneracy of the Parisian populace, and their want of parental affection!

Let us next turn to infants shut up in <92> this hospital. Of all animals, infants of the human race are the weakest: they require a mother's affection

---

3. "But I confine ... better provided separately": added in 2nd edition.
4. "The same almanack ... the foundling-hospital": added in 2nd edition.

to guard them against numberless diseases and accidents; a wise appointment of Providence to connect parents and children in the strictest union. In a foundling-hospital, there is no fond mother to watch over her tender babe; and the hireling nurse has no fondness but for her own little profit. Need we any other cause for the destruction of infants in a foundling-hospital, much greater in proportion than of those under the care of a mother? And yet there is another cause equally potent, which is corrupted air. What Mr. Hanway observes upon parish-workhouses, is equally applicable to a foundling-hospital. "To attempt," says he, "to nourish an infant in a workhouse, where a number of nurses are congregated into one room, and consequently the air become putrid, I will pronounce, from intimate knowledge of the subject, to be but a small remove from slaughter; *for the child must die.*" It is computed, that of the children in the London foundling-hospital, the half do not live a year. It appears by <93> an account given in to parliament, that the money bestow'd on that hospital from its commencement till December 1757 amounted to L. 166,000; and yet during that period, 105 persons only were put out to do for themselves.[5] Down then with foundling-hospitals, more noxious than pestilence or famine. An infant exposed at the door of a dwelling-house, must be taken up: but in that case, which seldom happens, the infant has a better chance for life with a hired nurse than in a hospital; and a chance perhaps little worse, bad as it is, than with an unnatural mother. I approve not indeed of a quarterly payment to such a nurse: would it not do better to furnish her bare maintenance for three years; and if the child be alive at the end of that time, to give her a handsome addition?

A house of correction is necessary for good order; but belongs not to the present essay, which concerns maintenance of the poor, not punishment of vagrants. I shall only by the way borrow a thought from Fielding, that fasting is the proper punishment of profligacy, not any punishment that is attended with shame. Pu-<94>nishment, he observes, that deprives a man of all sense of honour, never will contribute to make him virtuous.

Charity-schools may have been proper, when few could read, and fewer write; but these arts are now so common, that in most families children

---

5. "It is computed . . . do for themselves": added in 2nd edition.

may be taught to read at home, and to write in a private school at little expence. Charity-schools at present are more hurtful than beneficial: young persons who continue there so long as to read and write fluently, become too delicate for hard labour, and too proud for ordinary labour. Knowledge is a dangerous acquisition to the labouring poor: the more of it that is possessed by a shepherd, a ploughman, or any drudge, the less satisfaction he will have in labour. The only plausible argument for a charity-school, is, "That children of the labouring poor are taught there the principles of religion and of morality, which they cannot acquire at home." The argument would be invincible, if without regular education we could have no knowledge of these principles. But Providence has not left man in a state so imperfect: religion and mora-<95>lity are stamped on his heart; and none can be ignorant of them, who attend to their own perceptions. Education is indeed of use to ripen such perceptions; and it is of singular use to those who have time for reading and thinking: but education in a charity-school is so slight, as to render it doubtful, whether it be not more hurtful by fostering laziness, than advantageous by conveying instruction. The natural impressions of religion and morality, if not obscured by vitious habits, are sufficient for good conduct: preserve a man from vice by constant labour, and he will not be deficient in his duty either to God or to man. Hesiod, an ancient and respectable poet, says, that God hath placed labour as a guard to virtue. More integrity accordingly will be found among a number of industrious poor, taken at random, than among the same number in any other class.

I heartily approve every regulation that tends to prevent idleness. Chief Justice Hale says, "That prevention of poverty and idleness would do more good than all the gibbets, whipping-posts, and gaols in the kingdom." In that view, <96> gaming-houses ought to be heavily taxed, as well as horse-racing, cock-fighting, and all meetings that encourage idleness. The admitting low people to vote for members of parliament, is a source of idleness, corruption, and poverty. The same privilege is ruinous to every small parliament-borough. Nor have I any difficulty to pronounce, that the admitting the populace to vote in the election of a parish-minister, a frequent practice in Scotland, is productive of the same pernicious effects.

What then is to be the result of the foregoing enquiry? Is it from defect of invention that a good legal establishment for the poor is not yet discovered? or is it impracticable to make any legal establishment that is not fraught with corruption? I incline to the latter, for the following reason, no less obvious than solid, That in a legal establishment for the poor, no distinction can be made between virtue and vice; and consequently that every such establishment must be a premium for idleness. And where is the necessity, after all, of any public establishment? By what unhappy prejudice have people been led to think, that the Author of our na-<97>ture, so beneficent to his favourite man in every other respect, has abandoned the indigent to famine and death, if municipal law interpose not? We need but inspect the human heart to be convinced, that persons in distress are his peculiar care. Not only has he made it our duty to afford them relief, but has superadded the passion of pity to enforce the performance of that duty. This branch of our nature fulfils in perfection all the salutary purposes of charity, without admitting any one of the evils that a legal provision is fraught with. The contrivance, at the same time, is extremely simple: it leaves to every man the objects as well as measure of his charity. No man esteems it a duty to relieve wretches reduced to poverty by idleness and profligacy: they move not our pity; nor do they expect any good from us. Wisely therefore is it ordered by Providence, that charity should in every respect be voluntary, to prevent the idle and profligate from depending on it for support.

This plan is in many respects excellent. The exercise of charity, when free from compulsion, is highly pleasant. There is <98> indeed little pleasure where charity is rendered unnecessary by municipal law; but were that law laid aside, the gratification of pity would become one of our sweetest enjoyments. Charity, like other affections, is envigorated by exercise, and no less enfeebled by disuse. Providence withal hath scattered benevolence among the sons of men with a liberal hand: and notwithstanding the obstruction of municipal law, seldom is there found one so obdurate, as to resist the impulse of compassion, when a proper object is presented. In a well-regulated government, promoting industry and virtue, the persons who need charity are not many; and such persons may with assurance depend on the charity of their neighbours.*

---

* The Italians are not more remarkable for a charitable disposition, than their neigh-

It may at the same time be boldly affirmed, that those who need charity, would be more comfortably provided for by the plan of Providence, than by any legal establishment. Creatures loathsome by dis-<99>ease or nastiness, affect the air in a poor-house; and have little chance for life, without more care and kindliness than can be expected from servants, rendered callous by continual scenes of misery. Consider, on the other hand, the consequences of voluntary charity, equally agreeable to the giver and receiver. The kindly connection it forms between them, grows stronger and stronger by reiteration; and squallid poverty, far from being an obstruction, excites a degree of pity, proportioned to the distress. It may happen for a wonder, that an indigent person is overlooked; but for one who will suffer by such neglect, multitudes suffer by compelled charity.

But what I insist on with peculiar satisfaction is, that natural charity is an illustrious support to virtue. Indigent virtue can never fail of relief, because it never fails to enflame compassion. Indigent vice, on the contrary, raises indignation more than pity (*a*); and therefore can have little prospect of relief. What a glorious encitement to industry and virtue, and how <100> discouraging to idleness and vice! Will it be thought chimerical to observe further, that to leave the indigent on Providence, will tend to improve manners as well as virtue among the lower classes? No man can think himself secure against being reduced to depend on his neighbours for bread. The influence of that thought, will make every one solicitous to acquire the good will of others.[6] Lamentable it is, that so beautiful a structure should be razed to the foundation by municipal law, which, in providing for the poor, makes no distinction between virtue and vice. The execution of the poor-laws would be impracticable, were such a distinction attempted by enquiring into the conduct and character of every *pauper*. Where are judges to be found who will patiently follow out such a dark and intricate expiscation? To accomplish the task, a man must abandon every other concern.

---

bours. No fewer however than seventy thousand mendicant friars live there upon voluntary charity; and I have not heard that any one of them ever died of want.

(*a*) Elements of Criticism, ch. 2. part 7.

6. "Will it be . . . will of others": added in 2nd edition.

In the first English statutes mentioned above, the legislature appear carefully to have avoided compulsory charity: every measure for promoting voluntary charity was first try'd, before the fatal blow was struck, empowering parish-officers to im-<101>pose a tax for the poor. The legislature certainly did not foresee the baneful consequences: but how came they not to see that they were distrusting Providence, declaring in effect, that the plan established by our Maker for the poor, is insufficient? Many are the municipal laws that enforce the laws of nature, by additional rewards and punishments; but it was singularly bold to abolish the natural law of charity, by establishing a legal tax in its stead. Men will always be mending: what a confused jumble do they make, when they attempt to mend the laws of Nature! Leave Nature to her own operations: she understands them the best.

Few regulations are more plausible than what are political; and yet few are more deceitful. A writer, blind with partiality for his country, makes the following observations upon the 43° Elisab. establishing a maintenance for the poor. "Laws have been enacted in many other countries, which have punished the idle beggar, and exhorted the rich to extend their charity to the poor: but it is peculiar to the humanity of England, to have made their support a matter of <102> obligation and necessity on the more wealthy. The English seem to be the first nation in Europe in science, arts, and arms: they likewise are possessed of the freest and most perfect of constitutions, and the blessings consequential to that freedom. If virtues in an individual are sometimes supposed to be rewarded in this world, I do not think it too presumptuous to suppose, that national virtues may likewise meet with their reward. England hath, to its peculiar honour, not only made their poor free, but hath provided a certain and solid establishment to prevent their necessities and indigence, when they arise from what the law calls *the act of God:* and are not these beneficent and humane attentions to the miseries of our fellow-creatures, the first of those poor pleas which we are capable of offering, in behalf of our imperfections, to an all-wise and merciful Creator!" To this writer I oppose another, whose reflections are more sound. "In England, there is an act of the legislature, obliging every parish to maintain its own poor. Scarce any man living, who has not seen the <103> effects of this law, but must approve of it; and yet such are its effects, that the streets of London are filled with objects of misery beyond what is seen in any other city. The labouring poor, depending on this law to be provided in sickness and old age, are little solicitous to save, and become habitually profuse. The principle of charity is established by Providence in the human heart, for relieving those who are disabled to work for themselves. And if the labouring poor had no dependence but on the principle of charity, they would be more religious; and if they were influenced by religion, they would be less abandoned in their behaviour. Thus this seeming-good act turns to a national evil: there is more distress among the poor in London than any where in Europe; and more drunkenness both in males and females" (*a*).

I am aware, that during the reign of Elisabeth, some compulsion might be necessary to preserve the poor from starving. <104> Her father Henry had sequestered all the hospitals, a hundred and ten in number, and squandered their revenues; he had also demolished all the abbeys. By these means, the poor were reduced to a miserable condition; especially as private charity, for want of exercise, was at a low ebb. That critical juncture required indeed help from the legislature: and a temporary provision for the poor would have been a proper measure; so contrived as not to supersede voluntary charity, but rather to promote it. Unlucky it is for England, that such a measure was overlooked; but Queen Elisabeth and her parliaments had not the talent of foreseeing consequences without the aid of experience. A perpetual tax for the poor was imposed, the most pernicious tax that ever was imposed in any country.

With respect to the present times, the reason now given pleads against abolishing at once a legal provision for the poor. It may be taken for granted, that charity is in England not more vigorous at present, than it was in the days of Elisabeth. Would our ministry but lead the way, by showing some zeal for a reformation, ex-<105>pedients would probably be invented for supporting the poor, without unhinging voluntary charity. The following expedient is proposed, merely as a specimen. Let a tax be imposed by parliament on every parish for their poor, variable in proportion to the number; but not to exceed the half of what is necessary: directing the landholders

(*a*) Author of Angeloni's letters [[i.e., John Shebbeare]].

to make up quarterly, a list of the names and condition of such persons as in their opinion deserve charity; with an estimate of what each ought to have weekly. The public tax makes the half, and the other half is to be raised by voluntary contribution. To prevent collusion, the roll of the poor, and their weekly appointment, with a subscription of gentlemen for their part of the sum, shall be examined by the justices of peace at a quarterly meeting; who, on receiving satisfaction, must order the sum arising from the public tax to be distributed among the poor contained in the roll, according to the estimate of the landholders. As the public fund lies dead till the subscription be completed, it is not to be imagined that any gentleman will stand out; it would be a public imputation on his <106> character. Far from apprehending any deficiency, confident I am, that every gentleman would consider it as honourable to contribute largely. This agreeable work must be blended with some degree of severity, that of excluding from the roll every profligate, male or female. If that rule be strictly followed out, the innocent poor will diminish daily; so as in time to be safely left upon voluntary charity, without necessity of any tax.

But must miserable wretches, reduced to poverty by idleness or intemperance, be, in a Christian country, abandoned to diseases and famine. This is the argument, shallow as it is, that has corrupted the industry of England, and reduced multitudes to diseases and famine. Those who are able to work, may be locked up in a house of correction, to be fed with bread and water; but with liberty of working for themselves. And as for the remainder, their case is not desperate, when they have access to such tender-hearted persons as are more eminent for pity than for principle. If by neglect or oversight any happen to die of want, the example will tend more <107> to reformation, than the most pathetic discourse from the pulpit.

Even at the hazard of losing a few lives by neglect or oversight, common begging ought absolutely to be prohibited. The most profligate, are the most impudent and the most expert at feigning distress. If begging be indulged to any, all will rush into the public: idlers are fond of that wandering and indolent sort of life; and there is no temptation to idleness more successful, than liberty to beg. In order to be relieved from common beggars, it has been proposed, to fine those who give them alms. Little penetration must they have, to whom the insufficiency of such a remedy is not palpable.

It is easy to give alms without being seen; and compassion will extort alms, even at the hazard of suffering for it; not to mention, that every one in such a case would avoid the odious character of an informer. The following remedy is suggested, as what probably may answer. An officer must be appointed in every parish, with a competent salary, for apprehending and carrying to the workhouse every strolling beggar; under the penalty of losing his office, with what sa-<108>lary is due to him, if any beggar be found strolling four and twenty hours after the fact comes to his knowledge. In the workhouse such beggars shall be fed with bread and water for a year, but with liberty of working for themselves.

I declare resolutely against a perpetual tax for the poor. But if there must be such a tax, I know of none less subversive of industry and morals than that established in Scotland, obliging the landholders in every parish to meet at stated times, in order to provide a fund for the poor; but leaving the objects of their charity, and the measure, to their own humanity and discretion. In this plan, there is no encroachment on the natural duty of charity, but only that the minority must submit to the opinion of the majority.

In large towns, where the character and circumstances of the poor are not so well known as in country-parishes, the following variation is proposed. Instead of landholders, who are proper in country-parishes; let there be in each town-parish a standing committee chosen by the proprietors of houses, the third part to be changed annually. This committee with the <109> minister, make up a list of such as deserve charity, adding an estimate of what, with their own labour, may be sufficient for each of them. The minister, with one or two of the committee, carry about this list to every family that can afford charity, suggesting what may be proper for each to contribute. This list, with an addition of the sum contributed or promised by each householder, must be affixed on the principal door of the parish-church, to honour the contributors, and to inform the poor of the provision made for them. Some such mode may probably be effectual, without transgressing the bounds of voluntary charity. But if any one obstinately refuse to contribute after several applications, the committee at their discretion may tax him. If it be the possessor who declines contributing, the tax must be laid upon him, reserving relief against his landlord.

In great towns, the poor, who ought to be prohibited from begging, are less known than in country-parishes: and among a croud of inhabitants, it is easier for an individual to escape the public eye when he with-holds charity, than in country-pa-<110>rishes. Both defects would be remedied by the plan above proposed: it will bring to light, in great cities, the poor who deserve charity; and it will bring to light every person who with-holds charity.[7]

In every regulation for the poor, English and Scotch, it is taken for granted, that the poor are to be maintained in their own houses. Parochial poor-houses are creeping into fashion: a few are already erected both in England and Scotland; and there is depending in parliament a plan for establishing poor-houses in every part of England. Yet whether they ought to be preferred to the accustomed mode, deserves serious consideration. The erection and management of a poor-house are expensive articles; and if they do not upon the whole appear clearly beneficial, it is better to stop short in time.

Economy is the great motive that inclines people to this new mode of providing for the poor. It is imagined, that numbers collected at a common table, can be maintained at less expence than in separate houses; and foot-soldiers are given for an example, who could not live on their pay if they did not mess together. <111> But the cases are not parallel. Soldiers, having the management of their pay, can club for a bit of meat. But as the inhabitants of a poor-house are maintained by the public, the same quantity of provisions must be allotted to each; as there can be no good rule for separating those who eat much from those who eat little. The consequence is what may be expected: the bulk of them reserve part of their victuals for purchasing ale or spirits. It is vain to expect work from them: poor wretches void of shame will never work seriously, where the profit accrues to the public, not to themselves. Hunger is the only effectual means for compelling such persons to work.

Where the poor are supported in their own houses, the first thing that is done, or ought to be done, is to estimate what each can earn by their own labour; and as far only as that falls short of maintenance, is there place for

---

7. In the 1st edition the sketch ends here.

charity. They will be as industrious as possible, because they work for themselves; and a weekly sum of charity under their own management, will turn to better account, than in a poor-house, under the direction of mer-<112>cenaries. The quantity of food for health depends greatly on custom. Busbequius observes, that the Turks eat very little flesh-meat; and that the Janizaries in particular, at that time a most formidable infantry, were maintained at an expence far below that of a German. Wafers, cakes, boiled rice, with small bits of mutton or pullet, were their highest entertainment, fermented liquors being absolutely prohibited. The famous Montecuculi says, that the Janizaries eat but once a-day, about sun-set; and that custom makes it easy. Negroes are maintained in the West Indies at a very small expence. A bit of ground is allotted to them for raising vegetables, which they cultivate on Sunday, being employed all the rest of the week in labouring for their masters. They receive a weekly allowance of dry'd fish, about a pound and a half; and their only drink is water. Yet by vegetables and water with a morsel of dry'd fish, these people are sufficiently nourished to perform the hardest labour in a most enervating climate. I would not have the poor to be pampered, which might prove a bad example to the industrious: if they be sup-<113>ported in the most frugal manner, the duty of charity is fulfilled. And in no other manner can they be supported so frugally, as to leave to their own disposal what they receive in charity. Not a penny will be laid out on fermented liquors, unless perhaps as a medicine in sickness. Nor does their low fare call for pity. Ale makes no part of the maintenance of those in Scotland who live by the sweat of their brows. Water is their only drink; and yet they live comfortably, without ever thinking of pitying themselves. Many gentlemen drink nothing but water; who feel no decay either in health or vigour. The person however who should propose to banish ale from a poor-house, would be exclaimed against as hard-hearted and void of charity. The difference indeed is great between what is done voluntarily, and what is done by compulsion. It is provoking to hear of the petulance and even luxury of the English poor. Not a person in London who lives by the parish-charity will deign to eat brown bread; and in several parts of England, many who receive large sums from that fund, are in the constant custom of drinking tea twice <114> a-day. Will one incline to labour where idleness and beggary are so much encouraged?

But what objection, it will be urged, lies against adopting in a poor-house the plan mentioned, giving to no person in money more than what his work, justly estimated, falls short of maintenance? It is easy to foresee, that this plan can never answer in a poor-house. The materials for work must be provided by mercenary officers; who must also be trusted with the disposal of the made work, for behoof of the poor people. These operations may go on sweetly a year or two, under the influence of novelty and zeal for improvement; but it would be chimerical to expect for ever strict fidelity in mercenary officers, whose management cannot easily be checked. Computing the expence of this operose management, and giving allowance for endless frauds in purchasing and selling, I boldly affirm, that the plan would turn to no account. Consider next the weekly sum given in charity: people confined in a poor-house have no means for purchasing necessaries but at a sutlery, where they will certainly be <115> imposed on, and their money go no length.

We are now ripe for a comparison with respect to economy. Many a householder in Edinburgh makes a shift to maintain a family with their gain of four shillings *per* week, amounting to ten pounds eight shillings yearly. Seldom are there fewer than four or five persons in such a family; the husband, the wife, and two or three children. Thus four or five persons can be maintain'd under eleven pounds yearly. But are they maintain'd so cheap in the Edinburgh poor-house? Not a single person there but at an average costs the public at least four pounds yearly. Nor is this all. A great sum remains to be taken into the computation, the interest of the sum for building, yearly reparations, expence of management, wages to servants, male and female. A proportion of this great sum must be laid upon each person, which swells the expence of their maintenance. And when every particular is taken into the account, I have no hesitation to pronounce, that laying aside labour altogether, a man can make a shift to maintain him-<116>self privately at half of the expence that is necessary in a poor-house.

So far we have travelled on solid ground; and what follows is equally solid. Among the industrious, not many are reduced so low, but that they can make some shift for themselves. The quantity of labour that can be performed by those who require aid, cannot be brought under any accurate estimation. To pave the way to a conjecture, those who are reduced to poverty by dissoluteness or sheer idleness, ought absolutely to be rejected as unworthy of public charity. If such wretches can prevail on the tender-hearted to relieve them privately, so far well: they ought not to be indulged with any other hope. Now laying these aside, the quantity of labour may be fairly computed as half maintenance. Here then is another great article saved to the public. If a man can be maintained privately at half of what is necessary in a poor-house, his work, reckoning it half of his maintenance, brings down the sum to the fourth part of what is necessary in a poor-house.

Undistinguished charity to the deserving and undeserving, has multiply'd the poor; <117> and will multiply them more and more without end. Let it be publicly known that the dissolute and idle have no chance to be put on a charity-roll; the poor, instead of increasing, will gradually diminish, till none be left but proper objects of charity, such as have been reduced to indigence by old age or innocent misfortune. And if that rule be strictly adhered to, the maintenance of the poor will not be a heavy burden. After all, a house for the poor may possibly be a frugal scheme in England where the parish-rates are high, in the town of Bedford for example. In Scotland, it is undoubtedly a very unfrugal scheme.

Hitherto of a poor-house with respect to economy. There is another point of still greater moment; which is to consider the influence it has on the manners of the inhabitants. A number of persons, strangers to each other, and differing in temper and manners, can never live comfortably together: will ever the sober and innocent make a tolerable society with the idle and profligate? In our poor-houses accordingly, quarrels and complaints are endless. The family society and that of a nation <118> under government, are prompted by the common nature of man; and none other. In monasteries and nunneries, envy, detraction, and heart-burning, never cease. Sorry I am to observe, that in seminaries of learning concord and good-will do not always prevail, even among the professors. What adds greatly to the disease in a poor-house, is that the people shut up there, being secure of maintenance, are reduced to a state of absolute idleness, for it is in vain to think of making them work: they have no care, nothing to keep the blood in motion. Attend to a state so different from what is natural to us. Those who are innocent and harmless, will languish, turn dispirited, and tire of life. Those of a bustling and restless temper, will turn sour and peevish for want of occupation: they will murmur against their superiors, pick quarrels with their neighbours, and sow discord every where. The worst of all is, that a poor-house never fails to corrupt the morals of the inhabitants: nothing tends so much to promote vice and immorality, as idleness among a number of low people collected in one place. Among no set of people does profligacy more a-<119>bound, than among the seamen in Greenwich hospital.

A poor-house tends to corrupt the body no less than the mind. It is a nursery of diseases, fostered by dirtiness and crouding.

To this scene let us oppose the condition of those who are supported in their own houses. They are laid under the necessity of working with as much assiduity as ever; and as the sum given them in charity is at their own disposal, they are careful to lay it out in the most frugal manner. If by parsimony they can save any small part, it is their own; and the hope of encreasing this little stock, supports their spirits and redoubles their industry. They live innocently and comfortably, because they live industriously; and industry, as every one knows, is the chief pleasure of life to those who have acquired the habit of being constantly employ'd. <120>

SKETCH XI

A Great City considered in Physical, Moral, and Political Views

In all ages an opinion has been prevalent, that a great city is a great evil; and that a capital may be too great for the state, as a head may be for the body. Considering however the very shallow reasons that have been given for this opinion, it should seem to be but slightly founded. There are several ordinances limiting the extent of Paris, and prohibiting new buildings beyond the prescribed bounds; the first of which is by Henry II. *ann.* 1549. These ordinances have been renewed from time to time, down to 1672, in which year there is an edict of Louis XIV. to the same purpose. The reasons assigned are, "First, That by enlarging the city, the air would be rendered unwholesome. Second, That cleaning the streets would prove a great additional labour. Third, That adding to the number of inhabitants would raise the price of provi-<121>sions, of labour, and of manufactures. Fourth, That ground would be covered with buildings instead of corn, which might hazard a scarcity. Fifth, That the country would be depopulated by the desire that people have to resort to the capital. And, lastly, That the difficulty of governing such numbers, would be an encouragement to robbery and murder."

In these reasons, the limiting the extent of the city and the limiting the number of inhabitants are jumbled together, as if they were the same. The only reasons that regard the former, are the second and fourth;[1] and these,

---

1. Added in 2nd edition: "In these reasons . . . second and fourth." In 1st edition: "These reasons for confining the city of Paris within certain bounds are wonderfully

at best, are trifling. The first reason urged against enlarging the city, is a solid reason for enlarging it, supposing the numbers to be limited; for crouding is an infallible means to render the air unwholesome. Paris, with the same number of inhabitants that were in the days of the fourth Henry, occupies thrice the space, much to the health as well as comfort of the inhabitants. Had the ordinances mentioned been made effectual, the houses in Paris must all have been built story above story, ascending to <122> the sky like the tower of Babel. Before the great fire *anno* 1666, the plague was frequent in London; but by widening the streets and enlarging the houses, there has not since been known in that great city, any contagious distemper that deserves the name of a plague. The third, fifth, and last reasons, conclude against permitting any addition to the number of inhabitants; but conclude nothing against enlarging the town. In a word, the measure adopted in these ordinances has little or no tendency to correct the evils complained of; and infallibly would enflame the chief of them. The measure that ought to have been adopted, is to limit the number of inhabitants, not the extent of the town.

Queen Elisabeth of England, copying the French ordinances, issued a proclamation *anno* 1602, prohibiting any new buildings within three miles of London. The preamble is in the following words: "That foreseeing the great and manifold inconveniencies and mischiefs which daily grow, and are likely to increase, in the city and suburbs of London, by confluence of people to inhabit the <123> same; not only by reason that such multitudes can hardly be governed, to serve God and obey her Majesty, without constituting an addition of new officers, and enlarging their authority; but also can hardly be provided of food and other necessaries at a reasonable price; and finally, that as such multitudes of people, many of them poor who must live by begging or worse means, are heaped up together, and in a sort smothered with many children and servants in one house or small tenement; it must needs follow, if any plague or other universal sickness come amongst them, that it would presently spread through the whole city and confines, and also into all parts of the realm."

---

shallow. The most important of them conclude justly against permitting an increase of inhabitants: the second and fourth conclude only against enlarging the city" [2:62–63].

There appears as little accuracy in this proclamation, as in the French ordinances. The same error is observable in both, which is the limiting the extent of the city, instead of limiting the number of inhabitants. True it is indeed, that the regulation would have a better effect in London than in Paris. As stone is in plenty about Paris, houses there may be carried to a very great height; and are <124> actually so carried in the old town: but there being no stone about London, the houses formerly were built of timber, now of brick; materials too frail for a lofty edifice.

Proceeding to particulars, the first objection, which is the expence of governing a great multitude, concludes against the number of inhabitants not against the extent of the city. At the same time, the objection is at best doubtful in point of fact. Tho' vices abound in a great city, requiring the strictest attention of the magistrate; yet with a well-regulated police, it appears less expensive to govern 600,000 in one city, than the same number in ten different cities. The second objection, viz. the high price of provisions, strikes only against numbers, not extent. Beside, whatever might have been the case in the days of Elisabeth, when agriculture and internal commerce were in their infancy; there are at present not many towns in England, where a temperate man may live cheaper than in London. The hazard of contagious distempers, which is the third objection, is an invincible argument against limiting the extent of a great town. <125> It is mentioned above, that from the year 1666, when the streets were widened and the houses enlarged, London has never been once visited by the plague. If the proclamation had taken effect, the houses must have been so crouded upon each other, and the streets so contracted, as to have occasioned plagues still more frequently than before the year 1666.

The Queen's immediate successors were not more clear-sighted than she had been. In the year 1624, King James issued a proclamation against building in London upon new foundations. Charles I. issued two proclamations to the same purpose; one in the year 1625, and one in the year 1630.

The progress of political knowledge has unfolded many bad effects of a great city, more weighty than any urged in these proclamations. The first I shall mention, is, that people born and bred in a great city are commonly weak and effeminate. Vegetius (*a*) observing, that men bred to husbandry

(*a*) De re militari, lib. 1. cap. 3.

make the best soldiers, adds what follows. "Interdum tamen necessitas exigit, etiam urbanos ad ar-<126>ma compelli: qui ubi nomen dedere militiae, primum laborare, decurrere, portare pondus, et solem pulveremque ferre, condiscant; parco victu utantur et rustico; interdum sub divo, interdum sub papilionibus, commorentur. Tunc demum ad usum erudiantur armorum: et si longior expeditio emergit, in angariis plurimum detinendi sunt, proculque habendi a civitatis illecebris: ut eo modo, et corporibus eorum robur accedat, et animis."* The luxury of a great city descends from the highest to the lowest, infecting all ranks of men; <127> and there is little opportunity in it for such exercise as to render the body vigorous and robust.

The foregoing is a physical objection against a great city: the next regards morality. Virtue is exerted chiefly in restraint: vice, in giving freedom to desire. Moderation and self-command form a character the most susceptible of virtue: superfluity of animal spirits, and love of pleasure, form a character the most liable to vice. Low vices, pilfering for example, or lying, draw few or no imitators; but vices that indicate a soul above restraint, produce many admirers. Where a man boldly struggles against unlawful restraint, he is justly applauded and imitated; and the vulgar are not apt to distinguish nicely between lawful and unlawful restraint: the boldness is visible, and they pierce no deeper. It is the unruly boy, full of animal spirits, who at public school is admired and imitated; not the virtuous and modest. Vices accordingly that show spirit, are extremely infectious; virtue very little. Hence the corruption of a great city, which increases more and more in proportion to the number of inhabitants. <128> But it is sufficient here barely to mention that objection, because it has been formerly insisted on.

The following bad effects are more of a political nature. A great town is a professed enemy to the free circulation of money. The current coin is

---

* "But sometimes there is a necessity for arming the townspeople, and calling them out to service. When this is the case, it ought to be the first care, to enure them to labour, to march them up and down the country, to make them carry heavy burdens, and to harden them against the weather. Their food should be coarse and scanty, and they should be habituated to sleep alternately in their tents, and in the open air. Then is the time to instruct them in the exercise of their arms. If the expedition is a distant one, they should be chiefly employed in the stations of posts or expresses, and removed as much as possible from the dangerous allurements that abound in large cities; that thus they may be envigorated both in mind and body."

accumulated in the capital: and distant provinces must sink into idleness; for without ready money neither arts nor manufactures can flourish. Thus we find less and less activity, in proportion commonly to the distance from the capital; and an absolute torpor in the extremities. The city of Milan affords a good proof of this observation. The money that the Emperor of Germany draws from it in taxes is carried to Vienna; not a farthing left but what is barely sufficient to defray the expence of government. Manufactures and commerce have gradually declined in proportion to the scarcity of money; and that city which the last century contained 300,000 inhabitants, cannot now muster above 90,000.*[2] It may be observed beside, that <129> as horses in a great city must be provided with provender from a distance, the country is robbed of its dung, which goes to the rich fields round the city. But as manure laid upon poor land, is of more advantage to the farmer, than upon what is already highly improved, the depriving distant parts of manure is a loss to the nation in general. Nor is this all: The dung of an extensive city, the bulk of it at least, is so remote from the fields to which it must be carried, that the expence of carriage swallows up the profit.

Another bad effect of accumulating money in the capital is, that it raises the price of labour. The temptation of high wages in the capital, robs the country of its best hands. And as they who resort to the ca-<130>pital are commonly young people, who remove as soon as they are fit for work, distant provinces are burdened with their maintenance, without reaping any benefit by their labour.

But of all, the most deplorable effect of a great city, is the preventing of population, by shortening the lives of its inhabitants. Does a capital swell in proportion to the numbers that are drained from the country? Far from

---

* Is not the following inference from these premisses well founded, that it would be a ruinous measure to add Bengal to the British dominions? In what manner would the territorial revenues and other taxes be remitted to London? If in hard coin, that country would in time be drained of money, its manufactures would be annihilated, and depopulation ensue. If remitted in commodities, the public would be cheated, and little be added to the revenue. A land-tax laid on as in Britain would be preferable in every respect; for it would be paid by the East-India Company as proprietors of Bengal without deduction of a farthing.

2. "The city of . . . muster above 90,000": added (with note) in 2nd edition.

it. The air of a populous city is infected by multitudes crouded together; and people there seldom make out the usual time of life. With respect to London in particular, the fact cannot be dissembled. The burials in that immense city greatly exceed the births: the difference some affirm to be no less than ten thousand yearly: by the most moderate computation, not under seven or eight thousand. As London is far from being on the decline, that number must be supplied by the country; and the annual supply amounts probably to a greater number, than were needed annually for recruiting our armies and navies in the late war with France. If so, London is a greater enemy to population, than a <131> bloody war would be, supposing it even to be perpetual. What an enormous tax is Britain thus subjected to for supporting her capital! The rearing and educating yearly for London 7 or 8000 persons, require an immense sum.

In Paris, if the bills of mortality can be relied on, the births and burials are nearly equal, being each of them about 19,000 yearly; and according to that computation, Paris should need no recruits from the country. But in that city, the bills of mortality cannot be depended on for burials. It is there universally the practice of high and low, to have their infants nursed in the country, till they be three years of age; and consequently those who die before that age, are not inlisted. What proportion these bear to the whole is uncertain. But a guess may be made from such as die in London before the age of three, which are computed to be one half of the whole that die (*a*). Now giving the utmost allowance for the healthiness of the country above that of a town, children from Paris that die in the country <132> before the age of three, cannot be brought so low as a third of those who die. On the other hand, the London bills of mortality are less to be depended on for births than for burials. None are inlisted but infants baptised by clergymen of the English church; and the numerous children of Papists, Dissenters, and other sectaries, are left out of the account. Upon the whole, the difference between the births and burials in Paris and in London, is much less than it appears to be on comparing the bills of mortality of these two cities.

At the same time, giving full allowance for children who are not brought

---

(*a*) See Dr. Price [[*Observations on Reversionary Payments*]], p. 362.

into the London bills of mortality, there is the highest probability that a greater number of children are born in Paris than in London; and consequently that the former requires fewer recruits from the country than the latter. In Paris, domestic servants are encouraged to marry: they are observed to be more settled than when bachelors, and more attentive to their duty. In London, such marriages are discouraged, as rendering a servant more attentive to his own family than to that of his master. But a servant attentive to his own <133> family, will not, for his own sake, neglect that of his master. At any rate, is he not more to be depended on, than a servant who continues single? What can be expected of idle and pampered bachelors, but debauchery and every sort of corruption? Nothing restrains them from absolute profligacy, but the eye of the master; who for that reason is their aversion not their love. If the poor-laws be named the folio of corruption, bachelor-servants in London may well be considered as a large appendix. And this attracts the eye to the poor-laws, which indeed make the chief difference between Paris and London, with respect to the present point. In Paris, certain funds are established for the poor, the yearly produce of which admits but a limited number. As that fund is always pre-occupied, the low people who are not on the list, have little or no prospect of bread, but from their own industry; and to the industrious, marriage is in a great measure necessary. In London, a parish is taxed in proportion to the number of its poor; and every person who is pleased to be idle, is intitled to maintenance. Most things thrive by encou-<134>ragement, and idleness above all. Certainty of maintenance, renders the low people in England idle and profligate; especially in London, where luxury prevails, and infects every rank. So insolent are the London poor, that scarce one of them will condescend to eat brown bread. There are accordingly in London, a much greater number of idle and profligate wretches, than in Paris, or in any other town, in proportion to the number of inhabitants. These wretches, in Doctor Swift's style, never think of posterity, because posterity never thinks of them: men who hunt after pleasure, and live from day to day, have no notion of submitting to the burden of a family. These causes produce a greater number of children in Paris than in London; tho' probably they differ not much in populousness.

I shall add but one other objection to a great city, which is not slight.

An overgrown capital, far above a rival, has, by numbers and riches, a distressing influence in public affairs. The populace are ductile, and easily misled by ambitious and designing magistrates. Nor are there wanting critical times, in which such <135> magistrates, acquiring artificial influence, may have power to disturb the public peace. That an overgrown capital may prove dangerous to sovereignty, has more than once been experienced both in Paris and London.

It would give one the spleen, to hear the French and English zealously disputing about the extent of their capitals, as if the prosperity of their country depended on that circumstance. To me it appears like one glorying in the king's-evil, or in any contagious distemper. Much better employ'd would they be, in contriving means for lessening these cities. There is not a political measure, that would tend more to aggrandize the kingdom of France, or of Britain, than to split its capital into several great towns. My plan would be, to confine the inhabitants of London to 100,000, composed of the King and his household, supreme courts of justice, government-boards, prime nobility and gentry, with necessary shopkeepers, artists, and other dependents. Let the rest of the inhabitants be distributed into nine towns properly situated, some for internal commerce, some for foreign. Such a plan <136> would diffuse life and vigour through every corner of the island.

To execute such a plan, would, I acknowledge, require great penetration and much perseverance. I shall suggest what occurs at present. The first step must be, to mark proper spots for the nine towns, the most advantageous for trade, or for manufactures. If any of these spots be occupied already with small towns, so much the better. The next step is a capitation-tax on the inhabitants of London; the sum levied to be appropriated for encouraging the new towns. One encouragement would have a good effect; which is, a premium to every man who builds in any of these towns, more or less, in proportion to the size of the house. This tax would banish from London, every manufacture but of the most lucrative kind. When by this means, the inhabitants of London are reduced to a number not much above 100,000, the near prospect of being relieved from the tax, will make householders active to banish all above that number: and to prevent a renewal of the tax, a greater number will never again be permitted. It would require much political <137> skill to proportion the sums to be levied and distributed, so as to have their proper effect, without overburdening the capital on the one hand, or giving too great encouragement for building on the other, which might tempt people to build for the premium merely, without any further view. Much will depend on an advantageous situation: houses built there will always find inhabitants.

The two great cities of London and Westminster are extremely ill fitted for local union. The latter, the seat of government and of the noblesse, infects the former with luxury and with love of show. The former, the seat of commerce, infects the latter with love of gain. The mixture of these opposite passions, is productive of every groveling vice. <138>

⚭ SKETCH XII ⚭

Origin and Progress of American Nations

Having no authentic materials for a natural history of all the Americans, the following observations are confined to a few tribes, the best known; and to the kingdoms of Peru and Mexico, as they were at the date of the Spanish conquest.

As there has not been discovered any passage by land to America from the old world, no problem has more embarrassed the learned, than to account for the origin of American nations: there are as many different opinions as there are writers. Many attempts have been made for discovering a passage by land; but hitherto in vain. Kamskatka, it is true, is divided from America by a narrow strait, full of islands: and M. Buffon, to render the passage still more easy than by these islands, conjectures, that thereabout there may formerly have been a land-passage, swallowed up in later times by the ocean. <139> There is indeed great appearance of truth in this conjecture; as all the quadrupeds of the north of Asia seem to have made their way to America; the bear, for example, the roe, the deer, the rain-deer, the beaver, the wolf, the fox, the hare, the rat, the mole. He admits, that in America there is not to be seen a lion, a tiger, a panther, or any other Asiatic quadruped of a hot climate: not, says he, for want of a land-passage; but because the cold climate of Tartary, in which such animals cannot subsist, is an effectual bar against them.*

But to give satisfaction upon this subject, more is required than a passage

---

* Our author, with singular candor, admits it as a strong objection to his theory, that there are no rain-deer in Asia. But it is doing no more but justice to so fair a reasoner, to observe, that according to the latest accounts, there are plenty of rain-deer in the country of Kamskatka, which of all is the nearest to America.

from Kamskatka to America, whether by land or sea. An inquiry much more decisive is totally overlooked, relative to the people on the two sides of the strait; particularly, whether they have the same language. <140> Now by late accounts from Russia we are informed, that there is no affinity between the Kamskatkan tongue, and that of the Americans on the opposite side of the strait. Whence we may assuredly conclude, that the latter are not a colony of the former.

But further. There are several cogent arguments to evince, that the Americans are not descended from any people in the north of Asia or in the north of Europe. Were they descended from either, Labrador, or the adjacent countries, must have been first peopled. And as savages are remarkably fond of their natal soil, they would have continued there, till compelled by over-population to spread wider for food. But the fact is directly contrary. When America was discovered by the Spaniards, Mexico and Peru were fully peopled; and the other parts less and less, in proportion to their distance from these central countries. Fabry reports, that one may travel one or two hundred leagues north-west from the Missisippi, without seeing a human face, or any vestige of a house. And some French officers say, that they travelled more than a hundred leagues from the delicious country <141> watered by the Ohio, through Louisiana, without meeting a single family of savages. The civilization of the Mexicans and Peruvians, as well as their populousness, make it extremely probable that they were the first inhabitants of America. In travelling northward, the people are more and more ignorant and savage: the Esquimaux, the most northern of all, are the most savage. In travelling southward, the Patagonians, the most southern of all, are so stupid as to go naked in a bitter cold region.

I venture still farther; which is, to indulge a conjecture, that America has not been peopled from any part of the old world. The external appearance of the inhabitants, makes this conjecture approach to a certainty; as they are widely different in appearance from any other known people. Excepting the eye-lashes, eye-brows, and hair of the head, which is invariably jet black, there is not a single hair on the body of any American: no appearance of a beard.* Another distin-<142>guishing mark is their copper colour, uni-

---

* Some authors I am aware assert that the Americans would have beards like other

formly the same in all climates, hot and cold; and differing from the colour of every other nation. Ulloa remarks, that the Americans of Cape Breton, resemble the Peruvians, in complexion, in manners, and in customs; the only visible difference being, that the former are of a larger stature. A third circumstance no less distinguishing is, that American children are born with down upon the skin, which disappears the eighth or ninth day, and never grows again. Children of the old world are born with skins smooth and polished, and no down appears till puberty.

The Esquimaux are a different race from the rest of the Americans, if we can have any reliance on the most striking characteristical marks.[1] Of all the northern nations, not excepting the Laplanders, they are of the smallest size, few of them exceeding four feet in height. They have a <143> head extremely gross, hands and feet very small. That they are tame and gentle appears from what Ellis says in his account of a voyage, *anno* 1747, for discovering a north-west passage, that they offered their wives to the sailors, with expressions of satisfaction for being able to accommodate them. But above all, their beard and complexion make the strongest evidence of a distinct race. There were lately at London, two Esquimaux men and their

---

people; but that the men are at great pains to pluck them out, esteeming them unbecoming. But why are they esteemed unbecoming? Plainly from the grotesque figure that some men make by having a few downy hairs here and there appearing on the chin. These look as unseemly among them as a beard upon a woman among us. [[Note added in 3rd edition.]]

1. "The Esquimaux are . . . striking characteristical marks": added in 2nd edition. In 1st edition: "That the original inhabitants are a race distinct from others, I once thought demonstrable from some reports concerning the Esquimaux. The author of a history of New France, and several other writers report, that the Esquimaux are bold, mischievous, suspicious, and untamable; that it is not even safe to converse with them but at a distance; that no European skin is whiter; and that they are bearded up to the eyes. Supposing these facts to be true, had I not reason to believe, that the Esquimaux must have sprung from some nation in the north of Europe or Asia, though I could not pretend to say, whether the transmigration was by land or sea? From the same facts, however, I was forced to conclude, that the rest of the Americans could not have had the same origin; for if the Canadians or any other American nation were of Asiatic or European extraction, they must, like the Esquimaux, have had a beard and white skin to this day. But one cannot be too cautious in giving faith to odd or singular facts, reported of different nations. It was discovered by later accounts more worthy of credit, that the foregoing description of the Esquimaux is false in every particular" [2:72–73].

wives; and I have the best authority to affirm, that the men had a beard, thin indeed like that of a Nogayan Tartar; that they were not of a copper colour like the other Americans, but yellow like people in the North of Asia.[2]

It has been lately discovered, that the language of the Esquimaux is the same with that of the Greenlanders. A Danish missionary, who by some years residence in Greenland had acquired the language of that country, made a voyage with Commodore Palliser to Newfoundland *ann.* 1764. Meeting a company of about two hundred Esquimaux, he was agreeably surprised to hear the Greenland tongue. They received him kindly, and drew from him a promise <144> to return the next year. And we are informed by Crantz, in his history of Greenland, that the same Danish missionary visited them the next year, in company with the Rev. Mr. Drachart. They agreed, that the difference between the Esquimaux language and that of Greenland, was not greater than between the dialects of North and South Greenland, which differ not so much as the High and Low Dutch. Both nations call themselves *Innuit* or *Karalit,* and call the Europeans *Kablunet.* Their stature, features, manners, dress, tents, darts, and boats, are entirely the same. As the language of Greenland resembles not the language of Finland, Lapland, Norway, Tartary, nor that of the Samoides, it is evident, that neither the Esquimaux nor Greenlanders are a colony from any of the countries mentioned. Geographers begin now to conjecture, that Greenland is a part of the continent of North America, without intervention of any sea.* <145>

From the preceding facts it may be concluded with the highest probability, that the continent of America south of the river St. Laurence was

---

* The Danes had a settlement in Greenland long before Columbus saw the West Indies. Would it not appear paradoxical to say, that America was discovered by the Danes long before the time of Columbus, and long before they knew that they had made the discovery?

2. "But above all . . . North of Asia": added in 2nd edition. In 1st edition: "But what is most to the present purpose; they are of a copper colour, like the other Americans, only a degree lighter, occasioned probably by the intense cold of their climate; and they are altogether destitute of a beard. It is common indeed among them, to bring forward the hair of the head upon the face, for preserving it from flies, which rage in that country during summer; an appearance that probably has been mistaken by travellers for a beard" [2:72–74].

not peopled from Asia. Labrador on the north side of that river, is thin of inhabitants; no people having been discovered there but the Esquimaux, who are far from being numerous. As they have plenty of food at home, they never could have had any temptation to send colonies abroad. And there is not the slightest probability, that any other people more remote would, without necessity, wander far from home to people Canada or any country farther south. But we are scarce left to a conjecture. The copper colour of the Canadians, their want of beard, and other characteristical marks above mentioned, demonstrate them to be a race different from the Esquimaux, and different from any people inhabiting a country on the other side of Labrador. These distinguishing marks cannot be owing to the climate, which is the same on <146> both sides of the river St. Laurence.[3] I add, that as the copper colour and want of beard continue invariably the same in every variety of climate, hot and cold, moist and dry, they must depend on some invariable cause acting uniformly; which may be a singularity in the race of people (*a*), but cannot proceed from the climate.

If we can rely on the conjectures of an eminent writer (*b*), America emerged from the sea later than any other part of the known world: and supposing the human race to have been planted in America by the hand of

(*a*) Preliminary Discourse.
(*b*) M. Buffon.
3. "From the preceding . . . river St. Laurence": added in 2nd edition. In 1st edition: "One thing is certain, that the Greenlanders resemble the North-Americans in every particular: they are of a copper colour, and have no beard; they are of a small size, like the Esquimaux, and have the same language. And thus I am obliged to abandon my favourite argument, for proving the Americans, the Esquimaux excepted, to be indigenous, and not indebted to the old world for their existence. At the same time, the other arguments urged above remain entire; and from what is now said a circumstance occurs, that fortifies greatly the chief of them. People, who with a bold face surmount all difficulties rather than give up a favourite opinion, make light of the copper colour and want of beard, willing to attribute all to the climate. We want *data*, I acknowledge, to determine with accuracy what effects can be produced by climate. But luckily we have no occasion at present to determine that difficult point. It is sufficient that the climate of Labrador is much the same with that of the northern parts of Europe and Asia. From that circumstance I conclude with certainty, that the copper colour and want of beard in the Esquimaux cannot be the result of climate. And if so, what foundation can there be for making these circumstances depend on the climate in any other part of America? Truly none at all" [2:74–75].

God later than the days of Moses, Adam and Eve might have been the first parents of mankind, *i.e.* of all who at that time existed, without being the first parents of the Americans. The *Terra Australis incognita* is separated from the rest of the world by a wide ocean, which carries a ship round the earth without interruption.* How has that con-<147>tinent been peopled? There is not the slightest probability, that it ever has been joined to any other land. Here a local creation, if it may be termed so, appears unavoidable; and if we must admit more than one act of creation, even the appearance of difficulty, from reiteration of acts, totally vanisheth. M. Buffon in his natural history affirms, that not a single American quadruped of a hot climate is found in any other part of the earth: with respect to these we must unavoidably admit a local creation; and nothing seems more natural, than under the same act to comprehend the first parents of the American people.

It is possible, indeed, that a ship with men and women may, by contrary winds, be carried to a very distant shore. But to account thus for the peopling of America, will not be much relished. Mexico and Peru must have been planted before navigation was known in the old world, at least before a ship was brought to such perfection as to bear a long course of bad weather. Will it be thought, that any supposition ought to be embraced, however improbable, rather than admit a se-<148>parate creation. We are, it is true, much in the dark as to the conduct of creative providence; but every rational conjecture leans to a separate creation. America and the *Terra Australis* must have been planted by the Almighty with a number of animals and vegetables, some of them peculiar to those vast continents: and when such care has been taken about inferior life, can so wild a thought be admitted, as that man, the noblest work of terrestrial creation, would be left to chance? But it is scarce necessary to insist upon that topic, as the external characters of the Americans above mentioned reject the supposition of their being descended from any people of the old world.

It is highly probable, that the fertile and delicious plains of Peru and

---

* Late discoveries have annihilated the *Terra Australis incognita*. The argument however remains in force, being equally applicable to many islands scattered at a great distance from the continent in the immense South Sea.

Mexico, were the first planted of all the American countries; being more populous at the time of the Spanish invasion, than any other part of that great continent. This conjecture is supported by analogy: we believe that a spot, not centrical only but extremely fertile, was chosen for the parents of the old world; and there is not in America, a spot more centrical or more <149> fertile for the parents of the new world, than Mexico or Peru.

Having thus ventured to state what occurred upon the origin of the Americans, without pretending to affirm any thing as certain, we proceed to their progress. The North-American tribes are remarkable with respect to one branch of their history, that, instead of advancing, like other nations, toward the maturity of society and government, they continue to this hour in their original state of hunting and fishing. A case so singular rouses our curiosity; and we wish to be made acquainted with the cause.

It is not the want of animals capable to be domesticated, that obliges them to remain hunters and fishers. The horse, it is true, the sheep, the goat, were imported from Europe; but there are plenty of American quadrupeds no less docile than those mentioned. There is in particular a species of horned cattle peculiar to America, having long wool instead of hair, and an excrescence upon the shoulder like that of the East-India buffalo. These wild cattle multiply exceedingly in the fertile countries which the Missisippi traverses; <150> and Hennepin reports, that the Indians, after killing numbers, take no part away but the tongue, which is reckoned a delicious morsel. These creatures are not extremely wild; and, if taken young, are easily tamed: a calf, when its dam is killed, will follow the hunter, and lick his hand. The wool, the hide, the tallow, would be of great value in the British colonies.

If the shepherd-state be not obstructed in America by want of proper cattle, the only account that can or need be given, is paucity of inhabitants. Consider only the influence of custom, in rivetting men to their local situation and manner of life: once hunters, they will always be hunters, till some cause more potent than custom force them out of that state. Want of food, occasioned by rapid population, brought on the shepherd-state in the old world. That cause has not hitherto existed in North America: the inhabitants, few in number, remain hunters and fishers, because that state affords them a competency of food. I am aware, that the natives have been decreasing in number from the time of the first European settle-<151>ments. But even at that time, the country was ill-peopled: take for example the country above described, stretching northwest from the Missisippi: the Europeans never had any footing there, and yet to this day it is little better than a desert. I give other examples. The Indians who surround the lake Nippisong, from whence the river St. Laurence issues, are in whole but five or six thousand; and yet their country is of great extent: they live by hunting and fishing, having bows and arrows, but no fire-arms; and their cloathing is the skins of beasts: they are seldom, if ever, engaged in war; have no commerce with any other people, Indian or European, but live as if they had a world to themselves (*a*). If that country be ill peopled, it is not from scarcity of food; for the country is extensive, and well stored with every sort of game. On the south and west of the lake *Superior,* the country is level and fruitful all the way to the Missisippi, having large plains covered with rank grass, and scarce a tree for hundreds of miles: the inhabitants <152> enjoy the greatest plenty of fish, fowl, deer, &c.; and yet their numbers are far from being in proportion to their means of subsistence. In short, it is the conjecture of the ablest writers, that in the vast extent of North America, when discovered, there were not as many people, laying aside Mexico, as in the half of Europe.

Paucity of inhabitants explains clearly why the North-American tribes remain hunters and fishers, without advancing to the shepherd-state. But if the foregoing difficulty be removed, another starts up, no less puzzling, viz. By what adverse fate are so rich countries so ill peopled? It is a conjecture of M. Buffon, mentioned above, that America has been planted later than the other parts of this globe. But supposing the fact, it has however not been planted so late as to prevent a great population; witness Mexico and Peru, fully peopled at the era of the Spanish invasion. We must therefore search for another cause; and none occurs but the infecundity of the North-American savages. M. Buffon, a respectable author, and for that reason often quoted, remarks, that the males are feeble in their organs of genera-<153>tion, that they have no ardor for the female sex, and that they have few children; to enforce which remark he adds, that the quadrupeds of America, both native and transplanted, are of a diminutive size, compared

---

(*a*) Account of North America by Major Robert Rogers.

with those of the old world. A woman never admits her husband, till the child she is nursing be three years old; and this led Frenchmen to go often astray from their Canadian wives. The case was reported by the priests to their superiors in France: what regulation was made has escaped my memory. Among the males, it is an inviolable law, to abstain from females while they are engaged in a military expedition. This is pregnant evidence of their frigidity; for among savages the authority of law, or of opinion, seldom prevails over any strong appetite: vain would be the attempt to restrain them from spirituous liquers, tho' much more debilitating. Neither is there any instance, of violence offered by any North-American savage, to European women taken captives in war.

Mexico and Peru, when conquered by the Spaniards, afforded to their numerous inhabitants the necessaries of life in profu-<154>sion. Cotton was in plenty, more than sufficient for the cloathing needed in warm climates: Indian wheat was universal, and was cultivated without much labour. The natural wants of the inhabitants were thus easily supplied; and artificial wants had made no progress. But the present state of these countries is very different. The Indians have learned from their conquerors a multitude of artificial wants, good houses, variety of food, and rich cloaths; which must be imported, because they are prohibited from exercising any art or calling except agriculture, which scarce affords them necessaries; and this obliges a great proportion of them to live single. Even agriculture itself is cramped; for in most of the provinces there is a prohibition to plant vines or olives. In short, it is believed that the inhabitants are reduced to a fourth part of what they were at the time of the Spanish invasion. The savages also of North America who border on the European settlements, are visibly diminishing. When the English settled in America, the five nations could raise 15,000 fighting men: at present they are not able to raise 2000. Upon the whole, it is computed by <155> able writers, that the present inhabitants of America amount not to a twentieth part of those who existed when that continent was discovered by Columbus. This decay is ascribed to the intemperate use of spirits, and to the small-pox, both of them introduced by the Europeans.* <156>

---

* In all the West-Indian colonies, the slaves continually decrease so as to make frequent recruits from Africa necessary. "This decrease," says the author of a late account of Gui-

It is observable, that every sort of plague becomes more virulent by transplantation. The plague commits less ravage in Egypt, its native place, than in any other country. The venereal disease was for many ages more violent and destructive in Europe, than in America where it was first known. The people who sailed with Christopher Columbus, brought it to Spain from Hispaniola. Columbus, with thirty or forty of his sailors, went directly to Barcelona, where the King then was, to render an account of his voyage. All the inhabitants, who at that time tripled the present number, were immediately seized with the venereal disease, which raged so furiously as to threaten destruction to all. <157> The small pox comes under the same observation; for it has swept away many more in America, than ever it did in Europe. In 1713, the crew of a Dutch vessel infected the Hottentots with the small pox; which left scarce a third of the inhabitants. And the same fate befel the Laplanders and Greenlanders. In all appearance, that disease, if it abate not soon of its transplanted virulence, will extirpate the natives of North America; for they know little of inoculation.

But spirituous liquors are a still more effectual cause of depopulation. The American savages, male and female, are inordinately fond of spirituous

---

ana [[i.e., Edward Bancroft]], "is commonly attributed to oppression and hard labour; tho' with little reason, as the slaves are much more robust, healthy, and vigorous, than their masters. The true cause is, the commerce of white men with young Negro wenches, who, to support that commerce, use every mean to avoid conception, and even to procure abortion. By such practices they are incapacitated to bear children when they settle in marriage with their own countrymen. That this is the true cause, will be evident, from considering, that in Virginia and Maryland, the stock of slaves is kept up without any importation; because in these countries commerce with Negro women is detested, as infamous and unnatural." The cause here assigned may have some effect: but there is a stronger cause of depopulation, viz. the culture of sugar, laborious in the field, and unhealthy in the house by boiling, &c. The Negroes employ'd in the culture of cotton, coffee, and ginger, seldom need to be recruited. Add, that where tobacco and rice are cultivated, the stock of Negroes is kept up by procreation, without necessity of recruits. Because there, a certain portion of work is allotted to the Negroes in every plantation; and when that is performed, they are at liberty to work for themselves. The management in Jamaica is very different: no task is there assigned; and the poor slaves know no end of labour: they are followed all day long by the lower overseers with whips. And hence it is, that a plantation in Jamaica, which employs a hundred slaves, requires an annual recruit of no fewer than seven. [["Add, that where . . . fewer than seven": added in 2nd edition.]]

liquors; and savages generally abandon themselves to appetite, without the least control from shame. The noxious effects of intemperance in spirits, are too well known, from fatal experience among ourselves: before the use of gin was prohibited, the populace of London were debilitated by it to a degree of losing, in a great measure, the power of procreation. Lucky it is for the human species, that the invention of savages never reached the production of gin; for spirits, in that early period, would <158> have left not one person alive, not a single Noah to restore the race of men: in order to accomplish the plan of Providence, creation must have been renewed oftener than once.*

In the temperate climates of the old world, there is great uniformity in the gradual progress of men from the savage state to the highest civilization; beginning with hunting and fishing, advancing to flocks and herds, and then to agriculture and commerce. One will be much disappointed, if he expect the same progress in America. Among the northern tribes, there is nothing that resembles the shepherd-state: they continue hunters and fishers as originally; because there is no cause so potent as to force them from that state to become shepherds. So far clear. But there is another fact of which we have <159> no example in the old world, that seems not so easily explained: these people, without passing through the shepherd-state, have advanced to some degree of agriculture. Before the seventeenth century, the Iroquois or Five Nations had villages, and cultivated Indian corn: the Cherokees have many small towns; they raise corn in abundance, and enclose their fields: they breed poultry, and have orchards of peach trees. The Chickesaws and Creek Indians live pretty much in the same manner. The Apalachites sow and reap in common; and put up the corn in granaries, to be distributed among individuals when they want food. The Hurons raise great quantities of corn, not only for their own use, but for commerce. Many of these nations, particularly the Cherokees, have of late got horses, swine, and tame cattle; an improvement borrowed from the Europeans.

---

* Charlevoix says, that an Indian of Canada will give all he is worth for a glass of brandy. And he paints thus the effect of drunkenness upon them. "Even in the streets of Montreal are seen the most shocking spectacles of ebriety; husbands, wives, fathers, mothers, brothers, and sisters, seizing one another by the throat, and tearing one another with their teeth, like so many enraged wolves."

But corn is of an earlier date: when Sir Richard Greenville took possession of Virginia in the reign of Queen Elisabeth, the natives had corn; and Hennepin assures us, that the nations bordering on the Missisippi had corn long before they were visited by any European. Hus-<160>bandry, it is true, is among those people still in its infancy; being left to the women, who sow, who reap, who store up in public granaries, and who distribute as need requires. The inhabitants of Guiana in South America, continue to this day hunters and fishers. But though they have neither flocks nor herds, they have some husbandry; for the women plant cassava, yams, and plantains. They make a liquor like our ale, termed *piworee,* which they drink with their food. And tho' they are extremely fond of that liquor, their indolence makes them often neglect to provide against the want of it. To a people having a violent propensity to intemperance, as all savages have, this improvidence is a blessing; for otherwise they would wallow in perpetual drunkenness. They are by no means singular; for unconcern about futurity is the characteristic of all savages: to forego an immediate for a distant enjoyment, can only be suggested by cultivated reason. When the Canary Islands were first visited by Europeans, which was in the fourteenth century, the inhabitants had corn; for which the ground was prepared in the following <161> manner. They had a wooden instrument, not unlike a hoe, with a spur or tooth at the end, on which was fixed a goat's horn. With this instrument the ground was stirred; and if rain came not in its proper season, water was brought by canals from the rivulets. It was the women's province to reap the corn: they took only the ears; which they threshed with sticks, or beat with their feet, and then winnowed in their hands. Husbandry probably will remain in that state among American savages; for as they are decreasing daily, they can have no difficulty about food. The fact however is singular, of a people using corn before tame cattle: there must be a cause, which on better acquaintance with that people will probably be discovered.

America is full of political wonders. At the time of the Spanish invasion, the Mexicans and Peruvians had made great advances toward the perfection of society; while the northern tribes, separated from them by distance only, were only hunters and fishers, and continue so to this day. To explain the difference, appears difficult. It is still more difficult to explain, why the <162> Mexicans and Peruvians, inhabitants of the torrid zone, were highly polished in the arts of society and government; considering that in the old world, the inhabitants of the torrid zone are for the most part little better than savages. We are not sufficiently acquainted with the natural history of America, nor with that of its people, to attempt an explanation of these wonders: it is however part of our task, to state the progress of society among the Mexicans and Peruvians; which cannot fail to amuse the reader, as he will find these two nations differing essentially from the North-American tribes, in every article of manners, government, and police.

When the Spaniards invaded America, the Mexicans were skilful in agriculture. Maize was their chief grain, which by good culture produced great plenty, even in the mountainous country of Tlascalla. They had gardening and botany, as well as agriculture: a physic-garden belonging to the Emperor was open to every one for gathering medicinal plants.

The art of cookery was far advanced among that people. Montezuma's table <163> was for ordinary covered with 200 dishes, many of them exquisitely dressed in the opinion even of the Spaniards. They used salt, which was made with the sun.

The women were dextrous at spinning; and manufactures of cotton and hair abounded every where.

The populousness of Mexico and Peru afford irrefragable evidence, that the arts of peace were there carried to a great height. The city of Mexico contained 60,000 families;* and Montezuma had thirty vassals who could bring into the field, each of them, 100,000 fighting men. Tlascalla, a neighbouring republic, governed by a senate, was so populous as to be almost a match for the Emperor of Mexico.

The public edifices in the city of Mexico and houses of the nobility, were of stone, and well built. The royal palace had thirty gates opening to as many streets. <164> The principal front was of jasper, black, red, and white, well polished. Three squares, built and adorned like the front, led to Montezuma's apartment, having large rooms, floors covered with mats of different kinds, walls hung with a mixture of cotton-cloth and rabbit-

---

* We cannot altogether rely on what is reported of this ancient empire with respect to numbers. The city of Mexico, tho' considerably enlarged since the Spanish conquest, doth not at present contain more than 60,000 souls, including 20,000 Negroes and Mulattoes.

furs; the innermost room adorned with hangings of feathers, beautified with various figures in lively colours. In that building large ceilings were formed so artificially without nails, as to make the planks sustain each other. Water was brought into the city of Mexico, from a mountain at a league's distance.

Gold and silver were in so high esteem, that vessels made of these metals were permitted to none but to the Emperor. Considering the value put upon gold and silver, the want of current coin would argue great dulness in that nation, if instances did not daily occur of improvements, after being carried to a considerable height, stopping short at the very threshold of perfection. The want of current coin made fairs the more necessary, which were carried on with the most perfect regularity: judges on the spot decided mercantile <165> differences; and inferior officers, making constant circuits, preserved peace and order. The abundance and variety of the commodities brought to market, and the order preserved by such multitudes, amazed the Spaniards; a spectacle deserving admiration, as a testimony of the grandeur and good government of that extensive empire.

The fine arts were not unknown in Mexico. Their goldsmiths were excellent workmen, particularly in moulding gold and silver into the form of animals. Their painters made landscapes and other imitations of nature, with feathers so artfully mixed as to bestow both life and colouring; of which sort of work, there were instances no less extraordinary for patience than for skill. Their drinking-cups were of the finest earth exquisitely made, differing from each other in colour, and even in smell. Of the same materials, they made great variety of vessels both for use and ornament.

They were not ignorant either of music or of poetry; and one of their capital amusements was songs set to music relating <166> the atchievements of their kings and ancestors.

With such a progress both in the useful and fine arts, is it not surprising, that tho' they had measures, they knew nothing of weights?

As to the art of writing, it was no farther advanced than the using figures composed of painted feathers, by which they made a shift to communicate some simple thoughts; and in that manner was Montezuma informed of the Spanish invasion.

There was great ingenuity shewn in regulating the calendar: the Mexican year was divided into 365 days; and into 18 months, containing 20 days each, which made 360; the remaining five intercalary days were added at the end of the year, for making it correspond to the course of the sun. They religiously employ'd these five days upon diversions, being of opinion that they were appropriated to that end by their ancestors.

Murder, theft, and corruption in officers of state, were capital crimes. Adultery also was capital; for female chastity was in high estimation. At the same time, <167> consent was deemed a sufficient cause of divorce, the law leaving it to the parties concerned, who ought to be the best judges. In case of a divorce, the father took care of the male children, leaving the female children with the mother. But to prevent rash separations, it was capital for them to unite again.

It may be gathered from what has been said, that there was a distinction of rank among the Mexicans. So strictly was it observed, as to be display'd even in their buildings: the city of Mexico was divided into two parts, one appropriated to the Emperor and nobility, and one left to plebeians.

Education of children was an important article in the Mexican police. Public schools were allotted for plebeian children; and colleges well endowed for the sons of the nobility, where they continued till they were fit for business. The masters were considered as officers of state; not without reason, as their office was to qualify young men for serving their king and country. Such of the young nobles as made choice of a military life, were sent to the army, and made to suffer great hardships before <168> they could be inlisted. They had indeed a powerful motive for perseverance, the most honourable of all employments being that of a soldier. Young women of quality were educated with no less care, by proper matrons chosen with the utmost circumspection.

As hereditary nobility and an extensive empire, lead both of them to monarchy, the government of Mexico was monarchical; and as the progress of monarchy is from being elective to be hereditary, Mexico had advanced no farther than to be an elective monarchy, of which Montezuma was the eleventh king. And it was an example of an elective monarchy that approaches the nearest to hereditary; for the power of election, as well as the privilege of being elected, were confined to the princes of the blood-royal. As a talent for war was chiefly regarded in chusing a successor to the throne, the Mexican kings always commanded their own armies. The Emperor-elect, before his coronation, was obliged to make some conquest, or perform some warlike exploit; a custom that supported the military spirit, and enlarged the kingdom. From <169> every king was exacted a coronation-oath, to adhere to the religion of his ancestors, to maintain the laws and customs of the empire, and to be a father to his people.

Matters of government were distributed among different boards with great propriety. The management of the royal patrimony was allotted to one board; appeals from inferior tribunals, to another; the levying of troops and the providing of magazines, to a third: affairs of supreme importance were reserved to a council of state, held commonly in the King's presence. These boards, all of them, were composed of men experienced in the arts of war and of peace: the council of state was composed of those who elected the Emperor.

Concerning the patrimony of the crown, mines of gold and silver belonged to the Emperor; and the duty on salt brought in a great revenue. But the capital duty was a third of the land-rents, the estates of the nobles excepted; upon whom no tribute was imposed, but to serve in the army with a number of their vassals, and to guard the Emperor's person. Goods manufactured and sold were subjected to a <170> duty; which was not prejudicial to their manufactures, because there was no rival nation within reach.

Montezuma introduced a multitude of ceremonies into his court, tending to inspire veneration for his person; an excellent artifice in rude times, of however little significancy among nations enlightened and rational. Veneration and humility were so much the tone of the court, that it was even thought indecent in the Mexican lords, to appear before the King in their richest habits. Vessels of gold and silver were appropriated to his table, and not permitted even to the princes of the blood. The table-cloths and napkins, made of the finest cotton, with the earthen ware, never made a second appearance at the Emperor's table, but were distributed among the servants.

In war, their offensive weapons were bows and arrows; and as iron was not known in America, their arrows were headed with bones sharpened at the point. They used also darts and long wooden swords, in which were fixed sharp flints; and men of more than ordinary strength fought with clubs. They beside had <171> slingers, who threw stones with great force and dexterity. Their defensive arms, used only by commanders and persons of distinction, were a coat of quilted cotton, a sort of breast-plate, and a shield of wood or tortoise-shell, adorned with plates of such metal as they could procure. The private men fought naked; their faces and bodies being deformed with paint, in order to strike terror. They had warlike instruments of music, such as sea-shells, flutes made of large canes, and a sort of drum made of the trunk of a tree hollow'd. Their battalions consisted of great numbers crouded together, without even the appearance of order. They attacked with terrible outcries in order to intimidate the enemy; a practice prompted by nature, and formerly used by many nations. It was not despised even by the Romans; for Cato the elder was wont to say, that he had obtained more victories by the throats of his soldiers, than by their swords; and Caesar applauds his own soldiers, above those of Pompey, for their warlike shouts. Eagerness to engage is vented in loud cries: and the effects are excellent: they redouble the ardor of those <172> who attack, and strike terror into the enemy.

Their armies were formed with ease: the princes of the empire, with the cacics or governors of provinces, were obliged to repair to the general rendezvous, each with his quota of men.

Their fortifications were trunks of large trees, fixed in the ground like palisades, leaving no intervals but what were barely sufficient for discharging their arrows upon the enemy.

Military orders were instituted, with peculiar habits as marks of distinction and honour; and each cavalier bore the device of his order, painted upon his robe, or fixed to it. Montezuma founded a new order of knighthood, into which princes only were admitted, or nobles descended from the royal stock; and as a token of its superiority, he became one of its members. The knights of that order had part of their hair bound with a red ribbon, to which a tassel was fixed hanging down to the shoulder. Every new exploit was honoured with an additional tassel; which made the knights with ardor embrace every opportunity to signalize themselves. As no-<173>thing can be better contrived than such a regulation for supporting a military spirit, the Mexicans would have been invincible had they understood the order of battle: for want of which that potent empire fell a prey to a handful of strangers. I differ from those who ascribe that event to the fire-arms of the Spaniards, and to their horses. These could not be more terrible to the Mexicans, than elephants were at first to the Romans: but familiarity with these unwieldy animals, restored to the Romans their wonted courage; and the Mexicans probably would have behaved like the Romans, had they equalled the Romans in the art of war.

When that illustrious people, by their own genius without borrowing from others, had made such proficiency in the arts of peace, as well as of war; is it not strange, that with respect to religion they were no better than savages? They not only practised human sacrifices, but dressed and ate the flesh of those that were sacrificed. Their great temple was contrived to raise horror: upon the walls were crouded the figures of noxious serpents: the heads of persons sacrificed were stuck up <174> in different places, and carefully renewed when wasted by time. There were eight temples in the city, nearly of the same architecture; 2000 of a smaller size, dedicated to different idols; scarce a street without a tutelar deity; nor a calamity that had not an altar, to which the distressed might have recourse for a remedy. Unparallelled ignorance and stupidity obliged every Emperor, at his coronation, to swear, that there should be no unseasonable rains, no overflowing of rivers, no fields affected with sterility, nor any man hurt with the bad influences of the sun. In short, it was a slavish religion, built upon fear, not love. At the same time, they believed the immortality of the soul, and rewards and punishments in a future state; which made them bury with their dead, quantities of gold and silver for defraying the expence of their journey; and also made them put to death some of their servants to attend them. Women sometimes, actuated with the same belief, were authors of their own death, in order to accompany their husbands.

The author we chiefly rely on for an account of Peru is Garcilasso de la Vega: <175> though he may be justly suspected of partiality; for, being of the Inca race, he bestows on the Peruvian government, improvements of later times. The articles that appear the least suspicious are what follow.

The principle of the Peruvian constitution seems to have been an Agrarian law of the strictest kind. To the sovereign was first allotted a large proportion of land, for defraying the expences of government; and the remainder was divided among his subjects, in proportion to the number of each family. These portions were not alienable: the sovereign was held proprietor of the whole, as in the feudal system; and from time to time the distribution was varied according to the circumstances of families. This Agrarian law contributed undoubtedly to the populousness of the kingdom of Peru.

It is a sure sign of improved agriculture, that aqueducts were made by the Peruvians for watering their land. Their plough was of wood, a yard long, flat before, round behind, and pointed at the end for piercing the ground. Agriculture seems to have been carried on by united labour: lands <176> appropriated for maintaining the poor were first ploughed; next the portion allotted to soldiers performing duty in the field; then every man separately ploughed his own field; after which he assisted his neighbour: they proceeded to the portion of the curaca or lord; and lastly to the King's portion. In the month of March they reaped their maize, and celebrated the harvest with joy and feasting.

There being no artist nor manufacturer by profession, individuals were taught to do every thing for themselves. Every one knew how to plough and manure the land: every one was a carpenter, a mason, a shoemaker, a weaver, &c.; and the women were the most ingenious and diligent of all. Blas Valera mentions a law, named *the law of brotherhood*, which, without the prospect of reward, obliged them to be mutually aiding and assisting in ploughing, sowing, and reaping, in building their houses, and in every sort of occupation.

As the art was unknown of melting down metals by means of bellows, long copper pipes were contrived, contracted at the end next the fire, that the breath might <177> act the more forcibly on it; and they used ten or twelve of these pipes together, when they wanted a very hot fire. Having no iron, their hatchets and pick-axes were of copper; they had neither saw nor augre, nor any instrument that requires iron: ignorant of the use of nails, they tied their timber with cords of hemp. The tool they had for cutting stone, was a sharp flint; and with that tool they shaped the stone by continual rubbing, more than by cutting. Having no engines for raising stones, they did all by strength of arm. These defects notwithstanding, they erected great edifices; witness the fortress of Cusco, a stupendous fabric. It passes all understanding, by what means the stones, or rather great rocks, employ'd in that building, were brought from the quarry. One of these stones, measured by Acosta, was thirty feet in length, eighteen in breadth, and six in thickness.

Having neither scissars nor needles of metal, they used a certain long thorn for a needle. The mirrors used by ladies of quality were of burnished copper: but such implements of dress were reckoned too effeminate for men. <178>

With respect to music, they had an instrument of hollow canes glew'd together, the notes of which were like those of an organ. They had love-songs accompanied with a pipe; and war-songs, which were their festival entertainment. They composed and acted comedies and tragedies. The art of writing was unknown: but silken threads, with knots cast upon them of divers colours, enabled them to keep exact accounts, and to sum them up with a readiness that would have rivalled an expert European arithmetician. They had also attained to as much geometry as to measure their fields.

In war, their offensive arms were the bow and arrow, lance, dart, club, and bill. Their defensive arms, were the helmet and target. The army was provided from the King's stores, and no burden was laid on the people.

In philosophy, they had made no progress. An eclipse of the moon was attributed to her being sick; and they fancied the milky way to be a ewe giving suck to a lamb. With regard to the setting sun, they said, that he was a good swimmer, and that he pierced through the waves, to <179> rise next morning in the east. But such ignorance is not wonderful; for no branch of science can make a progress without writing.

The people were divided into small bodies of ten families each: every division had a head, and a register was kept of the whole; a branch of public police, that very much resembles the English decennaries.

They made but two meals, one between eight and nine in the morning, the other before sunset. Idleness was punished with infamy: even children were employ'd according to their capacity. Public visitors or monitors were appointed, having access to every house, for inspecting the manners of the inhabitants; who were rewarded or punished according to their behaviour. Moderation and industry were so effectually enforc'd by this article of police, that few were reduced to indigence; and these got their food and cloathing out of the King's stores.

With respect to their laws and customs, children were bound to serve their parents until the age of twenty-five; and marriage contracted before that time, without <180> consent of parents, was null. Polygamy was prohibited, and persons were confined to marry within their own tribe. The tradition, that the Inca family were children of the sun, introduced incest among them; for it was a matter of religion to preserve their divine blood pure, without mixture.

It was the chief article of the Peruvian creed, upon which every other article of their religion depended, that the Inca family were children of their great god the sun, and sent by him to spread his worship and his laws among them. Nothing could have a greater influence upon an ignorant and credulous people, than such a doctrine. The sanctity of the Inca family was so deeply rooted in the hearts of the Peruvians, that no person of that family was thought capable of committing a crime. Such blind veneration for a family, makes it probable, that the government of Peru under the Incas had not subsisted many years; for a government founded upon deceit and superstition, cannot long subsist in vigour. However that be, such belief of the origin of the Incas, is evidence of great virtue and modera-<181>tion in that family; for any gross act of tyranny or injustice, would have opened the eyes of the people to see their error. Moderation in the sovereign and obedience without reserve in the subjects, cannot fail to produce a government mild and gentle; which was verified in that of Peru; so mild and gentle, that to manure and cultivate the lands of the Inca and to lay up the produce in storehouses, were the only burdens imposed upon the people, if it was not sometimes to make cloaths and weapons for the army. At the same time, their kings were so revered, that these articles of labour were performed with affection and alacrity.

The government was equally gentle with regard to punishments. Indeed very few crimes were committed, being considered as a sort of rebellion against their great god the sun. The only crime that seems to have been punished with severity, is the marauding of soldiers; for death was inflicted, however inconsiderable the damage.

In this empire, there appears to have been the most perfect union between law and religion; which could not fail to produce obedience, order, and tranquillity, <182> among that people, tho' extremely numerous. The

Inca family was fam'd for moderation: they made conquests in order to civilize their neighbours; and as they seldom if ever transgressed the bounds of morality, no other art was necessary to preserve the government entire, but to keep the people ignorant of true religion. They had virgins dedicated to the sun, who, like the vestal virgins in Rome, were under a vow of perpetual chastity.

This subject shall be concluded with some slight observations on the two governments I have been describing. Comparing them together, the Mexican government seems to have been supported by arms; that of Peru by religion.

The kings of Peru were hereditary and absolute: those of Mexico elective. In contradiction however to political principles, the government of Peru was by far the milder. It is mentioned above, that the electors of the Mexican kings were hereditary princes; and the same electors composed the great council of state. Montesquieu therefore has been misinformed when he terms this a despotic monarchy (*a*): a monarchy can never be despo- <183>tic, where the sovereign is limited by a great council, the members of which are independent of him. As little reason has he to term Peru despotic. An absolute monarchy it was, but the farthest in the world from being despotic: on the contrary, we find not in history any government so well contrived for the good of the people. An Agrarian law, firmly rooted, was a firm bar against such inequality of rank and riches, as lead to luxury and dissolution of manners: a commonwealth is naturally the result of such a constitution; but in Peru it was prevented by a theocratical government under a family sent from heaven to make them happy. This wild opinion, supported by ignorance and superstition, proved an effectual bar against tyranny in the monarch; a most exemplary conduct on his part being necessary for supporting the opinion of his divinity. Upon the whole, comprehending king and subject, there perhaps never existed more virtue in any other government, whether monarchical or republican.

In Peru there are traces of some distinction of ranks, arising probably from office <184> merely, which, as in France, was a bulwark to the mon-

---

(*a*) L'Esprit des loix, liv. 17. ch. 2.

arch against the peasants. The great superiority of the Peruvian Incas, as demi-gods, did not admit a hereditary nobility.

With respect to the progress of arts and manufactures, the two nations differed widely: in Mexico, arts and manufactures were carried to a surprising height, considering the tools they had to work with: in Peru, they had made no progress; every man, as among mere savages, providing the necessaries of life for himself. As the world goes at present, our multiplied wants require such numbers, that not above one of a hundred can be spared for war. In ancient times, when these wants were few and not much enlarged beyond nature, it is computed that an eighth part could be spared for war: and hence the numerous armies we read of in the history of ancient nations. The Peruvians had it in their power to go still farther: it was possible to arm the whole males capable of service: leaving the women to supply the few necessaries that might be wanted during a short campaign; and accordingly we find that the Incas were great conquerors. <185>

The religion of the Peruvians, considered in a political light, was excellent. The veneration they paid their sovereign upon a false religious principle, was their only superstition; and that superstition contributed greatly to improve their morals and their manners: on the other hand, the religion of Mexico was execrable.

Upon the whole, there never was a country destitute of iron, where arts seem to have been carried higher than in Mexico: and, bating their religion, there never was a country destitute of writing, where government seems to have been more perfect. I except not the government of Peru, which, not being founded on political principles, but on superstition, might be more mild, but was far from being so solidly founded.

3 5282 00675 3415